ADAM SMITH'S
LEGACY

ADAM SMITH'S LEGACY

His place in the development of modern economics

Edited by
MICHAEL FRY

London and New York

First published 1992
by Routledge
11 New Fetter Lane, London EC4P 4EE

Simultaneously published in the USA and Canada
by Routledge
a division of Routledge, Chapman and Hall, Inc.
29 West 35th Street, New York, NY 10001

The Institute of Economic Affairs was set up as a research and
educational trust under a trust deed signed in 1955. It began regular
publication in 1957 with specialized studies of markets and pricing
systems as technical devices for registering preferences and apportioning
resources.

Typeset in September by
Leaper & Gard Ltd, England
Printed and bound in Great Britain by
Biddles Ltd, Guildford and King's Lynn.

British Library Cataloguing in Publication Data
Adam Smith's legacy : his place in the development
of modern economics.
I. Fry, Michael
330.153

ISBN 0–415–06164–4

Library of Congress Cataloguing in Publication Data
Adam Smith's legacy : his place in the development of modern economics
/ edited by Michael Fry.
p.   cm.
Proceedings of a conference held in the Usher Hall, Edinburgh, on
July 16–17, 1990, to mark the bicentenary of the death of Adam
Smith.
Includes bibliographical references and index.
ISBN 0–415–06164–4
1. Smith, Adam, 1732–1790–Congresses.   2. Economics–History
–Congresses.   I. Smith, Adam, 1723–1790.   II. Fry, Michael, 1947–
HB103.S6A6275   1992   91-25698
330.15′3—dc20   CIP

CONTENTS

v

FIGURES

TABLES

FOREWORD

Michael Fry

This book contains the proceedings of the conference held in the Usher Hall, Edinburgh, on 16–17 July 1990 to mark the bicentenary of the death of Adam Smith. It was not only for that reason a special occasion, but also because it brought together the largest number of Nobel laureates in Economic Science since the prize was instituted in 1969. Though not every one could be present personally, eleven of the laureates contributed in some way to the celebration. No less memorable was the collective participation of the audience. Drawn from thirty countries representing all continents, with notable delegations from Eastern Europe and Japan, it ranged from professors of economics through politicians, company chairmen, central bankers and journalists to schoolteachers and students.

The bicentenary was, however, far from just an act of respectful homage. In his native land, Smith has never ceased to be the subject of lively intellectual debate, even when his ideas were somewhat eclipsed elsewhere. And a generalist tradition of political economy has here survived the increasing technical sophistication of modern economics. So it has been especially gratifying to us to have seen, since the 1970s, the enormous revival of interest in what he had to say, not least in parts of the world where living advocates of freedom have been silenced.

Though at the conference we were on the whole spared attempts by ideologues to hijack Smith for their own causes, his legacy was still energetically disputed. The laureates, with the benefit of careers dating back in some cases to before the Second World War, yielded to nobody in their ability to fan the flames of controversy. To be sure, none declined to admit some debt in his own work to Smith, or denied the relevance today of the eloquent case made in *The Wealth of Nations* for economic liberty. In particular, everyone had profited from the grand design that Smith bestowed on their science from its outset, the scale of the synthesis into which he incorporated so many fruitful ideas. With a becoming modesty, they also conceded that, unlike some modern professors of economics, Smith had not sequestered himself in an ivory tower, but enriched his writings with concrete facts and the lessons of experience.

The organizers had invited the laureates to make their contributions under one of three headings. The first was to look again at *The Wealth of Nations* from today's perspective. Professor Paul Samuelson (Nobel laureate 1970) could not on medical grounds attend the conference in person, but we are delighted to publish here the paper he would have given. It summarizes a significant part of his endeavours during the past few years, in the course of which he has gone over the works of the classical political economists and tested their findings with the aid of modern techniques. From this scrutiny, Smith emerged with flying colours. Similarly, Professor Lawrence Klein (Nobel laureate 1980) demonstrated in his paper to the conference that, even without the aid of computers or much concept of statistics, Smith could produce remarkably acute analyses of the real economic world around him; if today we miss in him, for example, any consideration of business cycles, this was most likely because such cycles did not occur in the eighteenth century, not at least at any level above a local one.

Professor Maurice Allais (Nobel laureate 1988) addressed the conference in the usual language of scientific discourse during the eighteenth century, that is to say, in French. And to the proceedings he could thus bring a vivid sense of the contemporary intellectual universe. He pointed out that Smith was too much of a borrower from the ideas of his precursors and contemporaries to be objectively considered the founding father of political economy. Even so, he had strikingly formulated and given currency to one guiding idea, of the benefits in free decentralized action by economic agents within a competitive system. Allais continued with a spirited attack on modern economists for their obsession with the properties of efficiency, as embodied in general equilibrium theory. They should instead look at how markets become efficient in the search for surpluses, which they might find a far more dynamic and realistic means of explaining the operation of the economy.

Ill-health unfortunately prevented Sir Richard Stone (Nobel laureate 1984) from coming to Edinburgh. His paper, read for him, concerned what Smith had written about public economic policy and its limits, a subject of self-evident interest even two hundred years later. Sir Richard found a still more topical note in Smith in stressing how widely accepted his four maxims of taxation had become. Given that one of these required for the sake of fairness that everybody should contribute the same proportion of his income, the poll tax introduced in Britain appeared 'improper' – in Smith's words, typical of countries where 'the ease, comfort and security of the inferior ranks of people are little attended to'. This caused a stir in the audience, especially among the politicians. And when the opinions of the other laureates were solicited, it was found that most of those prepared to express an opinion thought as little of the poll tax as Smith.

In the second part of the programme, papers were invited under the rubric of modern applications of Smith's analysis. Professor Franco Modigliani (Nobel laureate 1985) is most renowned for his work on consumption function. He had shown that savings depend not on current income, but on what a person expects to earn over a lifetime. After confirmation by experience in the major economies during recent decades, this is now received wisdom. But it would have disconcerted Smith, who believed that saving depended on the victory of virtue in its eternal battles with vice. How could he have got savings so wrong, Modigliani wondered, when he was such a keen observer of people? He ought to have seen that people in a growing economy accumulate savings so that they can then dissave them, that is, run them down as the economy slows and they are less able to earn; this is the way in which income and expenditure are spread over their lifetimes. Perhaps Smith had erred in supposing that popular behaviour was what his own class did, and failed to notice that the labouring classes were not given to generous bequests for their offspring.

Virtue and vice also formed a point of departure in the paper from Professor James Buchanan (Nobel laureate 1986). He asked what was the economic basis for having a work ethic, a question that had first occurred to him three years ago when reflecting why he felt guilty watching American football games on the television for hour after hour. He had concluded that the drive to work and to keep working was rewarded by society with praise for ethical behaviour because the market was unable to put an economic value on it. But economic value there certainly was. If you went fishing, loafed around or took 'time to smell the flowers', you were withdrawing from the labour market. Not only were you reducing your pay, but selfishly taking the benefit of your specialization from everybody else in the economy, a vital matter in economies which had grown highly specialized. The work ethic, in other words, was a key economic component in its own right, and to be fostered for the common good.

Professor James Tobin (Nobel laureate 1981) told Buchanan not to worry: every leisure act had an economic pay-off for someone. This was one of the many details he skilfully blended into a wide-ranging paper which set out to trace the presence or otherwise of the invisible hand in modern macroeconomics. It led him to defend Smith against some of his self-proclaimed modern disciples: he was 'not responsible for excesses committed in his name'. In fact, he would probably not have been altogether unfriendly to activism against mass unemployment, which might enable principles he had favoured to reach their full potential.

The contribution of Professor Theodore Schultz (Nobel laureate 1979) stressed a related theme of human capital, the subject of increasing analytical attention. Smith himself had reckoned that the acquisition of abilities and skills should be counted as capital for it

> always costs a real expense, which is a capital fixed and realised, as it were, in the person.... The improved dexterity of the workman may be considered in the same light as a machine or instrument of trade which facilitates and abridges labour and which, though it costs a certain expense, repays that expense with a profit.

Schultz accused economists of having often ignored this simple truth, perhaps because they perceived a danger in treating a human being as a mere material component. Yet 'it is human capital, not space, cropland, energy or other physical properties of the Earth that is decisive in improving the income and welfare of people in the modernising economy.'

The third theme of the conference was the condition of modern economics. Professor Wassily Leontief (Nobel laureate 1973) launched a fiery attack on the abstruseness of many younger colleagues in the profession. At the time of Smith's death, he declared, economics had been in a splendid state, a science not dismal but highly fashionable. Now, despite prodigious output from an over-supply of economists, the returns were diminishing. He put this down to their increased bias towards hypothesis and abstract mathematical testing of it, as opposed to analysis of facts about activities and transactions of practical concern to those engaged in them. The pages of professional journals were crammed with theoretical models, of which the empirical validity could be neither proved nor disproved by conventional methods of statistical evidence. In fact such evidence as we had fell far short of what was needed for a realistic working model of a complex modern economy. The cure he prescribed was official financing of data collection on a large enough scale to allow economists to face the issues affecting the real economy. But his overall message was scarcely reassuring: 'Sometimes you see an old tree – very old and pretty rotten – with little shoots coming from the sides. It is my belief that is the state of economics as a science.'

The proceedings finally came full circle with the paper by Professor Jan Tinbergen, one of the recipients of the very first Nobel Prize in Economic Science. He is himself no longer able to travel, but this paper was read to the conference by Professor James Meade (Nobel laureate 1977). He looked back at what economics had been able to achieve for itself in finding a place among the universe of sciences, and took heart from the degree of theoretical rigour to which it had successfully aspired. Tinbergen yet returned, like so many of his fellow laureates, to the fact that economics has obviously failed to offer convincing solutions to a great many of the most pressing problems it sought to address.

At a conference held in the name, to the memory and to the honour of Adam Smith, nobody could fail to be impressed by how far economists had come since his day. Though there was much to be proud of in that, the leaders of the profession were still evidently much more concerned to maintain a clearer vision of their duties as citizens, not just scientists, and a suitable humility about scientific, as opposed to human, ends.

EDITORIAL NOTE

All references to *The Wealth of Nations* have been converted to the usages of the Glasgow edition (Oxford University Press: 1976, eds Campbell, Skinner and Todd). A reference thus (I, xi, a, 8) is to Book One, chapter xi, part I, paragraph 8. The editor is grateful to Professor Andrew Skinner for identifying the quotations.

1

THE OVERDUE RECOVERY OF ADAM SMITH'S REPUTATION AS AN ECONOMIC THEORIST

Paul A. Samuelson

Adam Smith had a powerful influence on the history of ideas, ideas of the educated non-economist public and most particularly of governmental policy-makers and their voter constituencies. David Ricardo's great influence was more narrowly focused on contemporaneous and subsequent economists. Macaulay's general schoolboy knew *The Wealth of Nations* but not Ricardo's *Principles of Political Economy*.

So to speak, Smith paid for his popularity with the lay public by being regarded among professional economists as 'old hat' and a bit prosaically eclectic. Ricardo, by contrast, wrote so badly as to provide that quantum of obscurity sufficient to evoke academic attention and overestimation. Karl Marx, it may be said, shared in the Ricardian tradition in more ways than is conventionally recognized.

As I reflect back upon what seems to have been a systematic undervaluation of Adam Smith in professional circles of six decades ago, I discern that a major responsibility for this lies with two scholars. It was David Ricardo himself who believed that Adam Smith's basic system was flawed at its core. Indeed, it was this critical view of Smith that caused Ricardo to write his *Principles*. The economists' world, blinded by Ricardo's reputation for brilliance and unable to recognize in his murky exposition the many *non sequiturs* contained there, accepted Ricardo's indictment at its face value.

The second authority influential in playing down Smith's worth was my old master, Joseph Schumpeter. Long before the Harvard days of his greatest reputation, the young Schumpeter's brilliant German work, *Economic Doctrine and Method* (1914), had patronized Smith with faint praise. Never did Schumpeter really alter this evaluation, as his posthumous classic of 1954 makes clear. Schumpeter seems to put ahead of

1

Smith as a theorist such predecessors as Cantillon, Hume and Turgot; and subsequent to him, Schumpeter would surely have regarded as Smith's superiors such diverse scholars as A.A. Cournot, Léon Walras, and (I vaguely remember from Schumpeter's 1935 Harvard lectures) Alfred Marshall. Whereas Ricardo regarded Smith as having defected from a proper labour theory of value, in Schumpeter's eyes Smith's crime was that of mediocrity, lack of originality, and excessive imitativeness. (When my colleague Robert L. Bishop prepared a definitive debunking of Ricardo's critique of Smith, he informed me that Schumpeter paradoxically proved to be one of the few scholars who correctly recognized Ricardo's lack of cogency and who defended Smith for his full due.)

Most economists of the generations between 1930 and 1990 have had limited interest in and knowledge of the history of economic analysis. They gladly go for whole hours without thinking about the subject.[1] Therefore, Schumpeter's evaluation was influential to them and set the climate of opinion.

Perhaps I ought to add a third name to the list of those who served to play down the merits of Smith relative to Ricardo: Karl Marx. Marx cannot be judged by twentieth-century economists to have been competent enough in economic theory to serve as a useful judge of Smith's analytical merits. But the fact that both neoclassical economics and Marxian economics trace back directly to Ricardo has undoubtedly raised his relative reputation. (As I once put it, the poet Robert Frost gained doubly when attracting both low-brow and high-brow readers).

If Marx is a third name, the temptation becomes strong to add Piero Sraffa as a fourth and recent name. I am not referring to the Sraffa who was a superb editor, but rather to the Sraffa who leads a school against 'marginalism' and 'mainstream economics' generally. Luigi Pasinetti, Pierangelo Garegnani, Nicholas Kaldor, and Joan Robinson, when they seek in classical economics a Kuhnian alternative paradigm to modern mainstream economics, are least attracted to Smith's and Mill's kind of supply-and-demand analysis and most attracted to Ricardian constructions.

In this brief exposition, I propose to audit a few of the most important criticisms of Smith, made by Ricardo and other authorities. My verdicts turn out mostly to be in Smith's favour; but more important is the analytic demonstration of why various indictments are invalid.

INDETERMINACY FROM TOO MANY 'RESIDUALS'?

My own failure as a student to accord to Smith the admiration he deserves as a theorist can be traced neither to Ricardo's criticisms nor to Schumpeter's faint praise. There was an oral tradition at the University of Chicago, hard for me to pin down more than half a century later, that Adam Smith had a correct but rather empty supply-and-demand theory of price, based on a cost-of-production equality that involved *indeterminate* factor-price variables.

Bluntly put, Smith was alleged to have too many 'residuals'. Labour got its subsistence wages; land rent got its residual rent; and interest or profit was also a residual return. When $A = B + C + D$, and only B is determinate in the equation, then to write successively $C = A - B - D$ and $D = A - B - C$ was still to be left with too many endogenous unknowns.[2]

Samuelson (1977), on the 200th anniversary of *The Wealth of Nations*, provided both a literary and mathematical vindication of Smith's system based on his tri-partite breakdown

$$price = wage\text{-}cost + rent\text{-}cost + interest\text{-}cost$$

No redundant residuals are left; and no inconsistencies are involved.

Population grows (algebraically) when the wage rises (algebraically) above the market cost of a specified basket of subsistence goods. Capital accumulates (algebraically) when interest or profit rate exceeds (algebraically) some specifiable minimum required yield. Land is fixed in supply: for simplicity it is needed only to produce corn. Other goods (manufactures) need only labour and corn as inputs. All production is time-phased. Landowners and capital-goods owners spend their rent and profit incomes according to their tastes, along with utilizing income for (algebraic) capital accumulation.

Smith is right to perceive that there is only one (real wage, profit rate, real rent/acre) that clears all supply–demand markets in the long run. He is right to perceive that land rent is a surplus that can be taxed without affecting real price ratios. He is right to perceive that the growth mode is the cheerful state for wages when capital accumulation precedes and drives up population. He correctly perceives that accumulation ultimately reduces the interest rate and raises the rent rate; also accumulation permits a higher subsistence wage if workers become more chary of reproducing. I say to Knight and to Samuel Hollander (1987: 78): there is no redundancy, and there is no self-contradiction in this Smith. QED. And I add for Ricardo, even if land were redundantly infinite in supply, accumulation of capital relative to population would compete down the profit rate (of course at the same time competing up the real wage). So what is the problem?

HOW SMITH WITHSTANDS MARX'S DOUBTS

One line of criticism of Smith's theoretical system traces peculiarly to Karl Marx. Few commentators seem to have noticed how repeatedly preoccupied Marx was by Smith's purported breakdown of price (and of national income) into the triad of components: wages, land rents and interest or profit. Marx accused Smith of omitting the fourth component of used-up raw materials or depreciation of durable capital instruments. Friedrich Engels, as editor for Marx, had to grapple with repetitive fragments of manuscript dealing with this accusation and adding up to what must involve tens and tens of thousands of words.

Actually, Smith is in the clear. He even uses the magic words 'value-added', deeming the used-up raw materials in a loaf of bread as being decomposable into the triadic wage–rent–interest components of previous stages of production. In one sentence Marx does seem to glimpse the correctness of Smith's taxonomy and accounting in a very special case. When labour and land alone produce wheat; and labour with wheat produces flour; and labour with flour produces finished bread – what today we would call the triangular Leontief input/output matrix of the simplest 'Austrian' case – then Marx conceives that Smith's value-added might work as a special trick. But, when iron produces coal and coal produces iron, Marx senses that an infinite regress without a finite beginning is involved. He complains that Smith is sending us from pillar to post and back again. Even though Smith is essentially right, any modern investigation must provide the rigour not to be expected in an eighteenth-century writer.

Actually, Marx's own Tableaux of Reproduction in *Capital*, Volume II, properly understood, provide the vindication of Smith against Marx's charge of circularity. V.K. Dmitriev (1898) shows Marxians and non-Marxians how the simultaneous equations of the input/output tableaux do vindicate Smith. I give Marx top marks for sensing that rigour is needed for auditing Smith's heuristics. (See Dorfman, Samuelson and Solow (1958) for discussion of the *convergent* infinite matrix-multiplier series, the so-called Cornfield–Leontief-

Gaitskell multiplier chains, that are shown to augment compatibly the Dmitriev–Marx simultaneous equations resolution of Smith's value-added accounting.)

The Marx of the labour theory of value came close to committing hara-kiri by pressing home the fallacy (sic) of Smith's infinite and illegitimate regression. For, as the 1958 analytics show, when land is free and the interest rate is zero – the rude early society in which Smith, Marx, Ricardo and Walras agree that the labour theory of value would be exact as a theory of competitive price – deer, beaver, coal and iron could not have their prices each equal to respective embodied total labour contents, ('live', direct labour plus 'dead', indirect labour) if a convergent infinite geometric progression did not justify Smith's labour value-added theory. Among writers sympathetic to Marx, Ian Steedman (1977) has noted this same point and properly faulted Marx for it.

SMITH AS MERELY A SUPPLY AND DEMAND MONGER

He who is Napoleonic is often paranoid. Having regarded Smith's supply-and-demand relations between price and wage-plus-rent-plus-interest components as emptily eclectic, Marx thought Smith's taut-ologies were not even genuine tautologies. It is ironical that Marxians and neoclassicists like Knight joined in the failure to perceive the genius of Smith's formulation of a general equilibrium model.

In recent times Samuel Hollander has been lampooned rather than praised for seeing supply and demand mechanisms everywhere in the classical writers. Even Mark Blaug (1978: 66) writes of Hollander as making Smith into more of a Léon Walras than a Ricardo, which I deem not to be a *reductio ad absurdum* but rather a merited compliment for Smith. (Given their respective dates, we might better compliment Walras for his Smith-like approach to general equilibrium.) Followers of Piero Sraffa or Marx, who are *not* identical sets, agree in their desire to reject mainstream equilibrium theory. In the sense of Thomas Kuhn's *The Structure of Scientific Revolutions* (1962), they want to regard the classical (i.e., the pre-1870) system as an alternative paradigm, a different and better paradigm to the modern ones. That is why they reproach Hollander for claiming to discern supply and demand content in the classical writers and why they prefer a Ricardo to a Smith.

Even before the 1951 and 1960 eruption into print of Sraffa, my reading of every one of the classical masters found in them an earlier and more primitive version of the Walras–Marshall–Wicksell system. As I once put it, 'Inside every classical writer there is a modern economist trying to get born.' Thünen is a notorious case where even marginalism is present; but Ricardo's numerical examples and concepts of external-margin and internal-margin land rent represent a significant advance beyond Smith's and Hume's excellent apperception that inelastically-supplied land earns a rent whose causation runs *from* rather than towards demand and competitive prices.

AVOIDING OVER-CONCRETE IMPLICIT INFERENCE

George Orwell would savour the Maoist dictum: What is not explicitly permitted is forbidden. Yet something like this doctrine can be espoused in setting up the rules of the game for commentators on any ancient writer such as Smith: if the writer does not explicitly say (in *his* language) 'I am stipulating that cost-prices are constant, regardless of changes in composition of demand', the commentator must abstain from writing that 'presumably' or implicitly' he 'means' that. This austere code is not one that I would insist on unconditionally. But departures from it should be dramatically earmarked, and made replete with caveats like 'This is a possible reading that seems consonant with the general tenor of the author's exposition; but of course it may never have occurred to him to make up his mind on the point – and at points A and B he does say X and Y.'

Against this background, I must strongly question statements by Blaug (1978) and Hollander (1987), that Smith's Book I chapters on price as determined by summed components of wage-cost, rent-cost and profit-cost, commit or predispose him to a constant-cost model that determines prices independently of the composition of demand. Logic neither requires nor makes likely such an inference. Thus, in 1933, Bertil Ohlin revolutionized Ricardian trade theory by explicit use of Smith–Walras–Cassel cost-price equations; and he did so for the explicit purpose of formulating a Heckscher–Ohlin model of non-labour factor endowments that negates the Ricardian comparative-advantage cost constancies.

Beyond logic, common experience reveals that the constant-cost case is the singular razor's edge instance. For almost all technologies, goods like cloth or wheat or copper or typewriters or claret use the thousands of factors of production in diverse combinations that may vary with intensity of demands and with both exogenous and endogenous variations in relative factor prices. Peppered through all of the books of *The Wealth of Nations* are Smithian examples of these realistic phenomena. Both Hollander and Blaug provide perceptive quotations from Smith on these points, Hollander being especially replete with apposite passages.

Relative to Ricardo, Smith deserves particular credit for not restricting his competitive possibilities. It was Ricardo, not Smith, who committed the egregious error of arguing that the complication of land and rent for the labour theory of value can be exorcised by our having recourse to external – or internal – margin no-rent lands. Ricardo's error is doubly egregious in that he perpetrates it as a purported correction of Smith for failure to recognize as a truth what we have known for almost a century to be a definite non-truth. (I fault great Ricardo scholars, such as Piero Sraffa and George Stigler, for not alerting their readers to Ricardo's bloomer; and I salute Knut Wicksell, Lionel Robbins and Ragnar Frisch for recognizing that where the external margin falls for land is an *endogenous* unknown that varies with intensities of relative demands.) By my *qualitative* count, Stigler's '93 percent labour theory of value for Ricardo' comes short by 50 per cent or more (both rent and time-intensity modify labour content); on my censorious days, after contemplating Sraffian examples in which corn is needed to produce corn, my *quantitative* bound on the inaccuracy of embodied-labour pricing verges on the infinite. The Ricardo who retreated back towards a labour theory of value was the Ricardo who believed that it was the scarcity of land that *alone* made possible diminishing returns for the equilibrium profit rate. Clio does have a sense of humour. Had Ricardo spent his adolescence off the floor of the stock exchange and in the classroom of mathematics, he would have realized the untenability of his schizoid attempt to divide off the theory of distribution from the complexities of the theory of value and the theory of value from the complexities of the theory of distribution. Two indecomposable halves cannot be summed to unity.

I am not scolding earlier writers for the *faux pas* of being born before the twentieth century. Rather I am scolding historians of thought who have written during these last six decades for repeating ancient *non sequiturs* – such as that 'goods, readily reproducible' imply, logically or empirically, horizontal *ss* supply curves (they do not); or that Smith's model is one of Marshallian partial equilibrium rather than Walrasian general equilibrium. What is relevant for the present purpose is to point out that Adam Smith is actually closer to articulated truth on many of these subleties than those who wrote in the half century after 1776.

RICARDO'S MAIN BEEF

Up front in the Preface to his *Principles*, Ricardo (1817–23: 6) states his critique: 'Adam Smith, not having viewed correctly the principles of rent, ... overlooked many important truths, which can only be discussed after the subject of rent is thoroughly understood.' Does Ricardo cogently convict Smith of failing to understand rent? I deny that Ricardo did, or that one more skilled than Ricardo could do so. Let me review some of the issues.

If the quantity of land is inelastically supplied, then there is a valid sense in which its rent is 'price determined', rather than price-determining. David Hume, writing at his life's end to congratulate Smith on the publication of *The Wealth of Nations*, gently reproaches him for overlooking the difference between price-determined rents and price-determining other costs. But what needs to be clearer than Smith's bald statement (I, xi, a, 8): 'High or low wages and profits, are the causes of high or low price; how or low rent is the effect of it'? Ricardo and Hume can have no valid complaint here, either of an error of commission or omission.

When I defend Smith on his treatment of rent, Blaugs, Stiglers, Hollanders, and other expert scholars rebut with the argument that Ricardo's exposition of rent is more extensive, subtle and deep. Yes, I do recognize that his treatment of the intensive as well as the extensive margin does go beyond Smith; and, as with Thünen somewhat later, Ricardo's numerical examples virtually arrive at the notion of marginal products and costs. But his increased definiteness does not make Ricardo's exposition of rent *definitive*: rather it reveals his understanding to be definitely wrong on some vital essentials – and most notably in his criticizing Smith for failing to agree that the need to pay positive rent cannot vitiate the truth that the prices of goods are proportional to their labour costs (when time intensities are neutral).

Ricardo does understand, and better than Smith, that a good's price is proportional to its *marginal* labour cost. But that saves only the face of his verbalistic labour theory of value and not his substantive theory. As soon as changed composition of demand for goods alters *endogenously marginal* labour embodiments, nothing substantive is left of the labour theory of value. The price of non-land-using cake

8

relative to land-using corn can fluctuate, not between 93 per cent and 100 per cent or between 89.5 per cent and 96.5 per cent, but between zero and infinity. (Try the Cobb–Douglas case with exponents [1.0,0] and [0.75, 0.25] or a von Neumann–Straffa similar example.)

Jacob Viner used to assign exam questions that showed how Ricardo's Chapter 2 recognized (in modern parlance):

$$P_2/P_1 = \frac{\text{marginal cost in labour}_1}{\text{marginal cost in labour}_2} = \frac{1/[\partial Q_1/\partial L_1]}{1/[\partial Q_2/\partial L_2]}$$

But, Viner insisted, this was compatible with rent's being 99 per cent of national income and labour's importance being derisory. Would that more historians of economic analysis had taken Viner's EC 301 or brooded more on Ricardo's text.

I risk the law of diminishing returns in expounding and rebutting Ricardo's many critiques of Smith. Sraffa's 1951 *Introduction* (pp. xxxvi–xxxvii) takes seriously a newfound 1818 letter to James Mill, explicating Ricardo's precise bone-picking. He charges (Chapter I, n.3: 22–3) Smith with erroneously (sic) believing that 'when profits and rent were to be paid, they could have some influence on the relative value of commodities independent of the mere quantity of labour that was necessary to their production.' Smith is right and Ricardo wrong under sensible definitions of necessary 'quantity of labour' and under identification of 'relative value of commodities' with relative competitive prices. To Mill, Ricardo defends himself, contrasting himself with Torrens: Ricardo (gratuitously?) charges Smith with believing that, when positive profit and rent arises, that '*raised* [R's italics] the prices or exchangeable value of commodities'. In opposition to Smith, Ricardo avers that 'exchangeable value varies ... owing only to two causes ... the ... quantity of labour required ... [and] the greater or less durability of capital'. This flat-footedly loses the possible effects of positive land rents; and it verbalistically niggles away at Smith's clear agreement that positive interest can affect prices of labour-intensive goods less than capital-intensive goods. It is cheek, cheap cheek, for Ricardo to insist that interest effects do not 'supersede' wage effects but only 'modify' them. Verbalisms aside, where are readers of Smith told that, when capital-goods inputs lower labour requirements, competitive price has to be *raised* by inclusion of an allowance for positive interest? Smith would have to be an idiot to have believed that; even to accuse him of that strikes me as almost self-accusatory, as if the accuser had been momentarily tempted to take the possibility seriously.

9

ADAM SMITH'S BLOOMER?

A subsidy on the export of grain surely will help land rents and corn production, while hurting manufacturers? From before Smith's time to after Ricardo's, this primitive theoretical proposition played a key role in the Corn Laws designed to protect agriculture. Yet the sage and eclectic Smith, on this issue, seemed to deny the obvious and to do so on the basis of the sweeping dogma that the price of corn determines the price of all goods.

Ricardo and the mob jumped on Smith for this aberration. Latter day commentators have generally sided with Ricardo against Smith. Hollander (1987: 85) even sounds a cosmic note: 'Ricardo's corrections make the transition to nineteenth-century classical theory.' I seek to defend Smith but not whitewash him. In the art of hagiography, it is sometimes expedient to cut one's losses, admitting that the hero is mortal and able to err. But, alas, this matter seems not to be open and shut. There is a legitimate long-run model – and one that both Ricardo and Smith occasionally found congenial – in which Smith seems to be essentially right.

> In it, a subsidy on corn has no longest-run effect on the real price of anything. (It does have effects on relative corn and cake productions.)
>   In it, the long-run *prices* of all commodities do bear an invariant relationship to the price of corn (and to *any* good's price!) regardless of subsidy-induced changes in tastes for corn, cake, ... on the part of landowners and *rentiers*.

This model being understood, we might choose to say that Smith leap-frogged the nineteenth century to catch a glimpse of today's 2-Primary-Factor Non-Substitution Theorem. See Samuelson (1959a and b) for an exegesis of the Ricardian system in strict Physiocratic terms. It is hard cheese to be pilloried by Ricardo and the mob for your brilliant anticipations. A revisionist Hollander might want to recast the roles of hero and captious pedant in the corn subsidy drama.

To take my point, contemplate a model of homogeneous land, labour and time-phasing. Corn is produced by land, labour and corn (seed). Other goods – silver, cake – are produced by labour alone in the first, simplest case. Labour supply is governed by a specifiable subsistence wage rate in terms of corn alone, $\bar{w}$. $W/P_{corn} \to \bar{w}$, and then population is in stationary equilibrium. Capital accumulation likewise grows until the profit or interest rate reaches its needed minimal yield, $\bar{r}$: when

$r \to \bar{r}$, net accumulation ends and stationary equilibrium obtains. For brevity, first suppose $\bar{r}$ is zero à la Schumpeter and not positive à la Fisher. To avert complication, in all industries inputs produce output after one time period. Finally, specify that landowners and profit-earners have the same tastes for corn and cake, spending specified fractions of their incomes on each. (The need for new-mined silver can be minimally positive, to ensure its production is sufficient to replace wear and disappearance of coins.)

The above model is close to the 'lost Atlantis' Ricardian model of around 1815, much beloved by neo-Ricardians (who would agree with Voltaire that, if it had never existed, we would have to invent it). Certainly it is a perfectly possible model that Smith, Ricardo and Mill could accept for purposes of analysis. Clearly all goods but corn obey the embodied-labour theory of value: their real prices, relative to each other and to labour (P_{cake}/P_{silver}, P_{cake}/W, ...) are invariant when technology is specified. In long-run equilibrium, $P_{corn}/W = 1/\bar{w}$, not because of technology but because population stability requires that each labourer command $\bar{w}$ of corn. Smith is right to relate all goods' prices to corn:

$$P_{cake}/P_{corn} = [P_{cake}/W] / [P_{corn}/W]$$
$$= \frac{a_{cake}(1+\bar{r})}{1/\bar{w}} = \bar{w}(1+\bar{r})a_{cake}$$

$$P_{corn}/P_{silver} = \frac{1/\bar{w}}{a_{silver}(1+\bar{r})} = \frac{1}{\bar{w}(1+\bar{r})a_{silver}}$$

Here (a_{silver}, a_{cake}) denotes labour coefficients of the respective industries.

What about corn's cost of production? That equals its per-unit wage outlay and rent outlay. What is the same thing, and *not* a contradiction, is that density of labour in corn production must grow until precisely its market-clearing real wage comes to equal the specified subsistence wage of $\bar{w}$. A post-Smithian writes this as

$$W/P = \bar{w} = \frac{\text{Intensive-margin wage productivity}}{1+\bar{r}}$$

The last numerator will decline as labour crowds the homogeneous corn land (as Smith perceives) and, at a unique L_{corn}/Land ratio, equilibrium obtains. (What is left over from labour's average productivity in excess of its marginal productivity – that is how post-1889 neoclassicists

11

described Smith's facts – constitutes the uniquely determined residual rent that equilibrium mandates.)

Now subsidize corn production for export. This is just like landowners changing their tastes from cake to corn. What happens? As Ricardo came to realize in his new chapter on machinery, all that happens in the long run is a decline in population needed for manufactures (cake production). Corn-land rent is unchanged by the subsidy or tastes change. All real prices stay the same. QED for a vindication of Smith. But what if the subsistence wage required a component of cake as well as corn? And what if cake and/or silver needed land as an input? Ricardo, having been scolded by Malthus for over-emphasizing corn in subsistence, scolds Smith for fabricating a special-case model.

As counsel for Smith, I reply to Ricardo. It does not matter how many goods use the homogeneous land as input. It does not matter if the subsistence-wage basket of goods has something of every good in it. Any subsidy merely boils down to a change in effective final demands; and, by the 1776–1959 2-Primary-Factor Non-Substitution Theorem involving a subsistence-wage for labour, all relative prices and the real rent rate per acre can be affected *only* by an alteration of subsistence needs or of technology or of long-run $\bar{r}$. (See Samuelson (1975: 41) for the factor-price frontier that, at each interest rate, makes homogeneous land rental a convex declining function of the real wage expressed in *any* market basket of goods. Then with $\bar{r}$ and $\bar{w}$ given, Smith's rent rate is uniquely determined independently of composition of demand. QED again.)

The classical economists were brilliant and creative minds who, if reborn among us today, would soon forge to the peak of our profession. But they lived in early times and had no access to the scientific knowledge and know-how that has accumulated over the centuries. Therefore, a modern graduate student is expected to improvize a more accurate account of the incidence of export subsidies than any classical writer ever managed to fabricate. In order to adjudicate the merits of the Ricardo and Smith litigants, I ought first to sketch a tolerably accurate, modern account of the incidence process.

Suppose tax moneys are used to subsidize each unit of corn exported; or what can come to the same problem, while avoiding the complications of what is to be assumed about the overall balance of exports and imports, suppose all corn sold to red-headed landowners and rentiers for their consumption gets a subsidy financed by lump-sum tax on all of their class. This does send up their relative corn expenditure relative to that on cake. In the short run this bids up $P_{corn}/\$W$, and it might (or might not) even bid up a bit the wage in silver units. (When prices in silver are to be emphasized, I use the '$' sign.) If it does, it must bid up P_{cake} a little. Since the price in ounces of silver itself stays by definition at unity, under constant labour productivity in silver mining, any rise in $W makes all silver mining shut down transiently. Short-run windfall profitability adjusts to all these transitions.

In the Smith–Ricardo subsistence-wage model, population must be declining when P_{corn}/$W stays above $1/\bar{w}$. When enough silver has worn away so that some positive mining resumes, $W must be back at the mine-cost level and cake price, P_{cake} must be back at the pre-subsidy level. Corn and all prices end back in pre-subsidy ratios, just as Smith had insisted. Cake production is permanently lowered as the permanent corn subsidy programme lowers its effective final demand relative to corn's; *all* of corn's transient rise in production has eroded away, and post-subsidy some of non-labourers' cake consumption has been cut by the new permanent taxation.

What complaint can Ricardo register? Having to accept Smith's prosaic facts, he must forge objections to Smith's dictum that the price of corn sets all the other prices. But this is mostly Schoolman verbalism: just as some scholars can be said to have an instinct for the jugular, too often I find Ricardo had an instinct for the capillary. Corn-cake price-ratio invariance is factual whatever the verbal gloss.

Smith is by no means in the clear after this defence. Glimpsing a truth is not the same as understanding all of it. Besides, when several varieties of land are involved – surely the realistic case always envisaged by all the classical writers – the qualified theorem loses its simplicity and its ability to exonerate Smith. But this brush that tars Smith also tars Ricardo's chapter on bounties. If heterogeneity of lands is posited, both savants are wrong. Ricardo's assertion that 'natural price' cannot change becomes false. Smith's constancy of P_{cake}/P_{corn} also becomes false when composition of demand changes. The time is ripe for Walras to be born! Still I think we do owe Smith some admiration where previously he was accorded condescension, and the bicentenary of his death is a good time to make amends.

NOTES

1   A true story dramatizes this point. In 1988 a Swedish scholar spent a sojourn at Harvard, during which time he sensibly audited the graduate macroeconomics seminar at MIT. He told me: 'I did not expect that much time would be spent on Knut Wicksell or Irving Fisher, but I confess to some surprise that the sizeable reading list contained no item before 1985.'

2   Jacob Viner's famous EC 301, during the years of 1930–8, certainly
    devoted attention to 'residual' theories of factor pricing – as for example
    Francis Walker's residual theory of wages. But I cannot remember Viner
    explicitly chastising Smith for at-least-one-too-many residuals. It was
    Frank Knight, I seem to recall, who threw that stone. See Douglas Irwin
    (1986) for discussion of the contents of Viner's 1930 course, as revealed
    by library copies of M. Ketchum's mimeographed notes.

REFERENCES

Blaug, Mark (1978) *Economic Theory in Retrospect*, third edition, Cambridge:
    Cambridge University Press.
Dmitriev, V.K. (1974) *V.K. Dmitriev: Economic Essays on Value Competition
    and Utility*, D.M. Nuti (ed.), Cambridge: Cambridge University Press.
Dorfman, P., Samuelson P., and Solow, R. (1958) *Linear Programming and
    Economic Analysis*, New York: McGraw-Hill Book Company Inc.
Hollander, Samuel (1987) *Classical Economics*, Oxford: Basil Blackwell Ltd.
Irwin, Douglas (1986) 'Jacob Viner's Price Theory Course', unpublished
    manuscript, Columbia University.
Kuhn, T.H. (1962) *The Structure of Scientific Revolutions*, Chicago:
    University of Chicago Press.
Marx, Karl *Capital*, Volume I (1867); Volume II (1885); Volume III (1894),
    Chicago: Charles H. Kerr & Company, 1909.
Ohlin, Bertil (1933) *Interregional and International Trade*, Cambridge, Mass.:
    Harvard University Press.
Ricardo, David (1951) *Works of David Ricardo, Volume I, On Principles of
    Political Economy and Taxation*, P. Sraffa (ed.), Cambridge: Cambridge
    University Press.
Samuelson, Paul A. (1959) 'A Modern Treatment of the Ricardian Economy:
    I. The Pricing of Goods and of Labor and Land Services', *The Quarterly
    Journal of Economics*, LXXIII (1), 1–35.
Samuelson, Paul A. (1959) 'A Modern Treatment of the Ricardian Economy:
    II. Capital and Interest Aspects of the Pricing Process', *The Quarterly
    Journal of Economics*, LXXIII (2), 217–31.
Samuelson, Paul A. (1975) 'Steady-State and Transient Relations: A Reply on
    Switching', *The Quarterly Journal of Economics*, LXXXIX (1), 40–7.
Samuelson, Paul A. (1977) 'A Modern Theorist's Vindication of Adam
    Smith', *The American Economic Review*, 67 (1), 42–29.
Samuelson, Paul A. (1984) *History of Economic Analysis*, Oxford: Oxford
    University Press.
Schumpeter, J.A. (1954) *History of Economic Analysis*, New York: Oxford
    University Press.
Schumpeter, J.A. (1914) *Economic Doctrine and Method, An Historical
    Sketch*, translation from the German, London, 1954.
Steedman, Ian (1977) *Marx After Sraffa*, London: New Left Books.

2

SMITH'S USE OF DATA

Lawrence R. Klein

Adam Smith was a professor of moral philosophy, and he is appropriately remembered for the underlying philosophical foundations that he provided for modern economics, yet *The Wealth of Nations* is full of quantitative analysis that is not explicitly philosophical, and I propose to look into his digressions into economic time series, in particular his analysis of wheat prices and related matters in Chapter XI, 'Of the rent of the land' which rounds out Book I.

In terms of modern economic discourse, one might say that Smith's argument is decidedly 'anecdotal'. He draws on a vast treasure of interesting facts, many of which are quantitative, down to numerical details. He refers (I, xi, b, 16) to the price of butcher's meat paid by Prince Henry (who died on 6 November 1612). He quotes a price of £9 10s. for 4 quarters of an ox weighing 600 pounds (31s. 8d. per hundred pounds weight). The argument of much of the book is supported by reference to many facts like these, some in precise numerical terms and some in general, such as the relation between the price of rice in China and the price of wheat in Europe. The philosophical base of *The Wealth of Nations* is implicit in all the explicit reasoning about the real world, which Smith has observed in minute detail, both contemporaneously and historically. My emphasis in this essay is, however, on Smith's use of systematic data in much the same way that modern quantitative economists look at such evidence.

At the end of Chapter XI, there is an extensive time series listing of wheat prices from 1202 to 1764. I am not going to analyse his use of data elsewhere, but simply will concentrate on this tabulation of wheat prices, although I do want, eventually, to relate this discussion to other statistical series of the eighteenth century in England in order to try to gain some perception of his appreciation of dynamic economics of his times.

The wheat data were not collected and prepared by Adam Smith. In modern parlance we would say that they are a secondary data listing, taken from two main sources: Bishop Fleetwood, *Chronicon Preciosum* (1707: 77–124) and supplemented by the accounts of Eton College. Two issues are of some interest. 1. How did Smith handle or interpret the data? 2. What are characteristics of these data that can be determined by modern time series analysis?

Smith did some very good and perceptive things with these data, but he also did some questionable things. First, it must be stressed that Smith realized the problem of changes in purchasing power when studying the behaviour of prices over long periods of time. Accordingly, he presented Fleetwood's time series of wheat prices in two modes, as nominal prices and as *real* prices. The latter mode was termed 'The average price of each year in money of the present times'. Very early in *The Wealth of Nations* (Chapter V, 'Of the real and the nominal price of commodities, or of the price in labour, and their price in money', he wrote,

> Labour, therefore, is the real measure of the exchangeable value of all commodities. (I, v, 1)

> labour, like commodities may be said to have a real and a nominal price. Its real price may be said to consist in the quantity of the necessaries and conveniences of life which are given for it; its nominal price, in the quantity of money. The labourer is rich or poor, is well or ill rewarded, in proportion to the real, not to the nominal price of his labour. (I, v, 9)

Fleetwood's nominal wheat prices were apparently transformed into real prices by using the table by Martin Folkes (*Table of English Silver Coins.* 1745: 142) The editorial notes of Edwin Cannan remark that the transformation was very approximate, with some margin of error.

Apart from some degree of numerical error, the main controversial aspect of Smith's use of these data is his splicing of the Fleetwood series, which ended with the entry for 1597. The entries for the next four years – 1598, 1599, 1600 and 1601 – were taken directly, without adjustment from the Eton College account. These prices were from Charles Smith (*Tracts on the Corn Trade*, 1766). The problem is that the Eton College quotations refer to the Windsor quarter, which consisted of 9 bushels; whereas a standard quarter was equal to 8 bushels. Also the Windsor market prices are for the best or highest priced wheat, and Smith makes no mention of quality differences. The splicing of the two series of wheat prices is not a major issue, however, because only four values are added to the Fleetwood time series, and the Eton College series are then tabulated separately from 1595 to 1764. Smith did not transform the Eton College series to real prices.

Smith's analysis of this price series was mainly descriptive. He commented on trend phases, some notable fluctuations (departures from trend) upwards or downward, and movements in relation to silver prices. He also commented from time to time about price movements in relation to prices of livestock or livestock products, but there are no lengthly or systematic listings of other prices in *The Wealth of Nations*.

Smith divided the series into 12–year averages and followed the smoother movements of the latter. He saw a declining trend in wheat prices from the thirteenth century to the middle of the sixteenth century and then rising towards the end of the sixteenth century. Fleetwood believed that silver was falling in value, but Smith attached much importance to the wheat prices and felt that they provided a better measure of value than prices of any other commodity. He also noted divergent movements of wheat and silver prices in various epochs and turned to such events as discoveries of new sources of precious metals in America as explanations for the divergences. His analysis of supply–demand balance in price determination was quite perceptive. He also invoked such events as Civil War, bounty on corn export, and debasement of coins as additional special factors that influenced the supply–demand balance for commodities.

Smith analysed price movements of the seventeenth and eighteenth centuries in relation to each other, to silver prices, and unusual supply factors, affecting either grain yields or availabilities of precious metals. In an earlier chapter, however, he provided a nice general analysis of price determination. He broke price into four components – intermediate materials component, a wage (labour) component, a profit component and a rent (land) component. He then worked with what amounts to a value-added concept of production and implicitly subtracted materials costs from gross output value. He was then left with three familiar inputs – land, labour and capital. The reward to land was rent, to labour was wage, and to capital (termed 'inspection and direction') was profit. This way of decomposing price into factor rewards was used for commodities such as corn and flax, but was also well suited for manufactured goods. This approach is the forerunner of present attachment to full-cost pricing in which all the factor costs are covered.

Let us suppose that Adam Smith had access to the facilities of modern hardware and software and also to the insightful techniques of twentieth-century statistical method. What might have been the kind of presentation at the end of Book I of *The Wealth of Nations*?

First, we can examine time series graphs of nominal and real prices, 1202–1594. These all come from Fleetwood. Nominal prices of wheat over this span of nearly four centuries show no decisive trend. There is an unusual peak at about 1270 and an intermediate peak near the end of the sixteenth century. There are fluctuations during this near 400–year period and more will be said of that below, but there is no trend and that may seem to be unusual to us who have lived in an inflationary era. We generally expect nominal prices to rise over very long stretches of time.

Smith wisely and daringly chose a very long time span, within which he analysed price movements. We can see from Figures 2.1–2.4 that prices rose *and* fell over several centuries. Nowadays, economists become overly preoccupied with short-run phenomena and translate recent experience to very long time periods – possibly forever. The general impression now is that prices rise endlessly. Some economic

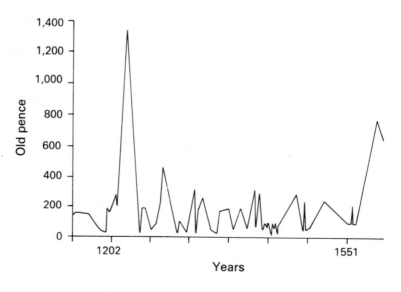

Figure 2.1 Nominal prices 1202–1594

18

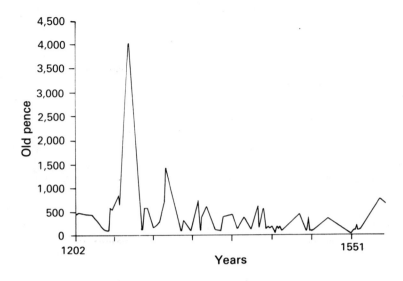

Figure 2.2 Real prices 1202–1594

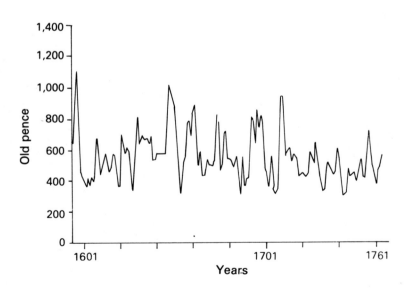

Figure 2.3 Nominal prices 1594–1764

19

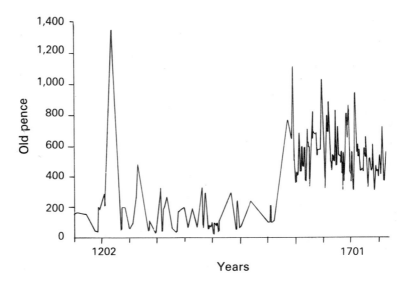

Figure 2.4 Nominal prices 1202–1764

historians write about large inflationary bouts in sixteenth-century Spain or other European centres. It is truly remarkable that both the real and the nominal series examined by Smith showed no long-term trend. He could comment on specific short-term movements in price, but he was not confronted with an implicit time graph that moved relentlessly upwards on a trend path.

Real prices of wheat, quoted in prices of Smith's time in the eighteenth century, are larger in value than the main run of nominal prices but the fluctuations are not very different. The same early peak that is found in the nominal series is plainly visible, but the tendency of the series to run up to an intermediate peak at the end of the sixteenth century is much subdued. In the later period 1594–1764 there are fewer missing annual observations and the data are not transformed into real prices. Again there is no pronounced trend, but if all the nominal data are put together in one time series diagram, it is clear that there are two statistical universes. The price graph from 1594–1764 is distinctly on a higher level than that part of the graph from 1202–1594.

What do these price data show? Interestingly enough, they show consistent systematic movement. A periodogram analysis of the Windsor wheat quotations from 1594–1764 (Figure 2.5) shows 3 peaks, at cycle lengths of 2–3 years, 6 years (the dominant peak) and at 42 years. A medium-term price cycle of 6 years seems to be plausible. Adam Smith commented on various particular price movements but he did not cite or notice empirical cyclical regularities. Although his data series show little sustained trend, they do have distinct cyclical properties. There are too many missing yearly values in the longer span of the other series, 1202–1594, to support a similar periodogram analysis.

It is interesting to focus on Smith's own century, the eighteenth. A subject of some consequence but one that is not taken up in depth by Adam Smith is the issue of cyclical regularity. As far as price is concerned, periodicity of fluctuation was present. Extensive documentation of the nineteenth century reveals deeply ingrained cyclical fluctuations. Smith commented at great length on particular movements in the price series but not to the point of drawing conclusions about regularity or commodity of fluctuations among many different series. The concept of 'the business cycle' came much later. It had its origins in the nine-

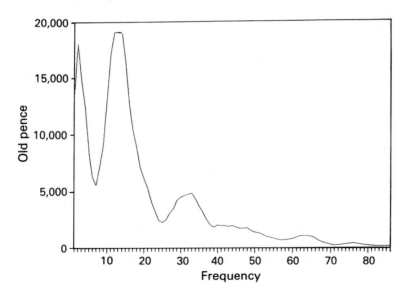

Figure 2.5 Periodogram: wheat price 1594–1764

teenth century, and it is worthwhile inquiring when this economic phenomenon first appeared and why it did not seem to occur earlier. There are many studies of business cycle movement beginning with the nineteenth century, mainly after 1850. In the United States, the period around the Civil War generally marks the start of serious quantitative research on business cycles. In Japan, the Meiji Restoration generally provides a convenient starting point. To a large extent, data availability is the primary constraining factor. In his encyclopedia article on 'Business Cycles', Arthur F. Burns cites cyclical turning points for four countries:

> United States, beginning 1834;
> Great Britain, beginning 1792;
> Germany, beginning 1866;
> France, beginning 1840.

In all cases, monthly dating precision begins after the middle of the century.

Sir William Beveridge (later Lord Beveridge) investigated the British trade cycle in the period before 1850. He found cyclical evidence in terms of physical production during the period 1785–1850.[2] His former research assistant J.H. Wilson (later Lord Wilson) reported a remarkable study on the period from 1717 to 1786.[3] Wilson raised some intriguing issues. If Beveridge and others had established the existence of the trade cycle, as we know it and analyse it in modern times, did it exist in similar form in the eighteenth century, in particular, in Adam Smith's time? Wilson did not relate his investigation to Adam Smith, rather to the eighteenth century, however, in the terms of reference of this paper, I am raising the question of the existence of the phenomenon in Smith's economic environment.

Both Beveridge and Wilson confined their investigation to physical indices of production and the latter notes specifically 'In no case have prices, or total values involving prices, been used.' It is, accordingly. interesting in the present context to examine the wheat price series used by Adam Smith for the corresponding period of the eighteenth century in relation to the output series of J.H. Wilson.[4]

Adam Smith, as noted above, was a keen observer of the economic events of his day and had an enormous grasp of economic history. Should one therefore have expected him to anticipate the industrial changes that were just beginning at the end of the eighteenth century and the characteristics of the economic system that they generated, in particular the business cycle? In a sense, these fluctuations are the outgrowth of the market economy whose foundations were being laid by Smith. Also, if there were regular rhythmical fluctuations with links distributed in time across many sectors of the economy, should they have been treated in more detail by Smith?

It is interesting that J.H. Wilson found no evidence of the business cycle in the eighteenth century comparable to that found by Sir William Beveridge in the nineteenth century. Wilson dated the modern cycle from the 1760s. He concluded: 'In the eighteenth century, fluctuations there were, but they were, in the main, localized to particular areas, or confined to individual industries.' Indeed, Adam Smith noted aspects of fluctuations in wheat prices in general and also other *particular* fluctuations in certain countries, areas or economic sectors. This is fully in keeping with our finding a significant periodicity in eighteenth-century wheat price movements. Not only do we find significant periodicities in the wheat price series used by Smith, but we also find evidence of periodicities in Wilson's series. He extracted trends from the series, and they show the following periodicities as illustrated in Figures 2.6–2.10:

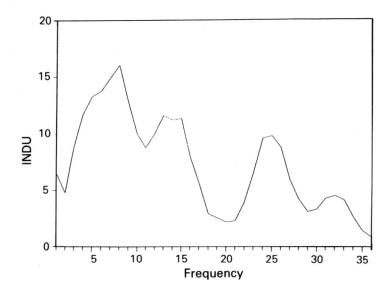

Figure 2.6 Periodogram: industrial index 1717–86

23

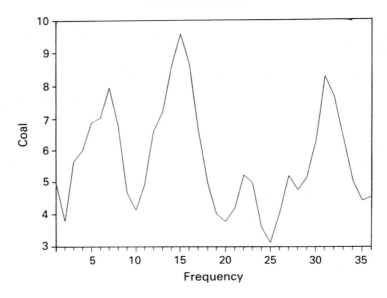

Figure 2.7 Periodogram: coal 1717–86

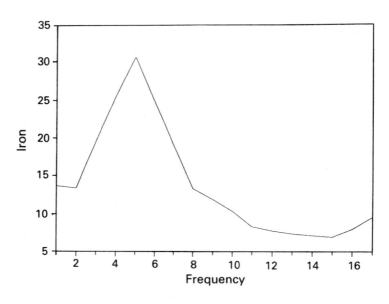

Figure 2.8 Periodogram: iron 1717–49

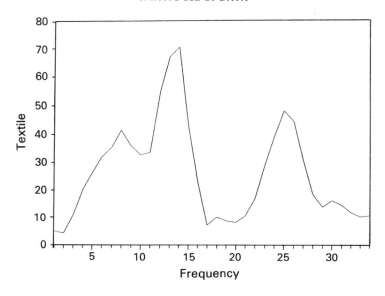

Figure 2.9 Periodogram: textile 1720–86

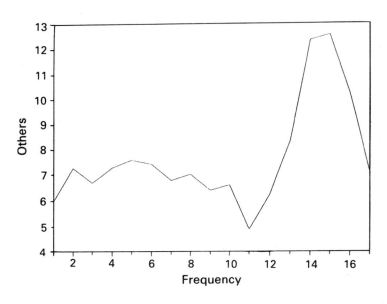

Figure 2.10 Periodogram: others 1717–49

Industrial index 4.4 years
(average of series) 2.3
Coal 5.0
2.3
Iron and steel 3.3
Textiles 2.4
Others 1.1

To substantiate his observation that a general business cycle in the modern sense did not exist prior to the late 1700s, Wilson calculated the correlation matrix for coal, iron and steel, and textiles. Of the six bivariate correlations, he found only one to be significant, namely, that between coal and textiles. This lack of correlation shows that there is not a general tendency among different series to fluctuate together, in a general business cycle pattern.

To amplify Wilson's work, I have considered the following additional calculations:

(i) Lead-lag correlation among interrelated series that are typical of modern business cycle movements.
(ii) The possible existence of general (multivariate) linear relationships among the variables instead of exclusively bivariate relationships.
(iii) Correlations between the wheat price data found in Smith's volume and various series from Wilson on physical production.

The significant correlation between textiles and coal production can be extended to the general lag relationship:

$$T_t = \alpha 0 + \sum_{i=0}^{3} \alpha_i \, C_{t-i} + u_t$$

In this equation, textiles production (T), a finished manufactured good, is related to prior inputs of coal (C) as a fuel or intermediate good in the manufacturing process. It is natural to look for a time lag here. For the period 1723–86, I confirm Wilson's finding of a significant relationship:

$$T_t = -27.24 + 0.51 \, C_t + 0.38 \, C_{t-1} + 0.26 \, C_{t-2}$$
$$(-0.59) \quad (2.78) \qquad (2.78) \qquad (2.78)$$

$$+ .13 \, C_{t-3} \qquad R^2 = 0.097$$
$$(2.78) \qquad DW = 1.82$$

$t-$ statistics are in parentheses below coefficient estimates, and they indicate that the estimated distributed lag coefficients differ significantly from zero.

26

On the other hand, iron and steel production is not significantly related to coal production, even with trial specifications of various time lags. Wilson constructed a broader measure of 'industrial' output, which averages coal, iron and steel, textiles, and *other* series. His industrial index series was correlated with the Eton College wheat price series, 1718–63, to see if there was any relationship between two cyclical series, one related to food prices and the other related to industrial output, broadly defined. There is no discernible relationship. Correlations estimated from

$$I_t = \alpha + \beta (WP)_{t-\theta} + u_t \qquad \theta = 0,1,2$$

or from

$$(WP)_t = \gamma + \delta I_{t-\theta} + v_t \qquad \theta = 0,1,2$$

show low correlation, high serial correlation of residuals, and very low $t-$ statistics for any of the parameter estimates $\hat{\alpha}$, $\hat{\beta}$, $\hat{\gamma}$ and $\hat{\delta}$. In this notion I_t stands of an index of industrial output, WP for wheat price; i_t and v_t are error terms.

Wilson smoothed the industrial index series with a three-year moving average. We, similarly, smoothed the wheat price series with a three-year moving average, but the smoothed series were no more closely correlated than the non-smoothed series.

Finally, the series from Wilson, on the one hand, and from Smith on the other, were considered from another point of view. The separate series for coal, iron and steel, textiles, and *other*, were analysed by the method of principal components, to see if there was a 'common factor' in these series that would be related in a cyclical sense to fluctuations in wheat prices, 1721–49. Here, the sample size is a lowest common denominator among the four which do not have identical observations points in all cases. The cumulative fractions of overall variance accounted for by the successive principal components are:

PC1	0.377
PC2	0.628
PC3	0.828
PC4	1.0

There is no single factor that can be identified with the concept of the business cycle that accounts for an overwhelming fraction of the variance. The four components are mutually orthogonal, and I regressed the wheat price on these as four independent variables

27

$$(WP)_t = 453.93 + 17.59 \, PC1 + 19.15 \, PC2$$
$$\quad\quad\quad (27.64) \quad (1.05) \quad\quad (1.15)$$

$$+ \, 8.07 \, PC3 + 8.03 \, PC4 \quad R^{-2} = 0.00$$
$$\quad (0.48) \quad\quad (0.48) \quad\quad DW = 0.97$$

No PCi is significant; the overall correlation is nonexistent; and the residual are serially correlated. The same equation with an estimated autoregressive transformation, or with a lagged dependent variable is no better in establishing an empirical relationship between wheat price and any principle component.

From this analysis, I draw the same conclusion as J.H. Wilson; there is no discernible common tendency for various statistical series to move together during the eighteenth century in what might be called a common business cycle, and the addition of wheat price to the set of production statistics does not alter that conclusion. There is little evidence that Adam Smith should have been able to observe business cycles in his professional life time. It is an open question as to whether he should have been able to see the makings of a business cycle in what was coming in the industrial age of the nineteenth century.

NOTES

Ms Matild Horvath supplied invaluable research support for this investigation.

1 Arthur F. Burns (1968) 'Business cycles', in David Sills (ed.), *International Encyclopedia of the Social Sciences*, 2, New York: Macmillan, 226–45.
2 Sir William H. Beveridge (1940) 'The trade cycle in Britain before 1850', *Oxford Economic Papers*, 3, February, 74–109.
3 J.H. Wilson (1940) 'Industrial Activity in the Eighteenth Century', *Economica*, n.s. 7, May, 150–60.
4 Wilson, *op. cit.*, notes that a satisfactory price index of the eighteenth-century period was being calculated on the basis of Sir William Beveridge's price tables in *Prices and Wages in England (The Mercantile Era)* but was not ready for the *OEP* article (see n.2 above). Of course, the standards of statistical information and precision would have been much higher than is exhibited in Smith's use of the Eton College accounts with respect to Windsor market prices, but the issue being investigated is Smith's data analysis, and this is what is being related to eighteenth century economic conditions.

3

THE GENERAL THEORY OF SURPLUSES AS A FORMALIZATION OF THE UNDERLYING THEORETICAL THOUGHT OF ADAM SMITH, HIS PREDECESSORS AND HIS CONTEMPORARIES

Maurice Allais

Adam Smith's work 'An Enquiry into the Nature and Causes of the Wealth of Nations' raises political economy to the level of the positive sciences, by the care he took never to base his reasoning other than on observation and experience ... If one were simply to jot down the number of truths that Smith established beyond doubt, the useful consequences he derived from the most firmly founded principles, the both shrewd and accurate insights revealed at every moment by his most accurately directed observations, the varied examples provided by his vast knowledge, one would fill a whole book.

> Jean-Baptiste Say (*Cours Complet d'Economie Politique Pratique*, 1829)

Economics, naturally complicated and therefore difficult, becomes easy when it is simplified, that is to say, when it is reduced to elementary ideas which, precisely defined, appear to be trivial as truths. Then this science develops under its own impetus. Its propositions generate one another, as if they were successively identical consequences and propositions; and the point at issue

demonstrates its solution so obviously that one discovers it almost
without having to reason.

Etienne Bonnot de Condillac
(Commerce and Government, 1776)

The purpose of this paper is to show, from the point of view of today's
economics, the fundamental concepts underlying the analyses of Adam
Smith, of his predecessors and of his contemporaries. It will show that
those concepts do correspond to an underlying model, which is actually
the one I have elaborated since 1943, the model of the economy of
markets,[1] founded on the general theory of surpluses. The paper consists
of three parts: Smith's underlying fundamental theoretical analysis in
the context of the economic thought of the eighteenth century; the
general theory of surpluses and the model of the economy of markets as
a formalization of Adam Smith's theoretical thought, together with that
of his predecessors and contemporaries; and the model of an economy
of markets versus the market economy model of the contemporary
literature.

SMITH'S UNDERLYING FUNDAMENTAL THEORETICAL ANALYSIS IN THE GENERAL CONTEXT OF ECONOMIC THOUGHT IN THE EIGHTEENTH CENTURY

For anybody who masters the modern sophistication of economics, it
is quite easy to detect the basic ideas and intuitions of the eighteenth
century, which, in a more or less explicit form, prefigured all the
developments which were to take place later. This remark is especially
valid in Smith's case. In *The Wealth of Nations* we can repeatedly
recognize the general concepts and bases of modern analysis. It is the
same for Smith's predecessors and contemporaries. It is true whether
we consider the concept of utility, the concept of 'surplus' realized in
the operations of exchange and production, or whether again we
consider the existence of an 'optimum' or a situation of a 'maximum'
produced by the interplay of competition. Everywhere in Smith we
discover analyses which were very promising, in that they really did
open the way to all the later developments.

This recognition may surprise us in two ways: first, in thus finding
the seeds of our fundamental knowledge present at the end of the
eighteenth century; second, at the inability of Smith, a man of vast
culture and of truly encyclopedic knowledge,[2] to confer a more precise

form on his analyses, especially in view of his wide knowledge of mathematics.

The Wealth of Nations

Almost immediately after the appearance of Smith's work, *An Inquiry into the Nature and Causes of the Wealth of Nations*,[3] all previous or contemporary economic writings were forgotten. This work, with its immense success and influence, was a guidebook for future generations of economists, and the starting point for most of their analyses.[4] *The Wealth of Nations* went through numerous English editions. There were several French and German translations, as well as others into Italian, Spanish, Dutch and Danish.[5]

For what reasons did Smith's work occupy this very exceptional place in the economic literature of the first part of the nineteenth century? There are at least three reasons. First, the work is enriched by concrete facts and the lessons of experience. Smith tackles his contemporaries' most pressing questions: the mercantile system, monetary organization, taxes, foreign trade, colonial administration, the role of the great commercial companies. The facts illustrate the arguments, and the arguments prompt reflection on the facts. Second, Smith's book constitutes a most remarkable synthesis of the economic thought of his age. Beyond a doubt, this synthesis powerfully contributed to its success. Finally, Smith's book brought to bear a stinging criticism of interventionism by governments, and provided a potent theoretical justification for the classical liberal ideology which largely dominated Europe in the following decades. The book became a veritable Bible.[6] Charles Rist stressed the point:

> Smith took all the important ideas of his predecessors in order to ground them in a more general system. By surpassing them, he made them useless, because he substituted for their fragmentary views a true social and economic philosophy. Those views thus acquire in his book an entirely new value. Instead of remaining isolated, they come to illustrate a general conception. In their turn, more light is cast on them. Smith, like almost all great writers, could borrow much from his predecessors or his contemporaries without losing his own originality. His work quotes or uses, without always acknowledging them, more than one hundred authors.[7]

This judgement is incontestable. Smith owes very much to his predecessors and contemporaries, notably to Hutcheson, Hume, Turgot and Quesnay,[8] whom he had often met personally. Though Schumpeter's general judgement may appear hard at first sight, one can only concur:

> But no matter what he actually learned or failed to learn from predecessors, the fact is that *The Wealth of Nations* does not contain a single analytic idea, principle or method that was entirely new in 1776.
>
> Those who extolled Adam Smith's work as an epoch-making, original achievement were, of course, thinking primarily of the policies he advocated – free trade, *laissez-faire*, colonial policy and so on. But, as should be clear by now and as will become clearer as we go along, this aspect would not lead to a different conclusion even if it were relevant to our subject.[9]

His judgement did not stop Schumpeter justly considering Smith as 'the most famous of all economists',[10] or from reaching this indisputable overall judgement: 'Though *The Wealth of Nations* contained no really novel ideas, ... it is a great performance all the same and fully deserves its success.'[11]

Still, Smith's exposition is not without its faults, some of them major. It is sometimes a little lacking in method, precision and clarity.[12] It contains many digressions, and it is certainly not didactic enough. The most important questions are in general dealt with incidentally and in connection with altogether subordinate questions. The best and perhaps most striking example of this is Smith's famous aphorism about 'the invisible hand', which is lost on a very lateral comment of Chapter 2 of Book Iv.[13, 14]

So great are his borrowings from his predecessors, that objectively Smith has no right to be considered the 'Founder of Political Economy'. One can only endorse the judgement made of him in France in the mid-nineteenth century by the *Dictionnaire de l'Economie Politique*: 'Adam Smith's name is the greatest in Political economy. He had the singular achievement of leaving an indelible mark on the world of ideas as clearly as on the world of facts.'[15]

The Wealth of Nations contains five books, on Labour, Capital, Economic Progress, the System of Political Economy, and on Public Finances. In its amplitude as in its general conception, the work can justly be considered as the first treatise of political economy.[16]

Smith's underlying fundamental theoretical thought

Without a doubt Smith's whole exposition rests on one fundamental guiding idea, namely that the free, decentralized action of economic agents in a system of competition and private property brings advantages for each of them. In Smith's own famous words, each one, moved by his selfish interest, is in reality led by an 'invisible hand' to satisfy the interests of all the others. In the light of our knowledge today and in modern language, what does that mean? What Smith's point of view actually implies is that the decentralized interplay of markets tends to bring the economy towards a situation of maximum efficiency at the frontier of the possible and the impossible. That is a theorem of convergence. At the limit, a situation of equilibrium in an economy of markets is a situation of maximum efficiency, and vice versa. There we have two theorems of equivalence. As a matter of fact, they are two asymptotic theorems.

It took more than two centuries for these three theorems to be proved. The proof rests fundamentally on three concepts: the concept of utility representing individual preferences; the concept of production function representing the operations of production; and the concept of surplus resulting either from exchange between two economic agents, or from the exchange on particular markets among several or among many economic agents.

The functioning of the economy rests on three elementary mechanisms and on one principle: each consumer seeks to maximize his index of preference; each producer seeks techniques of production likely to create surpluses of value; on each particular market (which may be an exchange between two agents, but equally may involve many participants) prices are fixed at a level such that each participant sees his situation improved and derives a surplus. The principle is that the realized surpluses are attributed to those who realize them. This is what may be called the principle of the private appropriation of surpluses.[17] The simultaneous interplay of these three mechanisms and the application of this principle constantly bring the economy towards a situation of maximum efficiency.

These are the guiding ideas which are always found, more or less explicitly, more or less clearly, more or less precisely, in the unfolding of Smith's work.

Smith as the forerunner of modern analysis

It is easy to illustrate Smith's underlying theoretical thought through quotations and I present some especially significant ones in my Appendix I (to be found at the end of this volume, see p. 166) but they could easily be multiplied. They show Smith to be a forerunner of modern analysis. Still, nowhere in *The Wealth of Nations* do we find a marshalling of the several fundamental principles which form its framework. The passage about 'the invisible hand' is justly famous. It prefigures the two theorems of equivalence and the theorem of convergence, but it does not amount to more than an entirely intuitive outline without any precise statement and without any real proof. Not till Edgeworth in 1881[18] and above all Pareto in 1906[19] were we given a real proof (though still only partial) of the two theorems of equivalence. As Pareto stressed, Walras was wrong to believe that he had proved the two theorems of equivalence. And he had only sketched a proof of the theorem of convergence with his theory of *tâtonnement*. Besides, as Edgeworth showed, his analysis is quite unrealistic, and indeed unacceptable.

Truth to tell, the three fundamental theorems only appear between the lines in Smith. We can only discover them because today we have precise knowledge of them, and even then we often have to look hard to find them.[20]   On the other hand, there is a central theme which dominates the whole of Smith's work with the greatest clarity: that economic freedom and the functioning of a decentralized economy are the necessary conditions for a prosperous economy and for economic development.

Smith's predecessors and contemporaries

As a matter of fact *The Wealth of Nations* ought not to be taken for a sudden miracle of human thought. When Smith wrote his work, he only presented, for the most part, a synthesis of the ideas of his time, ideas which in their essence were already accepted and widely diffused. The general conceptions and the positive knowledge which come together in *The Wealth of Nations* were already there. Indeed in all the economic writings from Boisguilbert to Turgot certain guiding ideas emerge:

- The idea that all economic phenomena are linked together, that they are interdependent.
- The idea that free competition is what makes production and exchange most advantageous for everyone.

- The idea that economic freedom is the condition of prosperity and growth.
- The idea that intervention by the state generally produces effects opposite to those which it claims to pursue.

Here we have the same ideas as those which underlie Smith's work.

There are other major ideas: the concept of utility, the concept of production function, the concept of surplus and the generation of surpluses, the intuitive concept of convergence in the economy, under the influence of multiple individual actions and reactions, towards a sort of collective optimum. But all these concepts are to be found, progressively elaborated, in Pierre de Boisguilbert (1646–1714), Richard Cantillon (1697–1734), David Hume (1711–76), François Quesnay (1694–1774), Robert Turgot (1727–81) and Etienne Bonnot de Condillac (1714–80). It is certain that authors such as Quesnay and Turgot profoundly influenced Smith.[21] Thus in Chapter 9 of Book IV of *The Wealth of Nations* he said of the physiocratic system:

> This system, with all its imperfections is, perhaps, the nearest approximation to the truth that has yet been published upon the subject of political economy, and is upon that account well worth the consideration of every man who wishes to examine with attention the principles of that very important science.[22]

Should we therefore value Smith any the less? Not at all, for he was able to avoid his predecessors' errors.

In many respects, for example, Quesnay's theory was a backward step in economic thought. To consider industry and commerce as 'sterile' activities was economically absurd. Smith's merit lies in his rejection of such a notion. As a general rule, he only retained what was fundamentally valid from the work of his predecessors and contemporaries.[23] Indeed, however much Smith borrowed from his predecessors and contemporaries, we can only endorse the judgement made of him by Charles Rist:

> His book still remains the most important document in one of the most important eras of economic thought. It is the happiest attempt to embrace in a single harmonious vision the infinite diversity of the world of economics ... To deal critically with Adam Smith would be to anticipate the history of economics in the nineteenth century. That is the highest praise one could bestow on him. The history of economic ideas for a hundred years hung, as it were, upon his book. Friend and foe alike took it as the

starting point for their own speculation; the former to develop, continue and correct it; the latter in bitter dispute with his main theories. All, by tacit consent, admitted that political economy began with him and that there was no point in going back further. It was, as his translator Garnier said, 'a complete revolution in the science'.[24]

On the generation of surpluses and on the existence of a spontaneous order generated by millions of independent actions, I have thought it useful to present in my Appendix I some very significant quotations from Smith, from his predecessors, and from his contemporaries (see p. 166).

Among all the works of Smith's contemporaries, there is one whose contribution to fundamental economic analysis is certainly outstanding, and who in this respect certainly surpasses Smith. This is Condillac, whose work, *Commerce and Government, considered in relation to one another*,[25] was published only a few weeks before *The Wealth of Nations*. Since these two works were written entirely independently, it is particularly significant to compare them. I thought it right therefore to present in the Appendix I (p. 170–3) some especially evocative quotations from Condillac which can usefully be placed side-by-side with those of Smith.

Condillac long remained an unrecognized author. The *Dictionnaire de l'Economie Politique* published in 1854 by Coquelin and Guillaumin is in general a remarkable work, yet it gives only a few paragraphs to the entry on Condillac.[26] The same is true of the *Dictionary of Political Economy* published by Ingris Palgrave in 1899.[27] Even Schumpeter could not see Condillac's contribution as fundamental, and devotes just a few lines to him. His general judgement is this:

> Condillac's work does not indeed quite merit the eulogies of W.S. Jevons, who called it 'original and profound', and of H.D. Macleod, who called it 'infinitely superior to Smith's'. The eulogies are amply accounted for by the enthusiasm of those two authors for what they believed to be an early formulation of their own theory of value. But there was nothing original about it and, considering all the predecessors on that path, we should wonder at Condillac's inefficient handling of it rather than at his sponsorship of it. Still, the book is a good if somewhat sketchy treatise on Economic Theory and Policy and much above the common run of its contemporaries.[28]

I think that Schumpeter, whose knowledge of economic literature was encyclopedic, read Condillac only very superficially.[29] If that is not so, I must conclude that he got him wrong. After all, mistakes are made, and will be made again, even by the greatest economists.

Our contemporaries have avoided Schumpeter's mistake. The *Encyclopedia of Social Sciences* (1968) devotes no less than two whole pages to a remarkable article on Condillac by Joseph J. Spengler.[30] *The New Palgrave* gives more than a page and a half to a very interesting article on Condillac by Peter Groenewegen.[31] Charles Gide rightly wrote:

> 'Commerce and Government, considered in relation to one another' is an admirable book, containing the seeds of the most modern theories. The unjust oblivion into which it has fallen is perhaps partly due to an awkward title which does not indicate its subject.... It is a true Treatise of Political Economy.... The enormous success of 'The Wealth of Nations' overshadowed the work of the French philosopher for a long time. Thus was Smith's theory to triumph, though inferior to Condillac's, and for many years thenceforward to provide the basis for the reflections of economists, in particular of British economists whose influence was preponderant during the first half of the nineteenth century.[32]

But if Condillac is definitely superior to Smith in theoretical analysis and logical systematization of ideas, Smith's work remains the more remarkable for the much greater amplitude of the subjects covered in it, for its abundance of ideas, and for its ability to fire the thoughts of so many readers, to stimulate their minds with different and even opposing views, and by the same token to hold the attention of economists of all schools of thought. In any event we can subscribe to Monjean's judgement in the *Dictionnaire d'Economie Politique* of 1854: 'Nobody before Smith had showed more clearsightedly and plainly the advantages of economic freedom, from the point of view of conciliation between the individual interest and the general market.'[33]

The several quotations given in my Appendix I, under similar headings in each section, show very clearly how identical Smith's fundamental ideas are to those of his predecessors and contemporaries. They doubtlessly also allow an appreciation of the clarity and pertinence of Condillac's thought.

The two central ideas of Smith's fundamental economic analysis

From an overall view of the underlying fundamental economic analysis in *The Wealth of Nations*, and generally in the literature of the eighteenth century, two major propositions emerge and assert themselves. The first proposition is that all operations of exchange and production have their origin in the search for the realization of surpluses, which through the interplay of the markets are distributed among all the participants. In the cases of both Smith and Condillac the unfolding of their ideas originates in this proposition, which is applied in each particular case. The second proposition which is only intuitive, but nevertheless asserts itself very strongly, is that the decentralized search for realizable surpluses, and their realization by millions of consumers and producers, constantly brings the economy towards a situation of coherent interdependence where a certain 'optimum' is realized. This is the proposition to which Smith's 'invisible hand' corresponds. These two propositions recur again more or less explicitly in all the authors of the nineteenth century, from Jean-Baptiste Say, a disciple of Smith, to Léon Walras.[34]

From the beginning of the seventeenth century to Walras, most analyses in economic literature rest on dynamic approaches concerned with causality, where the stress is placed essentially on the generation of surpluses. Though all the authors had the intuition to see that these chains of cause and effect brought the economy towards a situation felt to be optimal, none of them really tried to give a scientifically valid definition of it. Walras was the first to provide a definition of the situation to which the economy would tend, under constant structural conditions, as the outcome of a multiplicity of individual actions. This is a situation of general economic equilibrium.[35] Edgeworth was the first to define such a situation of equilibrium as a situation where every index of preference can be considered as a maximum, all the other indices of preference having given values.[36] Pareto – it remains unresolved whether independently or not – has given his name to this definition, considered as the definition of the situations of maximal efficiency, commonly called situations of Paretian optimum.[37]

At a conceptual level, it is necessary to distinguish between the concept of general economic equilibrium and the concept of maximum efficiency. Though the two theorems of equivalence are conducive to an identification of the situations of general economic equilibrium and the situations of maximum efficiency, we are in fact dealing with two different fundamental concepts. After Walras, economic analysis was devoted principally to the study of general economic equilibrium, that is to say, to the study of the frontier to which the economy in its development asymptotically tends. Analyses of the chain of cause and effect then passed down to a second level, even though they lay at the heart of all the previous analyses and are absolutely essential for a thorough analysis of economic reality.

In the second part of this paper I shall show how the general theory of surpluses, as I have elaborated it, allows us to represent all the chains of cause and effect studied by Smith, his predecessors, his contemporaries and his successors up until Walras. The analysis of the asymptotic situations of general economic equilibrium and of maximum efficiency is only a complementary analysis – certainly very important, but relatively secondary in the light of the concrete phenomena which constitute the reality, and which ought to represent in theory, the very foundation of economic analysis.

In the third part I shall also show that Walras's model of the market economy, which is usually considered in the literature, is entirely unrealistic, and that it is necessary to substitute for it the model of the economy of markets, which alone is capable of representing at the same time the chains of cause and effect in the real economy and the asymptotic situations of general economic equilibrium and of maximum efficiency.

THE GENERAL THEORY OF SURPLUSES AND THE MODEL OF AN ECONOMY OF MARKETS

This is presented as a formalization of the fundamental economic analysis of Adam Smith, his predecessors, his contemporaries and his followers up to Walras. As I have indicated, this analysis rests on two central ideas:

- The search for, achievement of, and the distribution of surpluses are the driving forces of the working of an economy of markets (*markets in the plural*).
- There exists indeed an order underlying the working of an economy of markets.

From this double point of view, the general theory of surpluses, as elaborated in my works since 1943, and the model of an economy of markets, on which it rests, allows us adequately to formalize the fundamental economic analysis underlying the work of Adam Smith and the works of his predecessors and contemporaries.[38]

Fundamental concepts and theorems of the general theory of surpluses

The concept of surplus

If economic agents engage in acts of exchange and production, it is because they thereby obtain certain benefits. For units of production these benefits in fact take the form of monetary gains. But for units of consumption the question is more complex. If I purchase a loaf of bread, this loaf has greater subjective value for me than the value which corresponds to the sum I give in payment. Similarly, and for the economy as a whole, transactions (and the corresponding productive operations) enable the economy, in the absence of external costs, to be placed in a preferable situation. In both cases, we are merely talking about propositions of a qualitative order. To give them a more precise form the concept of surplus, properly worked out, provides us with an operational definition of these advantages which in no way implies resort to the concept of cardinal utility, and is free of all consideration of prices, and of any hypothesis of continuity, derivability or convexity.

For the study of situations of economic equilibrium and maximum efficiency, and especially for the study of the dynamic evolution of the economy, the concept of surplus, appropriately defined, probably constitutes the most powerful. instrument of analysis in the entire theory of economics. It makes possible both the dynamic study of the evolution of the economy out of equilibrium and the study of equilibrium situations, and the analysis of conditions of maximum efficiency for the economy as a whole or for a particular sector of the economy, to be integrated in the same coherent whole. It also enables the foundations to be laid for the integration of money into theories of general economic equilibrium and of maximum efficiency.

Situations of maximum efficiency

A situation of maximum efficiency can be defined, following Pareto, as a situation in which it is impossible to improve the situation of some people without undermining that of others, i.e. to increase certain preference indices without decreasing others.

Distributable surplus

In 1943 I defined the distributable surplus relative to a given good and to a realizable modification of the economy which leaves all preference indexes unchanged, as the quantity of this good which can be released following this shift. The surplus considered here differs essentially from the concepts of consumer surplus as usually considered in the literature. The distributable surplus thus defined covers the whole economy, but this definition can be used for any group of agents.

Any exchange system, with the corresponding production operations it implies, is deemed advantageous when a distributable surplus is achieved and distributed, so that the preference index of any consumption unit concerned increases. If an exchange and production system is advantageous, there must be at least one system of prices which allows it, the prices used by each pair of agents being specific to them. The distribution of the realized surplus between agents is determined by the system of prices used in the exchanges between them.

Economic loss

I also defined in 1943 the loss for a given good which is associated with a given situation as the greatest quantity of this good which can be released in a transformation of the economy for which all the preference indexes remain unchanged. It is a well determined function of the preference indexes and of the disposable resources in the situation considered.

Two basic propositions

The reformulation of the general theory of equilibrium and maximum efficiency which is presented here rests essentially on two basic propositions. First, the necessary and sufficient condition for maximum efficiency is that the distributable surplus be negative or nil for any feasible modification of the economy. Second, the maximum value of distributable surplus in a given situation can be regarded as representing the loss associated with the situation considered. In fact, all the other concepts of surplus and loss which have hitherto been proposed in the literature run into major objections which only the concepts of distributable surplus and loss which I have just defined and which are analysed below entirely avoid.

41

Situations of stable economic equilibrium

In essence all economic operations of whatever type may be reduced to the search for, the achievement of, and the distribution of surpluses. Thus stable general economic equilibrium exists if, and only if, in the situation under consideration, there is no realizable surplus for any good. In such a situation the distributable surplus is zero or negative for all possible modifications of the economy compatible with its structural relations, and it is impossible to find a set of prices that would permit effective bilateral or multilateral exchanges (accompanied by the implied production operations) which are advantageous to all the agents concerned.

Equivalence of states of stable general equilibrium and states of maximum efficiency (equivalence theorems)

From the definitions of the situations of maximum efficiency and stable general economic equilibrium, it follows with the greatest generality and without any restrictive hypothesis of continuity, differentiability or convexity, that:

- Any state of stable general economic equilibrium is one of maximum efficiency (*first theorem of equivalence*).
- Any state of maximum efficiency is one of stable general economic equilibrium (*second theorem of equivalence*).

Since the essence of the economy is the pursuit, realization and allotment of distributable surpluses, there can be no stable general economic equilibrium if there is any distributable surplus. Every state of stable general economic equilibrium is therefore a state of maximum efficiency. Conversely, if there is maximum efficiency, there is no realizable surplus and, consequently, every state of maximum efficiency is a state of stable general economic equilibrium.

The set of states of maximum efficiency represents the boundary between the possible and the impossible. An immediate consequence of this property is that for any state of maximum efficiency the loss corresponding to any good is zero. It also follows that in such a situation the distributable surplus of any good is zero or negative for all possible modifications of the economy compatible with its structural relations. If a positive distributable surplus corresponds to a given modification of the economy, one can be certain that by suitably distributing this surplus, it will always be possible to act in such a way that in the new state of the economy which emerges from this modification and the distribution of this surplus, all the units of consumption will be in a preferable situation.

Integration of money into the analysis of economic equilibrium and maximum efficiency

The preceding definitions and theorems are extremely general and do not ascribe any special role to any good. However, in a complex economy, a particular good is used by all operators in their transactions. We will designate this good by the notation (U). It is in fact money, and it appears in all the preference functions and in all production functions. For this very reason, the theory of surpluses integrates money into the analysis of economic equilibrium and maximum efficiency.

The quantities of the good (U) which are used by units of consumption and by units of production can be considered as continuous variables. Once there exists a good (U) whose quantities are continuous variables appearing in *all* preference functions and *all* production functions, the condition of maximum efficiency for a determinate set of operators becomes simpler. Whereas in the general case the necessary and sufficient condition of maximum efficiency is that the maximum distributable surplus is nil for every good, it is now sufficient that this condition be fulfilled only for the good (U) used by all the operators.

The dynamic process of the economy: the decentralized search for surpluses and the model of an economy of markets

The logical inconsistencies and the unrealistic character of the model of the market economy (see pp. 45–54) led me in 1967 to replace it with a new model, that of the economy of markets (markets in the plural).

The model of the economy of markets

In their essence all economic operations, whatever they may be, can be basically reduced to the pursuit, realization and allotment of distributable surpluses. The corresponding model is that of the economy of markets.

In the model of the economy of markets the rules of behaviour of the economic agents are as follows. Every operator tries to find one or several other operators ready to accept a bilateral or multilateral exchange (accompanied by corresponding production decisions) which will release a surplus that can be shared out. In general, no exchange leads to general equilibrium of the economy, but every exchange brings it nearer. In contrast to the rules of behaviour of a market economy, the rules of behaviour of an economy of markets can *never* be at fault from the point of view of the theory of efficiency, for they always create an actually distributed surplus.

Theorem of convergence (third fundamental theorem)

Since, in the evolution of an economy of markets, surpluses are constantly being realized and allotted, the preference indexes of the consumption units are never decreasing, at the same time as some are increasing. This means that for a given structure, that is to say, for given psychology, resources and technical know-how, the working of an economy of markets tends to bring it nearer and nearer to a state of stable general economic equilibrium, and this state is a state of maximum efficiency. To any given initial situation whatsoever, assumed not to be a situation of equilibrium, there corresponds an infinite number of possible equilibrium situations, each corresponding to a particular path and each satisfying the general condition that no index of preference should take on a lower value than in the initial situation.

The economy of markets

Since the fundamental driving force of the economy and markets is the search for and realization of surpluses, a state of stable general equilibrium must be defined as one in which there is no possibility of generating any surplus whatsoever. A state of maximum efficiency remains defined as a situation in which any preference index can be considered as maximum for given values of all the other indexes.

The theory of the economy of markets shows how the achievement of a situation of maximum efficiency is made much easier by the decentralized search for all realizable surpluses and by the incentive resulting from their partial or total appropriation by the operators involved, and how this search cannot be effective without sufficient information about the opportunities for realizing surpluses. This theory highlights the conflict between the two points of view of ethics and efficiency since the private approximation of surpluses appears as a very useful, if not indispensable, driving force from the point of view of efficiency, whereas it may seem questionable from an ethical point of view, at least for some people. In fact the whole question is dominated by a very simple fact: one can share only what is produced; at all events, history contains no example of egalitarian societies which are efficient.

THE MODEL OF AN ECONOMY OF MARKETS VERSUS THE MARKET ECONOMY MODEL OF THE CONTEMPORARY LITERATURE

The tendencies of the contemporary literature

From Walras on, the literature became progressively – and unduly – concentrated on equilibrium analysis which, however interesting it might be, is less so than the analysis of the processes by which the economy tends at any time towards situations of equilibrium which in fact are never reached. Today there is a tendency to neglect the dynamic surpluses approach based on the consideration of value differences and in the name of so-called rigour it has been replaced by new theories. *A fortiori*, the general theory of surpluses which generalizes the classical analysis is simply ignored.

This development, which in reality, and despite the too-widely held belief to the contrary, represents an immense step backwards, basically stems from the domination of the literature by a totally unrealistic model, the market economy model, which rests on inadmissible hypotheses. In fact a short analysis of this model can help to shed much light on the approach presented of the general theory of surpluses and the economy of markets approach, which, rightly, underlay the whole economic thought of *The Wealth of Nations* and of economic literature of the eighteenth century in general.

Unreality of the market economy model of the contemporary literature

The market economy model

The model of the market economy on which, following Walras, nearly all the contemporary theories are based is grounded on two essential assumptions, not usually made explicit: the existence at every moment of a single set of prices for the whole economy, whether equilibrium obtains or not; and the transition from a non-equilibrium to an equilibrium situation through a system of exchange transactions (accompanied by the corresponding production decisions) accomplished simultaneously, once the system of equilibrium prices has been determined. It is assumed that at every moment and in any non-equilibrium situation a certain set of prices is announced. These prices being considered as given, each consumption unit maximizes its preference index and formulates the corresponding demands and supplies; each production unit maximizes its net income and formulates the corresponding demands and supplies. All the supplies and demands thus formulated, which correspond to the set of prices announced, are compared without a single exchange being realized. The price of any good whose demand exceeds its supply is assumed to rise and, conversely, the price of any good whose supply exceeds demand is assumed to drop. This produces a new set of prices. Then, still without any exchange being realized, new supplies and demands are formulated. A second set of prices is established, and the process continues until the announced set of prices actually equalizes the demand for and the supply of each commodity. This is the Walrasian process of *tâtonnement*.

For an initial situation characterized by a given distribution of resources among economic operators, the economic equilibrium of a market economy is essentially defined by three conditions: the preference index of every consumption unit is maximum, market prices being taken as given; the net income of each production unit is maximum, and positive or zero, market prices being taken as given; and for every good, supply is equal to demand at the market price. In the equilibrium situation, the value of every index of preference is greater than or equal to its initial value.

In reality, the first two principles do not hold generally in situations of maximum efficiency, and they can be non-valid.[40] The third principle of the equalization of supply and demand by the price, i.e. the exchange of all units using the same price system, is in no way a necessary condition for maximum efficiency, and can be in contradiction to the search for maximum efficiency. Since there is never a single set of prices for all operators in a situation which is not a state of equilibrium, the market economy model is totally unrealistic. Curiously enough, although, for instance, neither Edgeworth nor Pareto ever adopted this postulate as holding general value, the modern mathematical school places it as the foundation of its models.

The 'unicity' of prices and the equalization of demands and supplies through a single set of prices.

It is true that where quantities vary continuously (in the mathematical sense), and functions can be differentiated, the system of marginal prices in any situation of maximum efficiency is the same for all operators (equimarginal principle). But this condition is by no means a necessary feature of the dynamic evolution to a situation of maximum efficiency. Actually it does not follow from the conditions of equilibrium and maximum efficiency that in moving from the initial situation to the equilibrium situation it would be necessary that all units should be sold or bought at the same price (unicity of prices).[41] In reality, the condition of 'unicity' of prices is an ethical condition of equality of treatment which is not implied at all by the conditions of equilibrium and maximum efficiency. It may even be incompatible with the achievement of a situation of maximum efficiency.[42]

The hypothesis of general convexity

Although the theory of general economic equilibrium of a market economy was developed without difficulty, once the first-order conditions alone were examined, major problems arose in the study of the conditions of stability and in the attempt to secure rigorous analysis for the second-order conditions of the two theorems of equivalence. In order to dispense with these mathematical difficulties, and not because of any analysis of the data derived from introspection or from observation, many authors have assumed general convexity of the consumption units fields of choice and of the production units fields.

Indeed the two assumptions of general convexity of fields of choice and production actually play a key role in all demonstrations of the theories of equilibrium and maximum efficiency using the market economy model. In fact, it has been impossible until now to demonstrate with the set theory that, in the market economy, a state of equilibrium is equivalent to a state of maximum efficiency, and vice versa, without postulating the general convexity of fields of choice and production. However, the postulate of general convexity is formally contradicted both by introspective data on the fields of choice and by empirical study of the whole production sector. Economically the hypothesis of general convexity means that the marginal returns are never increasing. In fact this hypothesis implies absurd consequences: either the optimum size of the production units is nil and there is an infinity of production units for each good produced, or the optimum size and the number of production units remains indeterminate. It is, to say

47

the least, astonishing to see how many contemporary works use preference functions and production functions, and how few are devoted to a study of their real properties.

The abstract formalism of set theory

Over the past forty years, in economic research and even in teaching, there has been a steady trend towards the use of set theory and away from differential calculus to demonstrate the three fundamental theorems. However, as they rest on the market economy model and the hypothesis of general convexity, these theories suffer from serious weaknesses and internal inconsistencies from the standpoint of both logic and observed facts. In reality, their formal simplicity is obtained at a prohibitive cost. Essential concepts such as the generation of surpluses, economic loss and marginal equivalence, are no longer considered and have vanished totally from the analysis. As for the accepted assumption of continuity, the new theories are just as approximate and unrealistic as the theories based only on differential calculus, and they are actually incapable of coming to grips with the question of increasing returns or the fundamental problem of in-divisibility. By accepting the principle of general convexity, they lead to absurd results when applied to reality.

At any event, if we want to understand the real, what point is there in excluding differential calculus at the same time as continuity is accepted? It is absolutely unreasonable to proscribe the use of differential calculus in the name of formal rigour, and so have to rely on set theory alone. In fact, from a mathematical point of view, the future of economic theory rests on the *joint* use of differential calculus and set theory, wherever these two sectors of mathematics can yield essential results as simply and as rapidly as possible.

The economy of markets and the market economy

Table 3.1 compares the fundamental principles underlying the market economy model and the markets economy model analysed in the second part of this paper. Although the two models define situations of maximum efficiency in the same way, their definition of equilibrium is altogether different. The essential difference is that, in the latter, the exchanges leading to equilibrium take place successively at different prices and that, at any given moment, the price sets used by different operators are not necessarily the same. Whereas in the first model the

48

Table 3.1 Market economy and markets economy: fundamental principles underlying the two models and their implications

a) Assumptions and definitions

Market economy model	*Economy of markets model*
Assumptions	
(a) Transactions envisaged by operators are made in an undefined environment in which partners are not specified.	(a) Transactions are made between specific partners.
(b) The prices used by all operators are the same, whether general equilibrium obtains or not.	(b) The prices used are specific to every transaction.
(c) Supply and demand are virtual and do not result in actual exchanges as long as the condition that supply and demand be equal for all goods is not satisfied. The price of any good whose demand exceeds supply is assumed to rise, and conversely.	(c) Supply and demand result in actual exchanges if a surplus is realized.
(d) The transition from the initial situation to the final one is made in one single movement when and only when the set of prices implementing the overall equality of supply and demand for all goods has been found.	(d) Exchange transactions occur even though general equilibrium is not a consequence.
Definition of states of equilibrium	
Equilibrium exists if, under the set of prices considered, overall demand and supply are equal for each good.	Equilibrium exists if there is no realisable surplus for any good.

Definition of states of maximum efficiency

Maximum efficiency exists if every preference index is maximal for given values of the other indexes.

Fundamental theorems of equivalence and convergence

1. Every state of stable general economic equilibrium is a state of maximum efficiency.
2. Every state of maximum efficiency is a state of stable general economic equilibrium.
3. The working of an economy of markets leads to a state of stable general economic equilibrium and maximum efficiency.

Table 3.1 Continued

b) Approaches, criteria, proofs, and nature of the models

Market economy model	*Economy of markets model*
Approaches used	
Set theory	Set theory
● Assumptions of continuity and convexity for every consumption and production unit.	● No assumption at all.
Differential calculus	Differential calculus
● Assumptions of continuity and differentiability.	● Assumptions of continuity and differentiability.

Validity of the criteria for achieving a state of maximum efficiency

The two principles of	The dynamic principle of realizing surpluses is of absolutely general validity.
● maximization of the preference index of a consumption unit at given prices; and	
● maximization of income of a production unit at given prices;	
have no general validity and can be shown to lead to wrong decisions.	
The principle of equalization of demand and supply by a same price (non-discrimination principle) is in no way a necessary condition for maximum efficiency.	
The iterative price process which is considered to lead to a general equilibrium situation may not be convergent and may never bring about a state of maximum efficiency.	The process of the gradual realization of possible surpluses leads to a state of maximum efficiency in all cases.

Demonstration of the fundamental theorems of equivalence and convergence

Requires very restrictive and unrealistic conditions, whatever the approach.	Does not require any restrictive condition.

Nature of the model

The model applies only to an economy with perfect competition.	The model is general. It covers all cases from perfect competition to cartels and monopoly, whatever the economic system considered.

By stressing only the equilibrium price system, the model is purely static; only interdependences at equilibrium are considered.	By stressing the realization of surpluses, the model is essentially dynamic; it considers both causal sequences and the interdependence in the neighbourhood of the resulting general equilibrium.

---

final situation is determined totally by the initial situation, which correspondingly plays a privileged role without any real justification, in the second the final situation depends both on the initial situation and the path taken from it to the final situation. Whereas the market economy model postulates perfect competition and a large number, if not an infinity, of operators, the model of the economy of markets applies as well to cases of monopoly as to cases of competition.

Although in the market economy model the search for situations of general economic equilibrium is essentially focused on the determination of a particular system of prices, the model of the economy of markets centres all its analysis on the search for surpluses and their realization, and on the corresponding operations of exchange and arbitration (and on the production operations they imply). The specific prices used for each system of operations appear only as auxiliary parameters of relatively minor economic role; only the realized surpluses have real importance.

The evolutionary process of an economy of markets consists of a series of successive equilibria on partial markets. If the structure of the economy is assumed to remain the same over time and if its dynamic principles are observed, it will necessarily result in a state of stable general equilibrium which is also one of maximum efficiency, or at the very least very near to the set of the states of maximum efficiency. By its very nature, by emphasizing the realization of surpluses, the model of the economy of markets is essentially dynamic, whereas by stressing only the equilibrium price system, the model of the market economy is purely static. The model of the market economy only really takes into consideration the interdependence of economic phenomena in a situation of general economic equilibrium, whereas the model of an economy of markets focuses all its analysis on causal links, with the search for realizable surpluses and their realization constituting the fundamental and synthetic principle of the working of the whole economy. Interdependence in the neighbourhood of an equilibrium situation only appears as a consequence of this much more general process.

In fact the model of the economy of markets fundamentally corresponds to economic reality as it works in practice, whereas the model of the market economy is totally unrealistic. The theory of the markets model is in fact much simpler, for it makes it possible to demonstrate easily, without any restrictive hypothesis and in all cases, the tendency of the economy to approach a state of stable general equilibrium on the one hand, and on the other, the equivalence of states of stable general equilibrium and of maximum efficiency. The market economy model does give rise to considerable mathematical difficulties when an attempt is made to demonstrate the three fundamental theorems. Whether differential calculus or set theory is used, these theorems can be demonstrated only under extremely restrictive conditions, and the difficulties are, from an economic standpoint, completely artificial, for they arise solely from the unrealistic nature of the model used. Paradoxically, whereas these restrictive assumptions are totally unrealistic, most of the theoretical difficulties encountered disappear once they are discarded.

For the market economy approach to be considered satisfactory, conditions must be imposed which actually apply to a particular model and which are generally not fulfilled in reality, and for which, at all events, no rigorous justification can be found. Not only is the model of an economy of markets much more realistic than the model of a market economy, not only does it lend itself to much simpler and easier proofs, but these proofs can be made without being subject to any restrictive hypothesis of continuity, derivability or general convexity. In particular, they hold whether or not fields of choice and production are convex at all points, and there is no need to introduce any restrictive condition to demonstrate the stability of the general economic equilibrium. They do not even imply that in a situation of stable general equilibrium there is necessarily local convexity for each operator. Finally the simplicity of these proofs enables the basic reasons for a stable equilibrium to be seen easily, as well as the equivalence of states of stable general equilibrium and maximum efficiency.

The model of an economy of markets lends itself as readily to the analysis of the international economy as it does to that of national economies, and just as well to the analysis of eastern and Third World economies as to that of western economies. Once one realizes how utterly inadmissible, and indeed absolutely aberrant, is Walras's and his followers' model of the market economy, one conclusion is in any case unavoidable: the theories of general economic equilibrium and maximum efficiency, as they are still generally accepted and taught by the scientific 'establishment', must be radically overhauled, if not abandoned altogether. Another approach must be substituted for Walras's, and in fact, following Adam Smith, his predecessors and his contemporaries, the decentralized search for surpluses is really the only dynamic principle from which can be derived a realistic conception, both elaborate and fundamentally very simple, of the working of the economy.

The foundations of a realistic economic analysis

From the foregoing discussion a double conclusion emerges: fundamentally the approach of Adam Smith, of his predecessors and his contemporaries, i.e. the generation of surpluses approach, is essential to an understanding of the underlying nature of all economic phenomena; the general theory of surpluses allows us to represent adequately this approach in the most general case.

Important as the analysis of the conditions of general equilibrium and of maximum efficiency may be, the analysis of the dynamic processes which enable surpluses to be generated from a given situation is much more important. From this point of view the analyses by Adam Smith, his predecessors and his followers up to Walras appear much more realistic than the contributions which rest only upon the consideration of Walras's model of general economic equilibrium. In fact, what is really important is not so much the knowledge of the properties of a state of a maximum efficiency as the rules of the game which have to be applied for the real economy effectively to move nearer to a state of maximum efficiency.

The decentralized search for surpluses is truly the dynamic principle from which a thorough and yet very simple conception of the operation of the whole economy can be derived. Whereas in the market economy model the search for efficiency is essentially focused on the determination of a certain set of prices, the analysis of the economy of markets model is based on the search for potential surpluses and their realization. Not only is the economy of markets model much more realistic than the market economy model while lending itself to much simpler demonstrations, but these demonstrations are also not subordinated to any restrictive assumptions about continuity, differentiability of functions, or convexity. All of economic dynamics is brought back to a single principle: the minimization of loss for the economy as a whole.

The new theory of the economy of markets completely breaks with the current literature and essentially bases economic dynamics as a whole on the search for, the realization of, and the distribution of surpluses, in contrast to the current literature which bases it on the search for a system of equilibrium prices. The hypothesis of Walras's model of the existence at any one moment of a unique system of prices for all operators is completely rejected. With regard to the search for maximum efficiency situations, the economy of markets theory replaces the search for a certain system of prices, the same for all operators, with the search for a situation in which no surplus is realizable. The concept of prices is relegated to the background of the analysis and only plays a subsidiary role. It is the concept of surplus which plays the major role in the new formulation. Not only does this theory make possible a realistic representation of economic dynamics, disencumbered of all useless and arbitrary hypotheses, but it enables the real meaning of the working of the economy to be better understood, in its double aspect of management and distribution of income which it enables to be presented in an entirely different perspective.

By departing from the great tradition of the surpluses approach of Adam Smith, his predecessors and his contemporaries, and by adopting an unrealistic model with unrealistic assumptions, the contemporary theories, which are purely mathematical, have doomed themselves to sterility as regards the understanding of reality. Any model is necessarily an abstraction of reality. Obviously, no theory can represent all reality. But while abstraction is a necessity, the way it is used is not a matter of indifference.

The basic rule should be subordination to the data of observation and experience. Assumptions should not be chosen as a function of a theory; it is the theory that should be chosen so that its assumptions are in line with observed data. A theory should be selected not because of the aesthetic qualities of its mathematics and of its theorems, but as a function of a single criterion, analysis of and conformity to the facts. Any model that does not conform to reality either in its assumptions or in its results must be rejected as inappropriate, however aesthetically satisfying the mathematical reasoning used in the phase of logical deduction. For the economist, as for the physicist, the purpose is not to use mathematics as an end in itself, but primarily to grasp reality, and never to dissociate economic theory from its applications.

Today, complex theories are built on the model of the market economy and the postulate of general convexity, without their authors worrying about what relations the market economy model has, if any, to concrete reality and what fields of choice and production sets really are. Paradoxically, from the scientific point of view, infinitely more care has been lavished on the mathematical elaboration of models than on the discussion of their structure and assumptions as they relate to the analysis of facts. An immense flood of mathematics has relegated the discussion of essential assumptions to the background, and too many authors seem to be more preoccupied with the enunciation of theorems in pure mathematics than with analysing real facts. Nevertheless, as Pareto commented: 'Even from an exclusively theoretical standpoint the use of mathematics adds nothing to the rigour of proofs. If the premises are false, mathematically drawn deductions will be just as erroneous as those provided by ordinary logic.' Reality was the first concern of Adam Smith, of Turgot, of Condillac, and of so many other economists of the eighteenth century. We should never forget their example.

OVERVIEW

Today's tributes marking the bicentenary of Adam Smith's death show a double recognition. The first is a recognition of the essential part he played in the foundation of economic science by elaborating a vast synthesis of the positive knowledge of his time, and at the same time inspiring fruitful reflections of every sort. The second is a recognition of his role, no less essential, in the foundation of modern liberalism, in clarifying the fundamental advantages in the system of the economy of markets, in contrast to the general anti-economic consequences of all interventions by the state. Yet, in order to be recognised, Smith's work did not have to await our tributes to it. Contrary to the fears of his publishers in Scotland, in England and abroad, the market itself brought about its success, because it answered the need for a comprehensive presentation of the dominant ideas of his time, and for a justification of the system of a decentralized economy of markets. Perhaps Smith has been helped by events and by good luck. But if luck always has some part in every success, however great, equally there is never any great success without great merit.

The purpose of my paper has not been to present a comprehensive analysis of Smith's work. That would anyway have been an impossible task, and people other than myself are without doubt better qualified to do it. My purpose has been only to present and to analyse the underlying guiding principles in Smith's work, principles which were equally those of Turgot and of Condillac, and which indeed derive from two central ideas:

(i) The idea that all human economic actions are aimed at seeking, realizing and sharing surpluses.

(ii) The idea that all these actions do not cumulatively lead to chaos, but that, on the contrary, they lead to an underlying order by a process which Smith would immortalize in the phrase: 'the invisible hand'.

I have also shown that the general theory of surpluses and the model of the economy of markets, which since 1943 I have been elaborating from a critical analysis of all previous works in the literature, can represent, completely and validly, the underlying fundamental theoretical framework in the works of Smith, his predecessors and his contemporaries. I have completed this analysis by showing that the model of the market economy on which, since Walras, almost all the works of the last decades have rested, can in no way represent the approach, deducted from concrete reality, of Smith, his predecessors and his contemporaries, and that this model is totally unrealistic.

But I should not like, in this conclusion, to limit myself to the purpose of my paper. I should like finally to consider briefly two other prime aspects of Smith's work. The first is that Smith was above all preoccupied with the observation and analysis of facts. In our time, with its burgeoning of mathematical models as mere intellectual exercises quite divorced from reality, Smith's work takes on an exemplary value. It reminds us of what we should never forget, that submission to the data of experience is the golden rule for every scientific discipline. The second aspect is that Smith was not only a great economist, but equally a great scholar, constantly defending the essential idea that there is no economic development, no prosperous society, without economic freedom, and that it is only in a society founded on decentralized decision-making and on private property that men, all men, can flourish. Now that the collapse of the totalitarian economies of the east has shown, once again, the irreplaceable value of freedom in general, and of economic freedom in particular, Smith's defence of liberal ideas appears as a bequest of untold value.

NOTES

The appendices which accompany this chapter can be found in the Appendix at the end of this volume (p. 166).

1   See the second part of this chapter p. 39.

2   According to his biographers, Adam Smith, like Vilfredo Pareto later, had studied mathematics, physical science, ancient and modern literature, rhetoric, theology, logic, law, history, philosophy, ethics, metaphysics and the history of civilization. With equal facility he read Latin, Greek, French and Italian poets. He had not only literary talents, but

also those required for knowledge of the exact sciences. In his youth he showed a marked preference for the study of mathematics and physics. He knew their theories but more especially their history. His abilities are illustrated by his essays on the history of science, particularly by his commentaries on the 'History of Astronomy', of which Schumpeter remarked ((1954), *History of Economic Analysis*, New York: Oxford University Press, 182):

> Nobody, I venture to say, can have an adequate idea of Smith's intellectual stature who does not know these Essays. I also venture to say that, were it not for the undeniable fact, nobody would credit the author of the "Wealth of Nations" with the power to write them.

See especially, M. Monjean (1854) 'Smith (Adam)' *Dictionaire de l'Economie Politique*, II, Bruxelles: Meline, 683–90.; Courcelle-Seneuil (1888) 'Notice sur la Vie et l'Oeuvre d'Adam Smith', *Oeuvre choisies d'Adam Smith*, Paris: Guillaumin; Skinner (1987) 'Smith, Adam', 373–4).

3   During Smith's lifetime (1725–90), *The Wealth of Nations* ran through five editions in 1776, 1778, 1784, 1786 and 1789. The long index, which has since become familiar, appears only in the third edition of 1784. On the successive editions of *The Wealth of Nations* see the introduction of Edwin Cannan to his edition of 1904 (London: Methuen). See also Paul Gemähling (1933) 'Adam Smith' in *Les Grands Economistes*, Paris: Recueil Sirey, 93–6. In the following, citations to Smith refer to the very remarkable edition by Campbell and Skinner of 1976, beyond doubt the best (Oxford: Clarendon Press).

4   Even today Adam Smith's work is very often cited. Thus in the fourth edition of Samuelson's *Economics* (1948, London: McGraw-Hill) Smith's name is cited fifteen times, while J.S. Mill is only cited nine times, Alfred Marshall nine times, Pareto three and Walras just once.

5   On French translations, see Gemähling, op. cit., p. 95.

6   G.H. Bousquet is right to say:

> In certain respects the success of *The Wealth of Nations* recalls that of Marx's *Capital*. *The Wealth of Nations* was for classical economics what *Capital* was for socialism, a rallying point and a doctrinal manifesto. In other respects, the two books differ essentially. Smith was read and understood; Marx was hardly read by those who cite his authority, and not at all understood; Smith had disciples, Marx only worshippers; Smith's work was continued and developed by scientific minds, while Marx's was only expounded by theologians.

(1927), Essai sur l'Evolution de la Pensée Economique, Paris: Rivière, 58)

7   Charles Gide and Charles Rist (1926) *Histoire des Doctrines Economiques*, fifth edn, Paris: Recueil Sirey, 61.

8   Smith certainly owed much to Quesnay, to the point of wishing to make him the dedicatee of his work. It is not entirely clear why Quesnay's

death made Smith abandon the idea (on this point, see Monjean, op. cit., p. 686).

J.B. Say recalled hearing from Du Pont de Nemours how he had met Adam Smith in Parisian society, where all the most eminent personalities of the time gathered. By them he was regarded as a judicious and simple man, who still had to prove himself (J.B. Say (1928–29) *Cours Complet d'Economie Politique Pratique*, third edn, 1852, II, Paris: Guillaumin, 559. It is a matter of great regret that Adam Smith had his papers burned just before his death; they surely would have shown us the influence on his thought of the French school of economics.

A passage in a letter written by Turgot to Dr Price in 1778, two years after publication of the famous Scotsman's work, demonstrates what the former Intendant de Limoges thought of political economy among our neighbours:

> There is more enlightenment in France than you over there generally think and it will perhaps be easier than among you to lead the public to reasonable ideas.
>
> What makes me think so is your nation's infatuation with the absurd plan of subjugating America ... what makes me think so is the system of monopoly and exclusion favoured by all your political writers on commerce: I except Mr Adam Smith and old Tucker.
>
> G. Schelle (1914) *Introduction aux Oeuvres de Turgot*, vol. II, Paris: Alcan, 31)

9 Schumpeter (1954) *History of Economic Analysis*, New York: Oxford University Press, 184–5.
10 ibid., p. 181.
11 ibid., p. 185.
12 In his preface to the selected works of Adam Smith, Courcelle-Seneuil (1988, op. cit.) justly remarks that,

> The part of Adam Smith's account dealing with rent lacks thoughtfulness and clarity. In the long discussions on this matter which ensued, the two sides were equally able to appeal to the authority of the author of the *Inquiry into the Nature and Causes of the Wealth of Nations*.

Again, in his article on Adam Smith, Jacob Viner ((1968) *International Encyclopedia of the Social Sciences*, 14, New York) underlines the contradictions in his exposition of the link between value and labour (p. 327). On flaws in the composition of the book, see also the pertinent criticism by J.B. Say, a fervent admirer of Adam Smith, in *Traite d'Economie Politique* ((1819) Paris: Deterville, Calmann-Levy, 1972, lviii–lx).

13 One cannot help but compare the faults in exposition of Adam Smith's work with the technical clarity of a most remarkable but little known work by Condillac (1715–80), *Le Commerce et le Gouvernement* published in the same year of 1776 and dealing with the same subject as Adam Smith's (see Appendix pp. 170–2).

14   It is also worth stressing that Smith's work contains a very long index which, in volume 5 of the French translation by J.A. Roucher (1794) runs to 165 pages. In the edition by Campbell and Skinner this index runs to 62 closely printed pages. This was an innovation, one should note, in economic literature, but unfortunately it was not well done. It was happily completed in the edition of 1976 by Campbell and Skinner.

15   Monjean, op. cit.

16   In truth, the work could justly have been called 'Principles of Political Economy', but the title was doubtless avoided because it had been used in 1767 by James Steuart (see the introduction by Cannan (1950) to *The Wealth of Nations*). But the actual title 'An Inquiry into the Nature and Causes of the Wealth of Nations' probably made a greater contribution to the work's success.

17   Though the paternity of the term 'surplus' is generally attributed to Alfred Marshall, it was used by Adam Smith in the same sense. Thus he writes in chapter IX of Book IV (p. 671):

> According to this liberal and generous system, therefore, the most advantageous method in which a landed nation can raise up artificers, manufacturers and merchants of its own, is to grant the most perfect freedom of trade to the artificers, manufacturers and merchants of all other nations. It thereby raises the value of the *surplus* produce of its own land, of which the continual increase gradually establishes a fund which in due time necessarily raises up all the artificers, manufacturers and merchants whom it has occasion for.

Ten years, before, in 1766, Turgot had already used the word 'surplus' in the same sense, twice on the same page ('Réflexions sur la Formation et la Distribution des Richesses', *Oeuvres*, vol. II, Paris: Alcan, 571).

18   F.Y. Edgeworth (1881) *Mathematical Psychics*, London and New York: Kelley, 1953, 27; and M. Allais (1968) 'Pareto, Vilfredo: Contributions to Economics', *International Encyclopedia of the Social Sciences*, 11, New York, 404; and 1981, *La Theorie Générale des Surplus*, Grenoble: Presses Universitaires de Grenoble, 334.

19   V. Pareto (1909) *Manuel d'Economie Politique*, Paris: Giard et Brière. For a detailed commentary see Allais (1968) op. cit., pp. 403–6 and (1981) op. cit., pp. 323–4.

20   On the concept of general economic equilibrium P.A. Samuelson justly remarks 'Even in Adam Smith you can find the germ of the idea if you look hard enough' (Samuelson, op. cit., p. 614). The same observation might well be made of all the other contributions by Adam Smith to modern theory.

21   In volume II of the collected works of Turgot (pp. 31–2, n. 4), 1914, Gustave Schelle, the editor, thus recalls a comment by Morellet on Adam Smith's journey to France (1764–66):

> I got to know Smith during a journey he made to France in about 1762; he spoke our language very badly, but his *Theory of Moral Sentiments*, published in 1758, had given me a favourable impression

of his wisdom and depth. And truly, I still regard him today as one of the men who has made the fullest observations and analyses of all the questions he has dealt with.

M. Turgot, who like me loved metaphysics, thought a lot of his talent. We saw him several times. He was presented to Helvetius; we spoke of commercial theory, banking, public credit, and of several points in the great work he was planning, The Wealth of Nations. He made me a present of a very nice English wallet he had for his personal use, and which gave me good service for 20 years.

22 Adam Smith, *The Wealth of Nations*, II, p. 678.
23 In speaking of the physiocrats, J.B. Say writes, not without reason, in his *Traite d'Economie Politique*, (op. cit, I.411):

> The economists also claimed that Smith had obligations to them. But what do such claims mean? A man of genius has obligations to everyone around him, to the scattered notions that he has gathered up, to the errors that he has destroyed, even to the enemies who have attacked him, because everything helps to form his ideas; but then when he makes their conceptions his own, how vast they are, how useful to his contemporaries and to posterity. We should rather acknowledge what we owe him, and not reproach him for what he owes to others.

24 Gide and Rist, op. cit., pp. 119–20.
25 Though its content is analogous to that of *The Wealth of Nations*, Condillac's work is presented in a quite different way. It contains two parts, the first, a theoretical analysis (chapters I–XXX pp. 248–370), the other consisting of applications and illustrating the disastrous results of the obstacles of all kinds put in the way of economic freedom (chapters I–XIX, pp. 370–445). In Adam Smith, on the other hand, the applications are integrated into the theoretical analysis. Condillac indicated his eventual intention to publish a third part, but never did (see pp. 247 and 445).
26 H. Baudrillart (1853) 'Condillac (Etienne Bonnet de)' *Dictionnaire de l'Economie Politique*, I, Bruxelles: Meline, 502.
27 A. Courtois, Jr (1894) 'Condillac (Etienne Bonnot de)' in Inglis Palgrave (ed.) *Dictionary of Political Economy*, Second edn, 1987, I, 385.
28 Schumpeter (1954) op. cit., pp. 175–6.
29 While references to Adam Smith in the index of *History of Economic Analysis* runs to 60 lines (p. 1226), those to Condillac run to only two lines (p. 1212). This inquality of treatment really is quite unreasonable and unacceptable for anyone who has seriously read the works of both Adam Smith and Condillac.
30 Joseph J. Spengler (1968) 'Condillac, Etienne Bonnot de', *International Encyclopedia of the Social Sciences*, 3, New York, 211–13.
31 Here is the conclusion of the article 'Condillac, Etienne Bonnot de', by Peter Groenewegen (1987) *The New Palgrave, A Dictionary of Economics*, 1, London: Macmillan, 564–5):

> Condillac's economic work received a mixed reception from later

economists. J.B. Say (1805, p. XXXV) described it as an attempt 'to found a system of ... a subject which (the author) did not understand'.

Jevons (1871, p. XVIII) praised Condillac's 'charming philosophic work (because) in the first few chapters ... we meet perhaps the earliest distinct statement of the true connection between value and utility ...'

Macleod (1896, p. 73) described it as a 'remarkable work ... utterly neglected but in scientific spirit ... infinitely superior to Smith'.

Since then, it has remained neglected even though as 'a good if somewhat sketchy treatise on economic theory and policy (it was) much above the common run of its contemporaries' Schumpeter, 1954, pp. 175–76).

32 Gide and Rist, op. cit., pp. 55 and 86. It is an unfortunate fact that Condillac remains undervalued by most writers, and particularly by Anglo-Saxon writers. One is tempted to repeat here what Jevons wrote of Cournot in 1871 (*The Theory of Political Economy*, preface to 2nd edn, 28–9): 'One cannot blame English economists for their ignorance of Cournot's economic works when one sees that French writers do not know them any better.'

33 Monjean, op. cit., p. 688.

34 See Allais (1981) op. cit., pp. 295–332.

35 See M. Allais (1971) 'Les Théories de l'Equilibre Economique Général et de l'Efficacité Maximale', *Revue d'Economie Politique*, 3, May–June, 331–409, (1974a) 'Theories of General Economic Equilibrium and Maximum Efficiency' in G. Schwôdiauer (ed.) *Equilibrium and Disequilibrium in Economic Theory*, Dordreckt: D. Reidel Publishing Co.; and (1981) op. cit., pp. 336–9.

36 See note 18 above.

37 See note 19 above.

38 On the development of this second part of the chapter, see the Appendix pp. 175–87 at the end of this volume. See equally and principally M. Allais (1967) 'Les Conditions de l'Efficacité dans l'Economie' *Les Fondements du Calcul Economique*, I, Paris, Ecole Nationale Supérieure des Mines de Paris; (1971) op. cit.; (1974a) op. cit.; (1981) op. cit.; (1985) 'The Concepts of Surplus and Loss and the Reformulation of the Theories of Stable General Economic Equilibrium and Maximum Efficiency' in M. Baranzini and R. Scazzieri (eds) *Foundations and Dynamics of Economic Knowledge*, Oxford: Basil Blackwell; (1986) *The Equimarginal Principle. Meaning, Limits, and Generalisation*, Rivista Internazionale de Scienze Economiche e Commerciali, 1987; (1988) 'L'Economie des Infrastructures de Transport et les Fondements du calcul Economique', *Revue d'Economie Politique*, 2, 159–97.

39 On the following developments see principally Allais (1971) op. cit.; (1974a) op. cit.; (1986) op. cit.; and (1988) op. cit.

40 Allais (1971) op. cit., pp. 338–42 and notes 1–19, pp. 381–8; (1974a) op. cit., pp. 135–9 and notes 23–41, pp. 178–80.

41 See especially: Allais (1981) op. cit., pp. 346–52; (1986) op. cit.; Section IV, pp. 719–25, pp. 726–29; (1988) op. cit., pp. 162–4 and 176–8.

42 See especially: Allais (1986) op. cit., pp. 729–33; (1988) op. cit., pp. 178–83.

43 See especially: Allais (1986) op. cit., pp. 731–3 and (1988) op. cit., pp. 181–3.

44 On all points see Allais (1971) op. cit., pp. 359–64 and notes 1–21, pp. 395–7; (1974a) op. cit., pp. 153–7 and notes 155–75; (1986) op. cit., pp. 733–4; (1988) op. cit., pp. 183–4.

45 See Allais (1971) op. cit., pp. 372–3 and (1974a) op. cit., pp. 164–5.

46 On the following developments, see Allais (1971) op. cit., pp. 375–81; (1974a) op. cit., pp. 167–71; (1988) op. cit., pp. 190–2.

4

PUBLIC ECONOMIC POLICY: ADAM SMITH ON WHAT THE STATE AND OTHER PUBLIC INSTITUTIONS SHOULD AND SHOULD NOT DO

Richard Stone

INTRODUCTION

When I switched from law to economics in my third year as an undergraduate I knew very little about Adam Smith. I had heard that he was a great economic theorist, perhaps one of the greatest, but I was wholly ignorant of the breadth of the subjects – moral sciences and jurisprudence as well as economics – on which he lectured and wrote, and of his strong empirical streak, obtained from his wide reading in history, his travels in France and Switzerland, his discussions with Glasgow businessmen and his own acute powers of observation. I also did not realize that, despite his somewhat austere appearance, he seems to have been of an optimistic disposition and generally speaking to have been on the side of the underdog.

The question of efficiency was much considered by Smith. It was clear to him, as it had been to Petty more than a hundred years earlier, that the prosperity of a country depended on the goods and services available to its inhabitants rather than on the bullion and cash they possessed. This was the opposite of the mercantilist principle which led to policies designed to increase the inflow of precious metals by encouraging exports and discouraging imports as much as possible. He attached great importance to economic growth since with an increasing population it was only by this means that the great majority of the population, the workers, could hope to see better days. But how was this economic growth to be achieved?

63

Well, there was the division of labour, of course: we all know about the famous example of the pin factory with which he opens *The Wealth of Nations*. Then there was technical progress, which depended partly on engineers and scientists, or projectors as he terms them, and partly on the inventiveness of the workers themselves; a well-known case is that of the boy who devised a primitive form of valve gear which by dispensing with his labours gave him more time to play with his fellows. Then there was saving, needed to finance the new investment required by improved methods of production. And above all there was free trade.

Smith was passionately opposed to all laws and practices that tended to discourage production and increase prices. He strongly disapproved of the poor laws because, apart from the hardship they caused the poor, they impeded the mobility of labour. He viewed with suspicion all trade associations, both formal and informal: as he says, 'people of the same trade seldom meet together, even for merriment and diversion, but the conversation ends in a conspiracy against the public, or in some contrivance to raise prices' (I, x, c, 27). And he devotes chapter after chapter to exposing the harm caused by the combination of two things he particularly disliked: monopoly interests and government intervention in private economic arrangements. Government intervention was bad enough, since it was rarely based on an understnding of the country's economic needs, but it was far worse if it was promoted by powerful commercial interests intent not on the national welfare but on their own gains. Smith had very definite ideas about what the state should and should not do and it is these that I intend to discuss, starting with government expenditure and its finance.

GOVERNMENT EXPENDITURE

The first duty of the state is that of protecting the society from the violence and invasion of others; 'this means war' as Groucho Marx would have said. The second duty is that of protecting as far as possible every member of the society from the injustice and oppression of other members, which means establishing an efficient administration of justice. The third is that of promoting works and institutions which facilitate commerce. The fourth is encouraging the education of the people. And the fifth is supporting the dignity of the sovereign. Let us now see in more detail what Smith had to say about these duties.

Defence

In the early stages of society the state is involved in little expense. The important thing is that in times of war the fighters should show skill and dexterity in the use of arms. To help them to acquire this skill the state may find it necessary to provide an open space in which the citizens can practise their military exercises. But since the invention of firearms, skill has become less important, and regularity, order and prompt obedience to command are what matter. In other words, warfare has become more a social and less an individual activity. In these circumstances, the desired qualities can only be acquired by troops which are exercised in large bodies.

There are two main ways in which the state can provide for public defence. First, it can force the citizens of military age, perhaps with some exceptions, to practise military exercises in some measure and join the trade of a soldier to the trade they normally carry on; that is to say it may form a militia. Alternatively it may maintain a certain number of citizens in the constant practice of military exercises to the exclusion of any other trade; that is, it may form a standing army.

This issue had a contemporary relevance for Smith. *The Wealth of Nations* came out while the American War of Independence was going on. The English opposed the colonial militia with a standing army. But as Smith says, in a protracted war militias

> necessarily become in every respect a standing army, after they have passed a few campaigns in it. Should the war in America drag out through another campaign, the American militia may become in every respect a match for that standing army.... This distinction being well understood, the history of all ages, it will be found, bears testimony to the irresistible superiority which a well-regulated standing army has over every sort of militia. (V, 1, a, 27, 28)

Smith comments on the fact that warfare, and therefore defence, grows more and more expensive as society advances in civilization; this is largely due to the invention of firearms. But firearms are not such a bad thing after all: 'The invention of fire-arms, an invention which at first sight appears to be so pernicious, is certainly favourable both to the permanancy and to the extension of civilization', he says (V, i, a, 44). Pacifism was certainly no part of the moral equipment of the eighteenth-century intellectual. One wonders how Smith and his contemporaries would have reacted to the atom bomb.

Justice

The cost of providing justice varies greatly at different stages of society. In the early stages there is scarcely any property, and men can only injure one another in their persons by killing, wounding or defaming one another. In such circumstances potential offenders are generally restrained by prudential considerations without the intervention of the law. But with the growth of property, which is generally unequally divided, the position changes. The affluence of the rich excites the indignation of the poor, and the rich, surrounded at all times by unknown enemies, can only be protected by the powerful arm of the law. In Smith's words (V, i, b, 12), 'civil government, so far as it is instituted for the security of property, is in reality instituted for the defence of the rich against the poor, or of those who have some property against those who have none at all.'

In the Middle Ages the judicial authority of the sovereign was not a cause of expense but a source of revenue. A person who applied for justice was expected to bring a present; and he who applied with a large present was likely to get more than justice while he who applied with a small gift was likely to get something less. In the time of Henry II (1154–89) the instructions to the circuit judges show that they were sent round the country partly for the purpose of levying certain branches of the King's revenue. This inevitably led to abuses and eventually judges came to rely on fixed salaries.

Smith suggests that the cost of the administration of justice, including the salaries of judges, could be met from fees of court and adds, characteristically, that the diligence of the judges would be increased if they were not paid until after they had given their decision. He also would like to see a curb put on the extreme prolixity of legal language, traceable to the fact that all over Europe attorneys and clerks of court were paid according to the number of words they wrote, a practice which increased unduly the cost of legal proceedings (V, i, b, 22).

A final point is that the judicial and executive powers should not be united since, without being corrupt, a minister may sometimes imagine it necessary to sacrifice the interests of a private man to those of the state. Thus justice may be sacrificed to politics (V, i, b, 25).

Public works and institutions for facilitating commerce

Smith begins by considering public works such as roads, bridges, navigable canals and harbours and is anxious to ensure that as far as possible they should be self-financing and not burden the general revenue of society. This can be done by means of small tolls in the case of roads and of moderate port duties on tonnage in the case of harbours. Road tolls should be proportional to weight, at low rates for carts and wagons and higher rates for carriages of luxury, coaches, post-chaises, etc., so that the rich would be made to contribute to the relief of the poor by making cheaper the transport of heavy goods such as foodstuffs. But the temptation must be resisted of raising the charges for the purpose of contributing to general taxation; 'no raiding the road fund', as the cry was in the 1920s and 1930s.

Another question is who should maintain these works. In the case of a canal the toll or lock duty can be the property of an individual since if the canal were not kept in tolerable order it would be unusable and the owner would lose all the profit of the tolls. But the same cannot be said about a road: if it is neglected it does not become altogether impassable. For this reason the maintenance of roads should be put in the hands of commissioners or trustees answerable to the public authorities.

Works of local utility such as the lighting and paving of a town should be administered and financed by the local authority and not by the state. 'Were the streets of London', he says, 'to be lighted and paved at the expence of the treasury, is there any probability that they would be so well lighted and paved as they are at present, or even at so small an expense?' (V, i, d, 18)

The financing and running of public works and other institutions which are demonstrably of great commercial utility and require a large lay-out of capital can in some cases be entrusted to joint-stock companies. In general Smith was doubtful of the capacity of such companies to operate effectively; but where the money cannot be raised otherwise they have their use, provided the operations can be reduced to a routine. In his opinion the only activities which meet these conditions are banking, insurance, making and maintaining canals and supplying towns with water.

In short, wherever self-interest can be relied on to ensure efficiency, that is, where the consumer has a choice, large undertakings can be left in private hands. Where the consumer has no alternative, then the state must step in.

Education

Smith did not have a high opinion of the educational arrangements of his day. Indeed, considering his successful early career as a university teacher, his views on higher education are curiously negative.

He begins his discussion by considering how education should be paid for and what would stimulate the diligence of the teachers. His preference is for fees from the pupils, which as a stimulus add to emulation and to the reputation which can be gained by teaching well. Endowments may be useful but they should not be too large or teachers come to rely on them and lose all incentive to teach well. He is opposed to universities which pay salaries and do not allow the teachers to receive fees. Smith spent the years 1740–6 at Balliol after his university studies at Glasgow. His comment on this was that 'in the university of Oxford, the greater part of the publick professors have, for these many years, given up altogether even the pretence of teaching' (V, i, f, 8).'

So much for the case where the authority is vested in the institution. But things are likely to be even worse if the authority is vested outside the institution, say in the bishop or the lord-lieutenant of the county, as was often the case with grammar schools. The personage concerned can enforce a pretence at teaching but his supervision is ignorant and capricious, and the quality required from the teacher is not diligence but obsequiousness.

Schools and universities, Smith maintains, are not a good preparation for the real business of life. Universities, though, are better than nothing since without them there are subjects that could not be learnt anywhere; and they have excellent libraries, so that time there need not be entirely wasted. He has no opinion whatever of the educational value of the Grand Tour as a substitute for university. The only good that he can see in it is that 'a father delivers himself, at least for some time, from so disagreeable an object as that of a son unemployed, neglected and going to ruin before his eyes' (V, i, f, 36). This is Smith at his most dismal on the subject of upbringing. It can hardly have been true of the travels of the young Duke of Buccleuch to France and Switzerland with Smith as his tutor.

In spite of the inefficiency of private institutions Smith does not contemplate intervention by the state in secondary or higher education; but he thinks that something should be done for the children of the common people. He recognizes that by the division of labour the work of the great body of the people comes to be confined to a very few simple operations so that in the end the individual 'becomes as stupid and ignorant as it is possible for a human creature to become' (V, i, f, 50). To counteract this he advocates little schools where children could be taught at a cost so small that even the common labourer could afford it. The state might make a contribution to the pay of the master, but not too much or he would soon learn to neglect his business. The children would be taught to read, write and account. And if instead of a smattering of Latin, which can scarcely ever be of any use to them, they were taught the elements of geometry and mechanics, these would be useful in almost any trade. It might even be a good idea for employers to require a competence in these most essential parts of education.

Smith continues

> The more they are instructed, the less liable they are to the delusions of enthusiasm and superstition.... An instructed and intelligent people besides are always more decent and orderly than an ignorant and stupid one. ... They are more disposed to examine, and more capable of seeing through, the interested complaints of faction and sedition, and they are, upon that account, less apt to be misled into any wanton or unneccessary opposition to the measures of government. (V, i, f, 61)

As I said at the beginning, Smith was an optimist.

Supporting the dignity of the sovereign

This is taken for granted and Smith does not waste many words on it. In an opulent and improved society where all classes are daily growing more expensive in their houses, furniture and everything else, we cannot expect the sovereign to prove the exception to the rule. He too, therefore, becomes more expensive and 'we naturally expect more splendour in the court of a king, than in the mansion house of a doge or burgomaster' (V, i, h, 3). Thus speaks the loyal subject and 'regular guy'.

GOVERNMENT FINANCE

The finance needed to defray goverment expenditures may be obtained from three sources. The first is taxation; the second, which Smith calls 'sources belonging to the sovereign or commonwealth', is the income arising from Crown lands and from commercial enterprises run by the state; and the third is borrowing.

Smith opens his discussion of taxation by laying down four maxims (V, ii, b, 3–6).

(i) 'The subjects of every state ought to contribute towards the support of the government, as nearly as possible, in proportion to their respective abilities, that is, in proportion to the revenue which they respectively enjoy under the protection of the state.'

(ii) 'The tax which each individual is bound to pay ought to be certain, and not arbitrary. The time of payment, the manner of payment, the quantity to be paid, ought all to be clear and plain to the contributor, and to every other person.'

(iii) 'Every tax ought to be levied at the time and in the manner in which it is most likely to be convenient for the contributor to pay it.'

(iv) 'Every tax ought to be so contrived as both to take out and to keep out of the pockets of the people as little as possible, over and above what it brings into the publick treasury of the state.'

Smith does not claim originality for these maxims, which he says have recommended themselves more or less to the attention of all nations. He does not include among them the concept of progressiveness, though he remarks that 'it is no bad thing if the rich man contributes a larger share than the poor man to the expenses of the state.' His concept of fair taxation is simply that everyone should contribute the same proportion of his income. This is essentially the same idea as that put forward by Petty a hundred years earlier, except that Petty proposed a common proportion of capital, human as well as physical, and in *Verbum Sapienti* gave an example of how £1 million might be raised in this way. A little later, in 1695, another political arithmetician, Gregory King, did allow for progression: his scheme for raising £1 million is based on income tax, and in it the tax goes up threefold every time the income doubles, because, as he says, 'it may be better spared'. The poll taxes in the late seventeenth century also attempted to introduce progression in a rough way; for instance peers paid, according to rank, enormously more than the common man, and shareholders in some of the major trading companies were separately assessed.

I have always thought it a pity that Smith had little faith in political arithmetic (IV, v, b, 30). He had ideas about equity but they were less precise and perhaps for this very reason less liberal than those of his predecessors in the seventeenth century. Let us now see what he thought about the fiscal arrangements of his day.

Direct taxes

Smith considers four types of direct tax: taxes on rent, taxes on profits, taxes on wages, and the poll tax.

Taxes on the rent of land may either vary with the current rent and thus rise or fall with the improvement or decline of the property; or they may be fixed according to the rent obtaining at a given date, a practice which with time inevitably leads to inequalities and even absurdities (V, ii, c). Nevertheless this was the practice followed in Britain, where land taxes were based on assessments made in the reign of William and Mary, some seventy or more years earlier; in nearly all cases rents had risen since that time and so the constancy of the valuation had been advantageous to the landlord and injurious to the state. An alternative is to levy taxes not on the rent of the land but on its produce, in which case the tax is advanced by the tenant but claimed back from the landlord. In general Smith approves of land taxes but thinks that landowners who carry out improvements should enjoy a measure of exemption.

Taxes on the rent of houses are not easy to assess because house rent has two components which do not stand in a uniform ratio to each other (V, ii, e). The first is the rent of the house itself, which is equivalent to the ordinary profit of building and is regulated by the ordinary interest of money. The second is ground rent, which tends to be low in the country and higher in towns, particularly in the fashionable quarters of the capital. Thus a tax on house rents is likely to fall heaviest on the rich, no unreasonable thing in Smith's opinion.

Given the difficulty of ascertaining with any exactness the real rent of houses, various substitutes had been adopted which were thought to bear some proportion to the rent. The first tax of this kind was hearth money, in which a tax of two shillings was laid on every hearth. But this was very unpopular because it involved 'the odious visit of the tax-gatherer' and it was abolished at the beginning of the reign of William and Mary as 'grievous to the People'. It was later replaced by the so-called window tax, the idea being that the taxman need not enter the house to count the windows. The basic rate was two shillings for every inhabited house; a house with ten to twenty windows paid four shillings more, one with twenty to thirty paid 10 shillings and one with thirty and over paid £1 (V, ii, e, 18).

Smith did not much like window taxes. His main objection was that they offend against his first maxim, indeed they are regressive: a house that rents for £10 in a country town may sometimes have more windows than one which rents for £500 in London. Another objection is that they might be expected to lower rents, though he adds that in his own time the increase in the demand for houses 'has raised the rents more than the window-tax could sink them; one of the many proofs of the great prosperity of the country, and of the increasing revenue of its inhabitants' (V, ii, e, 20).

As regards the taxation of profits Smith has considerable misgivings. He divides profit into two parts, one which repays the interest on the capital invested and one which is net gain. 'This latter part of profit', he says 'is evidently a subject not taxable directly' (V, ii, f, 2). In most cases it is not more than a very moderate compensation for the risk and trouble of employing the stock, which the employer must have otherwise he will turn his capital to other uses. I find it difficult to follow this argument, since if all profits were taxed there would be little point in a shift of investment; some temporary advantage might be obtained from moving into a less competitive trade but this would soon drive down the profit of it, as Smith is constantly reminding us.

Whatever may be the position in theory, Smith tells us that attempts at taxing profits do not work well in practice. 'If', he says, 'most of the lands of England are not rated to the land-tax at half their actual value, the greater part of the stock is scarce rated, perhaps, at one fiftieth part of its actual value' (V, ii, f, 8). This is tax evasion on a pretty large scale.

Sometimes taxes are laid on the profits of particular branches of trade. There was an idea for a uniform tax on shops, but this was given up as it would have been much to the advantage of large shops which as soon as they had got rid of their small competitors would have found themselves in a monopoly position.

Smith's attitude to profits is somewhat contradictory. On the one hand profits are the main source of saving, since in general wage-earners are too poor and landowners too profligate to contribute much; and saving is the source of investment which makes technical progress possible. On the other hand profit-makers are less than honest. 'Our merchants', he says in one place, 'complain that the high price of labour is the cause of our manufacturers being undersold abroad; they are silent on their own profits.' 'The rise of wages', he says elsewhere, 'operates like simple interest. The rise of profits operates like compound interest. Our merchants and master manufacturers are silent with regard to the pernicious effect of their gains' (I, ix, 24). Why, then, did he not think it right that profit-makers should pay tax 'in proportion to their respective abilities', according to his first maxim of taxation?

Wages should not be taxed. A man living on ten shillings a week has no money to spare, so if a tax is laid on him his wage must be increased proportionately; this increase will be advanced by his employer and it, together with the profit on it, will ultimately be paid by the consumer. Nor should the earnings of 'ingenious artists and men of liberal professions' be taxed; if they are, 'the professions will be deserted unless their recompense is raised by somewhat more than the tax.' Michelangelo would have been rather surprised to hear the matter put in this way.

On the other hand there is no harm in taxing the emoluments of 'persons in office'. They are not regulated by competition but by personal favour and are generally regarded with dislike. For instance, when the land tax was four shillings in the pound it was a popular move to lay a tax of five shillings and sixpence in the pound on official salaries which exceeded £100.

As for poll taxes, Smith has no patience with them. If they are made to depend on a man's fortune, which changes the whole time, they are arbitrary unless an intolerable inquisition is made at least once a year. If on the other hand they depend on rank they are very unequal since people of the same rank may have very different fortunes. They are indiscriminate and oppressive, especially for the ordinary working man. In short they are 'improper taxes', typical of countries where 'the ease, comfort and security of the inferior ranks of the people is little attended to' (V, ii, j, 9).

This is a very condensed version of what Smith has to say about direct taxes. Three principles emerge from it. Taxes which cannot be assessed fairly, such as the window tax and the poll tax, are iniquitous. Taxes which discourage production or lead to price increases, such as taxes on profits and on wages, are unwise. The only taxes which are justified are those laid on the unproductive members of society such as people in official positions and landowners who do nothing but collect rent from their tenants. He even sympathizes with the Irish idea of imposing a tax on absentee landlords, though he concludes that it is not practicable.

Indirect taxes

Taxes on expenditure arise out of the difficulty of taxing income directly and proportionably. Smith divides consumable commodities into necessaries and luxuries (V, ii, k, 2). Luxuries can be taxed but necessaries should not be because they call forth a rise in wages and consequently a rise in prices. Necessaries are not only those commodities which are indispensable to support life but are also whatever the custom of the country requires even the lowest ranks of society to possess. thus in

England men are expected to possess a linen shirt and both men and women are expected to possess leather shoes. The existing tax on leather should be abolished and so should those levied on salt, soap and candles.

Beer, though not strictly a necessary, is an important part of an Englishman's diet, and excise duties on drink always get special attention from English writers on taxation. Smith points out that if the common man wanted a drink he had to buy it in an alehouse, where it was subject to duty. But in the country it was the usual practice among all the rich and many of the well-to-do to brew their own beer, and no duties were levied on home-brewing to avoid families being troubled with the odious visits of the tax-gatherer. As a consequence the rich got their drink cheaper than the poor. He demonstrates that if the malt duty were tripled and all other duties on beer and ale were done away with, the tax burden would be more fairly distributed and the tax yield about 10 per cent higher than under the existing system.

Fuel is a necessity not only for the private consumer but also for industry, and so manufacturies were largely confined to the coal counties. Much as Smith disapproved of subsidies – or bounties as they were called – he thinks a case could be made for subsidizing the transport of coal from those parts of the country in which it is mined to those where it is needed. In fact quite a high duty was imposed on coal carried coastwise though not on coal carried by road, river or canal. Thus the tax system may have a considerable influence on the location of industries.

Such cases were rare, however; in Great Britain, Smith remarks, inland trade is almost perfectly free. This freedom is perhaps one of the principal causes of the prosperity of the country and he would like to see it extended to imports. Not that he wanted to do away with customs duties altogether. He accepted revenue duties since there was no less reason to tax imports than to tax domestic produce. The duties he objected to were protective duties, which inevitably raise prices and stimulate smuggling. As to export bounties, they simply mean subsidizing the foreign buyer at the expense of the domestic taxpayer.

Another point stressed by Smith is ease of payment. Taxes on perishables are relatively painless, being advanced by the dealer and then included in the price. Taxes on expensive durables, which are high and might put off the potential buyer, would be less discouraging if they could be paid by instalments.

Again, three principles emerge from all this. Indirect taxes must not throw an undue burden on the common man. They must not hinder the free circulation of commodities whether domestic or foreign. And they must not be so high or so inconvenient to pay as to discourage buyers and thus defeat their own purpose.

Taxes on the transfer of property

These were taxes on capital, of which Smith did not approve. Where the possession of property does not change hands, he says, taxes on it are never intended to take away any part of its capital value but only some part of the revenue arising from it. Where property changes hands by legacies, gifts *inter vivos* or sale, taxes have frequently been imposed which take away some part of the capital value.

These taxes are levied by means of stamp duties or duties of registration. Both these methods of taxation were in Smith's day of very modern invention. But, he says

> In the course of little more than a century ... stamp duties have, in Europe become almost universal, and duties upon registration extremely common. There is no art which one government sooner learns from another than of draining money from the pockets of the people. (V, ii, h, 12)

'Sources belonging to the sovereign or commonwealth'

These will usually take the form of stock or land. Crown lands, in Smith's opinion, do not yield a quarter of the rent which could be obtained if they were in private hands. If they were sold and the proceeds used to reduce the national debt there would be both an immediate and a future gain, since the interest on the proceeds of the sale would exceed the present value of the produce and the increase in productivity would increase future population and tax yields.

There are also mercantile projects to be considered. A post office is profitable and seems suitable for every sort of government. Small republics have benefited from shops: thus Hamburg has a public wine cellar, an apothecary's shop and even a pawn shop which yields a revenue of over £30,000 a year. The Canton of Berne gains considerably by lending abroad. A public bank has provided profit for Hamburg, Venice and Amsterdam but Smith does not recommend it for England whose government 'whatever may be its virtues, has never been famous for good economy' (V, ii, a, 4).

The public debt

This was a very sore subject with Smith. What alarmed him was not wartime borrowing, of which he saw the necessity, but peacetime waste. As he says,

> The want of parsimony in time of peace imposes the necessity of contracting debt in time of war [V, iii, 4]. . . . In Great Britain, from the time we had first recourse to the ruinous expedient of perpetual funding, the reduction of the publick debt in time of peace has never borne any proportion to its accumulation in time of war. (V, iii, 41)

The requirements in wartime are usually some three or four times the normal expenditure in peacetime. It is impossible all of a sudden to raise taxes to this extent and even if it could be done there would be a delay between the immediate need for money and the gradual returns from the new taxes. The moneyed man gains by lending to the government. The state knows this and is glad to dispense with the duty of saving. The man in the street, far away from the scene of war, enjoys the amusement of reading in the newspapers about the exploits of his fleets and armies and does not worry too much how they are financed.

And so the bad habit of public borrowing becomes ingrained. In 1691, during the War of the League of Augsburg, the national debt was £3.1 million; by 1776 it had reached £131.2 million. There had been some wars in between, but also periods of peace. Even allowing for some depreciation in the value of money the figure seemed enormous. What would Smith say if he saw its present size?

THE GOVERNMENT ACCOUNTS IN 1776

I shall conclude this summary by showing the order of magnitude of the revenue from different taxes, the net borrowing and the amount of public expenditure on different items in Smith's day. Figures for 1776 are given in Table 4.1.

These figures all come from Brian Mitchell's admirable *Abstract of Historical Statistics* which in turn is based as far as my table is concerned on official publications appearing in the last century. I have left the original terminology alone and hope it is not too obscure. The table shows that indirect taxes contribute to revenue far more than direct ones, and that the military establishment and the debt charges largely incurred on its account form the bulk of the expenditure. I should add that in my table, in order to simplify matters, net

Table 4.1 Net public income, borrowing and expenditure of Great Britain, 1776 (£ millions)

Customs	2.7	Army	4.2
Excise	5.4	Navy	2.7
Stamps	0.4	Ordnance	0.5
Post office	0.2	Debt charges	
Land and assessed taxes	1.9	funded	4.0
		terminable annuities	0.4
Net income	10.6	unfunded	0.2
		Civil list	0.8
Net borrowing	(3.4)	Other	(1.2)
Net expenditure	14.0		
		Net expenditure	14.0

borrowing is obtained as a residual. Mitchell gives a direct estimate of £3.1 million.

MONOPOLIES

Public expenditure and its finance, whether well or badly managed, are the legitimate concern of the state and this is a principle which Smith, not being an anarchist, would not have dreamt of disputing. But there is an aspect of government policy which he considered both illegitimate and harmful, and this is the establishment and encouragement of private monopolies.

The practice whereby the Crown issued letters patent conferring on the recipients, on payment of an adequate sum, the exclusive right of dealing in a particular commodity or following a particular trade went back many centuries. Under the Tudors monopolies came to be a serious abuse; for instance at one stage the price of monopolized salt rose from 16 to 180 pence a bushel, an increase of more than tenfold. On his accession James I suspended all existing monopolies but before the end of his reign they were being issued as freely as they had been by his predecessors. Finally in 1624 a bill passed both houses of parliament in which all monopolies were declared illegal with two exceptions: inventions were protected for twenty-one years and great companies trading abroad were exempted. Town and city trade corporations were not considered, although they too were monopolies in the sense that no inhabitant of the town could exercise the incorporated trade without first obtaining the freedom of the corporation.

Foreign trade was mainly carried on either by regulated companies, in which each member traded on his own stock at his own risk, or by joint-stock companies in which profits and losses were shared in proportion to the capital contributed by each member. Either type of company might or might not have exclusive privileges which entitled them to keep out of their territory all independent merchants, the so-called inter-lopers. In general Smith thought large companies cumbersome and inef-ficient, but what he really objected to were their privileges, which not only prevented competition but often were stretched to include func-tions which properly belonged to the state.

In *The Wealth of Nations* he mentions five regulated companies for foreign trade, namely the Hamburgh Company, the Russia Company, the Eastland Company (which traded in the Baltic), the Turkey Company and the Africa Company (V, ii, e, 8). Though essentially engaged in trade, the Turkey Company contributed to maintain an ambassador and two or three consuls 'who', as Smith says, 'lile other public ministers, ought to be maintained altogether by the state, and the trade laid open to all his majesty's subjects' (V, i, e, 10). As to the Africa Company, when it was established in 1750 the merchants were expressly charged with main-taining British forts and garrisons between Cape Blanc and the Cape of Good Hope. The arrangements did not work out well, however, and many of the installations were eventually taken over by the state. The Hamburgh, Eastland and Russia companies were much less powerful but, says Smith, 'though such companies may not, in the present times, be very oppressive, they are certainly altogether useless. To be merely useless, indeed, is perhaps the highest eulogy which can ever justly be bestowed upon a regulated company' (V, i, e, 9).

Joint-stock companies, being more tightly knit, were more of a menace. The most famous example is the East India Company. Smith gives a circumstantial account of its history and has not words strong enough to expose its misdeeds. The original East India Company was established in 1600 as a regulated company by an exclusive charter from Queen Elizabeth; this was not confirmed by parliament, and was there-fore of doubtful validity. In 1612 the members united into a joint-stock company but by the end of the century, in consequence of their dubious charter, they found themselves nearly driven out of business by inter-lopers. In 1698 a deal was struck with parliament: in exchange for a loan of £2 million which they advanced to the government at an interest of 8 per cent, a new exclusive charter was granted for the formation of a new company, though the old company was allowed to continue trading until 1701. A somewhat confused situation now arose which was finally cleared up in 1711, when a single joint-stock company with sole exclusive rights was established.

In the course of the eighteenth century the company made further loans to the government and enormously extended its commercial activities. This was done at very great cost, however. The company became involved in an endless succession of wars with its French rivals in Pondicherry and with the Indian rulers who, having entered into what they at first thought profitable commercial deals with the company, gradually found their authority over their subjects undermined and their foreign policies interfered with by an organization which at times did not even respect its financial obligations.

Thus an institution that had begun as a trading company took over the functions of government, with disastrous results. On the financial side, in spite of large profits, the company's debts in 1773 were larger than ever and it had recourse to the state for assistance; the same happened in 1784 (V, i, e, 26). On the economic side its policy was both shortsighted and dishonest. It discouraged production by paying very low prices to the native producers while charging very high prices to its customers in England. It destroyed whole crops of valuable produce such as spices – a monstrous practice to which the Dutch East India Company was also addicted – in order to push resale prices even higher. Furthermore, the servants of the company carried on a brisk inland trade on their own account, amassing great fortunes of which neither the shareholders nor the Treasury back in England ever saw a penny. In Smith's own words,

> the monopoly of the company can tend only to stunt the natural growth of that part of the surplus produce which, in the case of free trade, would be exported to Europe. That of the servants tends to stunt the natural growth of every part of the produce in which they choose to deal. (IV, vii, c, 105)

Smith compares the attitudes to government of a monarch and of a company of merchants. The former, he says, will want to see the quantity and value of the produce as large as possible, thereby maximizing his own revenue. But the latter will see trading as their principal business and so will want to buy as cheaply and sell as dearly as possible. As sovereigns their interest would be the same as that of their subjects but as merchants it is quite the reverse. He continues

> It is a very singular government in which every member of the administration wishes to get out of the country, and consequently to have done with the government, as soon as he can, and to

whose interest, the day after he has left it and carried his whole fortune with him, it is perfectly indifferent though the whole country was swallowed up by an earthquake. (IV, vii, c, 106)

He concludes 'such exclusive companies, therefore, are nuisances in every respect: always more or less inconvenient to the countries in which they are established, and destructive to those which have the misfortune to fall under their governments' (IV, vii, c, 108). Many people agreed with this, but powerful interests were involved and several decades were to pass before the East India Company was finally wound up.

COLONIAL POLICY

The position was quite different in the West Indies and the thirteen provinces on the American mainland. Smith has some very interesting things to say on this subject. In order to follow his argument it must be remembered that he was writing in the mid-1770s when these provinces were still colonies and the War of Independence could still be referred to as 'the present disturbances' (V, iii, 90).

In these colonies, then, trading rights were not confined to exclusive companies but there were monopolistic restrictions of another kind. In 1651, under the Commonwealth, a Navigation Act was passed which prohibited the carrying of colonial produce to England unless in English or colonial vessels with an English captain and crew. After the union of Scotland with England the privileges accorded to the English were extended to the Scots. Under this act, which was still in force in Smith's day, colonial commodities were divided into 'enumerated' and 'non-enumerated'. The former were either goods not produced in Britain, such as molasses, coffee and tobacco, or not produced in sufficient quantities, such as timber, tar and pig-iron. The non-enumerated commodities, for instance grain and salted meats and fish, could be exported freely by the colonists.

These arrangements had good and bad points. They gave British seamen wide opportunities for employment. They provided Britain with raw materials and exotic consumption goods, though probably at a higher price than if there had been free trade. And British merchants could count on a handsome supply of valuable goods for re-export, tobacco being a particularly profitable item. On the other hand much of the capital that would otherwise have financed trade with Europe and North Africa was tied up in the colonial trade, and this meant that owing to the distance of America the returns were slow; and they were further slowed down by the fact that the colonists, who were always short of capital, obtained it as far as they could by delaying payment for the goods they imported from Europe.

On balance, however, trade with America was a good thing. In Smith's words,

> we must carefully distinguish between the effects of the colony trade and those of the monopoly of that trade. The former are always and necessarily beneficial; the latter always and necessarily hurtful. But the former are so beneficial, that the colony trade, though subject to a monopoly, and notwithstanding the hurtful effects of that monopoly, is still upon the whole beneficial, and greatly beneficial; though a good deal less so than it otherwise would be. (IV, vii, c, 47)

This is the strictly private, commercial point of view. But there is another, opposite point of view which Smith is at pains to stress, namely the public interest. The American colonies were a sink of public money. Not only did they entail a considerable outlay on the civil establishment but very expensive wars had been entered into because of the need to protect them. And the colonies themselves refused to contribute to these expenses. They might have done so if approached in the right way. Their refusal was not so much a matter of money as of politics: they were loyal to the king but did not accept the jurisdiction of the British parliament. Each province had its own assembly, which they considered equivalent to that parliament, and if the king wanted assistance then he should apply for it through their own legislative bodies. If he would not do so, then they would not pay.

As Smith saw it, there were two possible solutions to this impasse: one was total union with Britain, the other total separation. The *status quo* was untenable.

> The rulers of Great Britain have, for more than a century past, amused the people with the imagination that they possessed a great empire on the west side of the Atlantic. This empire, however, has hitherto existed in imagination only. It has hitherto been, not an empire, but the project of an empire; not a gold mine, but the project of a gold mine; a project which has cost, which continues to cost, and which, if pursued in the same way as it has been hitherto, is likely to cost immense expence without being likely to bring any profit. (V, iii, 92)

The one thing that could give substance to this imperial illusion was a union of the two countries on a footing of complete equality. Doubtless its realization would encounter great difficulties and strong prejudices but none that appeared to Smith insurmountable. And he went a step further: Ireland too should be brought in.

> By a union with Great Britain, Ireland would gain, besides the freedom of trade, other advantages much more important, and which would much more than compensate any increase of taxes that might accompany that union. By the union with England, the middling and inferior ranks of people in Scotland gained a compleat deliverance from the power of an aristocracy which had always before oppressed them. By a union with Great Britain the greater part of the people of all ranks in Ireland would gain an equally compleat deliverance from a much more oppressive aristocracy; an aristocracy not founded, like that of Scotland, in the natural and respectable distinctions of birth and fortune; but in the most odious of all distinctions, those of religious and political prejudices. (V, iii, 89)

In this empire each of the three countries would be represented in a central parliament in proportion to their tax yield. Petty, a hundred years earlier, had had the same vision, though in his day America was much less developed and Ireland only half subdued. But not even Petty, bold as he was, went the whole length of Smith, who concludes

> Such has hitherto been the rapid progress of that country in wealth, population and improvement, that in the course of little more than a century, perhaps, the produce of American might exceed that of British taxation. The seat of the empire would then naturally remove itself to that part of the empire which contributed most to the general defence and support of the whole. (IV, vii, c, 79)

The other solution, that of separation, would mean granting America independence without delay. At this point Smith's optimism deserts him:

> To propose that Great Britain should voluntarily give up all authority over her colonies ... would be to propose such a measure as never was, and never will be adopted, by any nation in the world.... Such sacrifices, though they might frequently be agreeable to the interest, are always mortifying to the pride of every nation, and what is perhaps of still greater consequence, they are always contrary to the private interest of the governing part of it, who would thereby be deprived of the disposal of many places of trust

and profit, of many opportunities of acquiring wealth and distinction. . . . The most visionary enthusiast would scarce be capable of proposing such a measure, with any serious hopes at least of its ever being adopted. If it was adopted, however, Great Britain would not only be immediately freed from the whole annual expence of the peace establishment of the colonies, but might settle with them such a treaty of commerce as would effectually secure to her a free trade, more advantageous to the great body of the people, though less so to the merchants, than the monopoly which she at present enjoys. By thus parting good friends, the natural affection of the colonies to the mother country, which, perhaps, our late dissentions have well nigh extinguished, would quickly revive. It might dispose them not only to respect, for whole centuries together, that treaty of commerce which they had concluded with us at parting, but to favour us in war as well as in trade, and, instead of turbulent and fractious subjects, to become our most faithful, affectionate, and generous allies; and the same sort of parental affection on the one side, and filial respect on the other, might revive between Great Britain and her colonies, which used to subsist between those of ancient Greece and the mother city from which they descended. (IV, vii, c, 66)

Unfortunately, as Smith had anticipated, 'the rulers of Great Britain' did not see it that way.

THE PROGRESS OF FREE TRADE

Free trade might be characterized as a macroeconomic approach to increasing the wealth of nations, in which the attempt is made to improve the welfare of the whole community, in contrast to the microeconomic approach, which concentrates on improving the welfare of individuals and building up the total welfare as the sum of individual welfare. The trouble with the latter scheme is that only a limited part of the community, namely the traders and manufacturers, will be gainers.

Free trade benefits the community in two ways. It tends to increase the size of the market, thus giving more scope to the division of labour and technical progress, and it also tends to reduce prices. Thus the product will be larger and prices will be lower. This was the burden of Smith's argument. But he was not sanguine about its success:

to expect, indeed, that the freedom of trade should ever be entirely restored in Great Britain, is as absurd as to expect that an Oceana or Utopia should ever be established in it. Not only the prejudices of the publick, but what is much more unconquerable, the private interests of many individuals, irresistibly oppose it. (IV, ii, 43)

But events proved him wrong. His advocacy of free trade was taken up by Pitt, who in 1786, only ten years after the first publication of *The Wealth of Nations*, concluded a commercial treaty with France which swept away many of the protective duties between the two countries. During the short period before the outbreak of the war with France this piece of legislation seems to have been accepted and successful, but the country had to wait until the next century before sustained progress could be made.

In 1820 Alexander Baring presented to a receptive House of Commons a petition of the merchants of the City of London. This document, which contains an admirable statement of the principles of free trade, was drafted by Thomas Tooke. It was to support these principles that in 1821 Tooke, Ricardo, Malthus, James Mill and others founded the Political Economy Club. Another step forward was taken in 1823 when William Huskisson was appointed president of the Board of Trade. He carried his Reciprocity of Duties bill which modified the effects of the Navigation Acts. He reduced the duty on silk and lowered the import and export duty on wool.

These were important steps in the development of a free trade policy but there remained the burning question of the restrictions on the importation of corn. Between 1773 and 1822 numerous acts had been passed to regulate its price. These had not worked well and in the years of commercial panic, 1825–6, the privy council was authorized to suspend them and allow the importation of corn in case of necessity. There were now doubts about the soundness of protection and the desirability of the Corn Laws. Canning, in his short administration in 1827, carried in the House of Commons a number of resolutions for a more liberal policy and a bill was passed by the Commons based on them; but Canning died and the bill was defeated in the Lords as a result of Wellington's opposition. In 1828, when the Duke came into office with Peel and Huskisson among his colleagues, the duties on imported corn were regulated on a new sliding scale which fell as the average price in England rose.

The Commercial Society, established in Manchester in 1794, had been reconstituted in 1820 as the Manchester Chamber of Commerce. One of its first acts had been to protest against the abandonment in the previous year of the provision for the complete liberation of trade between Great Britain and Ireland. The protest was put forward by a deputation to the government and by a petition to parliament. Thereafter opinions against protection, and in particular duties on foreign grain, hardened among the merchants and manufacturers of Manchester. Late in 1838 the Chamber denounced the policy of protection, and shortly afterwards the National Anti-Corn Law League was founded. The names of John Bright and Richard Cobden appear from the beginning. The League was immensely active, ran a journal and raised large sums of money to promote its ends. C.P. Villiers, an early supporter, presented each year to parliament his resolution in favour of free trade; it regularly fell through but he was not discouraged.

In 1845 Peel brought forward the budget in which he proposed to devote the surplus to reducing or abolishing a number of duties. But the reductions did not go far enough for the advocates of the League and Lord Stanley and some other ministers refused to support total abolition. Peel resigned. Lord John Russell tried to form a government and failed. Peel was recalled and accepted office, calculating that he could carry a bill abolishing the Corn Laws with the help of his own tory friends and the whigs and free-traders. Lord Stanley was replaced in the government by Gladstone.

The voting on the bill for the Abolition of the Corn Laws which Peel brought forward early in 1846 is of interest. It cut completely across parties. Of the 556 who voted in the House of Commons, 57 per cent were in favour, of whom almost a third were conservatives and the remaining two thirds whigs and liberals. The 229 opponents were almost all conservatives. The majority in the Commons was 98; in the Lords it was 47.

In 1849 the Navigation Laws were repealed, and from 1853 on, Gladstone removed the remaining impediments to free trade. And so eighty years after the first appearance of *The Wealth of Nations* the battle was practically won – at least for the time being.

5

ON THE WEALTH OF NATIONS

Franco Modigliani

I must begin with a confession: my title is intended to be a bit misleading – a play on words. For when I refer to 'the wealth of nations', the title of Adam Smith's famous book, I am using the expression 'wealth of nations' in the modern sense of the stock of national net worth, whereas he means the flow of the annual produce or essentially what we now mean by national income (except that, in contrast with the modern western practice, he maintains that services should not be included in income).

SMITH'S VIEW OF THE DETERMINANTS OF SAVING

What does Smith have to say about the determinants of wealth, the flow by which it is accumulated, or saved, and about its role in the economy? First, he is a strong supporter of the view that productively employed capital plays an essential role in determining the growth of Smithian weath –

> The annual produce ... of any nation can be increased in its value by no other means but by increasing either the number of its productive labourers or the productive power of those labourers who had before been employed. The number of its productive labourers, it is evident, can never be much increased, but in consequence of an increase in capital.(II, iii, 32)

And to increase the productive power of the same number of labourers 'an additional capital is almost always required' (pp. 274–5). This investment and hence saving is necessary and sufficient for the growth of output, at least as long as labour is in elastic supply.

This view of the essential role of saving in economic development is of course broadly shared today, though it has not always been accepted. Probably the best known dissenting view was expressed in the course of the Keynesian revolution, as the General Theory set forth the so-called 'paradox of thrift': 'In the absence of investment opportunities, more saving leads to less, not more, output.'

What then, according to Smith, determines the behaviour of this variable so crucial for economic development? Somewhat surprisingly, the answer to this question occupies but a very modest portion of *The Wealth of Nations*, basically some two pages. Smith sees saving as the resultant of a continuous tug-of-war between 'two principles' (instincts). On the one hand is 'the principle that prompts to save, which is the desire of bettering our condition' and results in frugality, on the other is the 'passion for present enjoyment, the principle which prompts to expense', which results in 'profusion' or 'prodigality'. Fortunately in this struggle 'the principle of frugality seems not only to predominate but to predominate very greatly' and 'in spite both of the extravagance of government and the great errors of administration'. The reason for this confidence in vigorous positive net national saving is that the passion for present enjoyment, 'though sometimes violent and very difficult to restrain, is, in general, only momentary and occasional', whereas the desire of bettering our condition, 'though generally calm and dispassionate, comes with us from the womb, and never leaves us till we go into the grave'. Mankind continuously struggles to improve its condition and an 'augmentation of fortune is the means by which the greater part of men propose and wish to better their condition ... and the most likely way of augmenting their fortune'. To this end they 'save and accumulate some part of what they acquire, either regularly and annually or upon some extraordinary occasion' (II, iii, 28).

Thus, in essence, private saving is the result of a dispassionately and rationally planned accumulation, reflecting the uniform, constant and uninterrupted effort of every man 'to better his condition' (p. 275), routing a blind, irrational and destructive impulse to spend. It is interesting that in this paradigm there is no reference to other major factors affecting either individual or national saving behaviour, not even to income nor to the role of bequests. One can of course think of plausible explanations for these omissions, e.g. Smith may have been thinking of the upper classes and not of the labourers; similarly, by improving oneself, he may have been thinking of oneself as including one's heirs. But there is no hint whatever to authorize such an interpretation.

Smith, however, is quite aware of the fact that fiscal policy has also a role to play in national saving. 'Great nations are never impoverished by private, though they sometimes are by public prodigality and misconduct' (II, iii, 30). But what impoverishes nations according to Smith is not fiscal deficits as such, but rather, excessive expenditure. At first sight this view seems to concord with that set forth recently by R. Barro (see p. 96). What causes the burden is the expenditure as such, and it makes no difference whether it is financed by taxes or deficit. But while the conclusions look similar, the underlying reasoning is quite different. Smith's proposition is directly related to his view about productive and unproductive labour.

> Public revenue is ... employed in maintaining unproductive hands.... Such people, as they themselves produce nothing, are all maintained by the produce of other men's labour. When multiplied, therefore, to an unnecessary number, they ... may consume so great a share of their whole revenue, and thereby oblige so great a number to encroach upon their capitals, upon the funds destined for the maintenance of productive labour, that all the frugality and good conduct of individuals may not be able to compensate the waste and degradation of produce occasioned by this violent and forced encroachment. (II, iii, 30)

The views of Smith about saving, virtue and vice may appear somewhat unusual and even surprising from the vantage point of current academic thinking about these issues. But it should be realized that they are still popular among the lay public, the press and politicians, if one can judge from the public reaction to the recent crumbling of the private saving rates in the US. The decline was frequently viewed as reflecting the demise of virtuous thrift and the taking over of instant gratification.

Having reviewed Smith's conception, I propose to contrast it with two later views on the determinant of saving. One is Keynes's paradigm, which reigned supreme for a couple of decades following the publication of *General Theory*. The other is the paradigm associated with the so-called 'new theories of the consumption' function and embodied in the 'permanent income' hypothesis of Milton Friedman and the life cycle hypothesis developed by myself and Richard Brumberg with the collaboration of several other authors.

THE KEYNESIAN PARADIGM

In Chapter 9 of *General Theory*, Keynes starts by listing 'eight main motives ... of a subjective character which lead individuals to refrain from spending out of their income'. Each of the motives is given a summary descriptive label. Of these motives, one corresponds to Smith's single motive, 'improvement', and is so-labelled by Keynes. Its purpose is to 'enjoy a gradually increasing expenditure since it gratifies a common instinct to look forward to a gradually increasing standard of life.' Two more motives have a vague relation to the one suggested by Smith, and might be regarded as elaborations thereof. One, labelled 'enterprise', is 'to secure a masse de manoeuvre to carry out speculative or business projects'. The other, called 'independence', is to 'enjoy independence and the power to do things, though without a clear idea of definite intention of specific action'.

Three motives then follow that can be grouped together under the heading of transfer of resources over time or hump saving (see p. 92) This involves spending less now in order to spend more later, or in order to make up for past overspending. The motives are as follows:

(i) Foresight – 'essentially to provide for later needs of the individual and his family such as old age, family education and the maintenance of dependants'.
(ii) Precaution – to build a reserve against unforeseen contingencies.
(iii) Calculation – to postpone consumption to a later time because, with a positive return on capital, one can obtain later a larger consumption than what is given up now.

This leaves two reasons: the bequest motive labelled 'pride', and 'to satisfy pure miserliness' (p. 108) labelled 'avarice'.

This is clearly an extensive and well-thought-out catalogue, though its usefulness suffers greatly from the absence of any judgement as to the empirical importance of different motives. We are only told of a hunch that 'the strength of these motives will vary enormously according ... [to such factors as] institutions, ... and according to habits formed by race, education, convention, religion, and current morals, ... and the pevailing distribution of wealth and the established standard of life' (p. 109).

But at this point Keynes makes a strange and unexpected twist: he tells us that

> Since ... the main background of subjective and social incentives changes slowly, [we can take them as given, and therefore] we are

left with the conclusion that in the short-run changes in consumption depend largely on the rate at which income is being earned, and not on changes in the propensity to consume out of a given income. (p. 110)

In other words, for all practical purposes what determines consumption or saving is just income. Thus the explanation of saving finally reduces to his purely empirical 'psychological law': 'Men are disposed, as a rule and on the average to increase their consumption as their income increases, but not by as much as the increase in their income.' This twist is perhaps understandable considering that what Keynes was really interested in was to show that, in the final analysis, what determines income (and saving) is investment; and for that purpose it was enough to establish that saving depends on income. But it was none the less an unfortunate switch from the point of view of truly understanding saving behaviour. In fact his proposition, though valid, was uninformative, just like the proposition, say, that to a good approximation, petrol consumption can be accounted for just by the number of miles driven. Certainly in the short run (for given technology) the proposition is true, but it is not very enlightening in understanding the important issue of how and why there are variations in petrol consumption for given miles, i.e. in petrol consumption per mile. Similarly, Keynes's hypothesis does not come to grips with the real issue of changes in saving which reflect variation in the proportion of income saved, as between different families or between different countries, or different phases of the cycle.

The only hypothesis suggested by Keynes in this regard, at the aggregate level, is that the saving ratio is likely to move cyclically (p. 97), and that a greater portion of income will be saved as real income rises, presumably at both the individual and the national level. As will be seen, the first of these hypotheses is consistent with later developments of the theory of saving, while the second is not, at least at the national level.

The Keynesian generation took over his simplified message, accepting the proposition that saving and the saving ratio depended on income across families and across countries, though they frequently pushed the simplification further by postulating a linear consumption function with a positive intercept, which insured that the saving ratio would rise with income. But there was a general tendency to base the hypothesis on the empirical proposition announced by Keynes in his psychological law with no attempt to understand its economic justification. And the empirical tests undertaken by many, though they got off to a good start, soon turned to grief.

THE NEW THEORIES

The new theories of the consumption function start from an entirely different angle, namely by relying on the classical theory of the allocation of available resources among alternative uses, an approach pioneered by Irving Fisher. In the theory of saving, of course, what is available to allocate is (the present value of) life resources, and the alternative uses are consumption at different periods of life.

The first basic implication of the approach is that, contrary to the post-Keynesian formulation, consumption at any point of time (in the short run) depends, not on current income as such, but on life resources and allocation preferences. Thus individual saving over a short interval is the residual difference between the chosen consumption, based on life income, and what income happens to be at that time. This point of departure is common to both the permanent income and the life cycle hypothesis; the difference springs from the fact that Friedman postulates an infinitely long and therefore also monotonously uniform life. Consumption is determined by the resources available over the infinite life, called permanent income, and does not change except because of revisions in anticipated permanent income. Thus he is concerned with analysing the implication for saving by individual or groups of random deviations of current from permanent income (so-called transitory income). In the life cycle model (LCH), instead it is recognized that life is finite and varied, and that there are systematic life cycle variations in planned consumption and income as an individual passes from youth to working age and to old age with more or less complete retirement. The LCH can therefore study the implications of deviations of income and on consumption from its life average that occur systematically over the life cycle.

It should already be apparent that there is a deep chasm between the LCH and the Smithian paradigm; not only is *saving* rationally planned, but (most) dissaving is rationally planned, too. In the permanent income hypothesis (PYH) it is a rationally planned response to transitory disturbances, and in the LCH it is a response to that and also to foreseen life cycle variations in income and need. But in neither case is it the result of an uncontrollable urge to buy. In fact, according to the LCH, a major (if not the only) reason for the accumulation of wealth is to consume it later. Note that this kind of saving gives rise to a holding of wealth which is transitory (even though possibly long lasting) in the sense that it will, eventually, be largely drawn down to support consumption. The importance of this type of accumulation was first suggested by Sir Roy Harrod, who labelled it 'hump saving' – though a more descriptive terminology is 'hump wealth'.

Some interesting evidence in support of the LCH's hump saving is provided by tabulations of the size distribution of saving. Under Smith's hypothesis, one would expect that the number of savers should greatly exceed that of dissavers; similarly, the standard Keynesian view should imply that there is little dissaving in the upper income classes and less saving and more dissaving in the lower classes. Under the LCH, however, net saving and large dissaving, and balance between numerous and large saving and large dissaving, and the frequency and relative size of dissaving should be largely independent of income.

One such tabulation was reported in a study by Proctor, 'Survey of Changes in Family Finances', in which saving was defined as the change in assets. The results are striking.

(i)   For all the respondents the proportion not saving was 31 per cent, of which 7 per cent reported zero saving and 24 per cent dissaving.
(ii) When respondents are classified by wealth, this proportion was not very different in each wealth class, but tended to be somewhat smaller at lower wealth than in the highest wealth brackets.
(iii) Very large dissaving (over $5,000 in 1963 prices) increases in frequency as one moves up the wealth scale.
(iv) If respondents are classified by income brackets, it is still true that the frequency and magnitude of dissaving in the top bracket is above the average for the whole group.

As a result of their common foundation, the LCH and the PYH have essentially the same implication with respect to short-run individual behaviour. However, for the LCH the systematic life cycle variations in income, saving and wealth provide the foundation for modelling *aggregate* saving behaviour, a subject on which the permanent income hypothesis is essentially mute. Hereafter we will focus on the aggregative implications, since these are relevant to an understanding of the recent developments.

IMPLICATIONS OF THE LIFE CYCLE HYPOTHESIS FOR AGGREGATE SAVING

The national saving ratio of a country does not depend on how rich or poor it is, a view that was taken for granted before the LCH. It depends instead on its income growth trend: it will be zero for zero growth and rise as the growth of the economy increases. In addition, it responds to those forces that impinge on the life profile of wealth and thus on the wealth income ratio.

To illustrate how these results can be established, assume at first that there are no bequests. Then all wealth arises from life cycle induced accumulation, followed by later dissaving, i.e. it is 'hump' wealth. But can hump wealth alone possibly account for the whole of national wealth in the absence of bequests? It was shown in Modigliani and Brumberg (1954) that, even if the only reason for the hump wealth was accumulation to support retired consumption, and assuming a stylized life cycle consumption constant through life and income constant till retirement – one could account for a wealth income ratio of around 5, somewhat larger than the actual ratio estimated for the US since the beginning of the century.

Next, it should be apparent that, provided the preferred allocation of life resources to consumption over the life cycle is stable over time and independent of income, then for any given path of life earning, the age path of wealth relative to life resources, and hence the wealth–income ratio will be independent of per capita income.

Consider now the case of a stationary economy; here per capita as well as aggregate income is constant, hence the wealth–income ratio must be constant; but with stationary income it follows that wealth must also be constant. If wealth is constant, then saving, which is the change in wealth, must be *zero* – in a stationary society there is no saving. Furthermore, saving will be zero independently of the level of income.

There will be saving if, and only if, the economy is growing. Suppose it is growing exclusively through population growth. Positive saving will then occur, because, even though each age group continues to save (or dissave) an unchanged fraction of its income, population growth will reduce the proportion of old people relative to other groups, and the old retired people can be expected to save less than the younger population. An alternative way of formulating this result is to remember that, with steady growth there is a fundamental relation between saving, growth and wealth, namely the portion of income saved must be equal to the rate of growth multiplied by the wealth–income ratio. (This relation is of course a variant of the famous Harrod–Domar proposition that the investment–income ratio must be equal to the product of the rate of growth, of growth of output and the capital output ratio.) This shows again that in a stationary society with zero rate of growth, wealth must be constant and saving must be zero.

If the wealth–income ratio were independent also of growth, then the saving ratio would be strictly proportional of growth, no matter what its sources, with the proportionality factor given by the wealth–income ratio. However, one can show that, in general, the ratio of wealth to income will not be constant, but instead will tend to decline with growth, though only moderately, in the relevant range. This means that the saving ratio can be expected to rise with growth but at a declining rate.

The life path of hump wealth, and hence the path of wealth and the wealth–income ratio, will be affected not only by retirement habits but also by a host of other factors such as (i) the chosen path of consumption, 'the life path of earned income', (ii) provisions for children's education; (iii) the extent of uncertainty and the need to build up precautionary reserves which interacts with the availability of various types of public and private insurance; (iv) the rate of return on capital – though there is still no generally acceptable evidence as to the sign of this effect; and last, but not least, (v) credit rationing, which should have a positive effect on saving by forcing postponement of consumption. In addition it should largely rule out the possibility of growth of productivity reducing saving (as suggested by Friedman) by leading to large dissaving on the part of the young. The quantitative importance of these other forces in affecting the saving ratio is still under investigation.

THE ROLE OF BEQUESTS AND FISCAL POLICIES

There remains the question of bequests, or more generally of inter-generational transfer. Here we must make a clear distinction between transfers arising from a bequest motive and those arising from a precautionary motive. Considering that the length of life is uncertain, one would expect people with risk aversion to behave so as to control the risk of running out of retirement resources by holding reserves, a portion of which will, on average, be bequeathed. But such bequests, like all other sources of LCH accumulation, will be proportional to life resources. Therefore they do not change the implications of the basic model that the saving rate is independent of income and dependent on growth.

However, some bequests presumably arise from a bequest motive which leads a person to allocate part of their resources to leave an estate to their heirs. But this motive too will not change the properties of the basic model if we postulate that the bequest process is such that the ratio of bequeathed to total wealth is stable in time for given tastes. This assumption is unequivocally supported by the evidence, at least in the US, since the beginning of the century. One simple formulation that will ensure this property, while allowing for the fact that richer people will tend to leave relatively more, is to postulate that the proportion of life resources bequeathed will tend to rise with the level of resources, including inherited wealth. There is some evidence for this proposition. But even if bequests can be accommodated in the model, one may raise the question of how large a fraction of wealth, and hence saving, might be accounted for by hump saving versus bequests. This is an issue that has been hotly debated, the life cycle portion having been estimated anywhere between 20 and 80 per cent. My own conclusion based on a great deal of evidence is that the share of life cycle wealth in total is around 75 per cent.

There remains one further influence on saving: fiscal policy. Though there are rather sharp differences on this issue, all agree that fiscal policy has some effects on national saving. The still-prevailing Keynesian framework has the implication that a dollar of government deficit reduces national saving by a dollar if it arises from higher expenditure, while if the deficit comes from cutting taxes, national saving declines somewhat less than a dollar, namely by the marginal propensity to consume; the fall of national saving is less in this case because, though the government increases its deficit by one dollar, the private component of saving is increased by the propensity to save.

To see the implications of the LCH, consider the case of deficit arising from a cut in taxes and financed by public borrowing. This increases the resources of the current generation, leading to higher consumption; but by how much? If the current generation is informed and rational, it should realize that the gain is less than the tax cut, because higher future taxes will have to be levied to pay interest (and eventually principal). Therefore the resources are increased only by the difference between the tax cut and the present value of the increased taxes to be paid. If all members of the living cohorts had an infinite lifespan, then of course the present value of the future taxes would be precisely equal to the tax cut. Hence the current generation would be no better off as a result of the tax rebate; it should not increase its consumption and should save the entire tax cut. The result would be an unchanged level of national saving, as the dissaving of the government is offset by the higher private saving. But of course life is finite, and therefore each individual gains the difference between the tax cut and the present value of future taxes that will fall on them over their lifetime. The private sector should therefore be expected to increase consumption to an extent that depends on such things as life expectancy, interest rates and credit rationing. It has been estimated that with fully rational (smoothing) behaviour, on average, saving might rise by 30 per cent of the deficit, resulting in a reduction of national saving by 70 per cent.

Barro has recently advanced the proposition that national saving should not be affected at all by taxes or deficit, but only by government expenditure. As noted earlier, this is a conclusion quite similar to that set forth by Smith, though it rests on an entirely different consideration, basically a life cycle model with infinite life. Barro reaches his conclusion, though recognizing that life is finite, by hypothesizing that individuals behave as though life were infinite because their utility includes the welfare of an infinite chain of heirs. But this hypothesis can be rejected as a description of aggregate behaviour because of several logical flaws and inconsistency with empirical evidence on bequests and attitudes towards heirs. However, it could have some validity for some restricted sector of the population.

TESTS OF SAVING THEORIES

There have been numerous tests of saving theories; I would like to report briefly here on a very recent one that illustrates how the LCH can throw light on a very remarkable development of the last thirty years or so which would be hard to account for by either Smith's or Keynes's view: namely the dramatic and generalized decline of the saving rates between the decade of the 1960s and that of the 1980s (through 1987), at least for the twenty-one OECD countries for which reliable information is available. For this period the average national saving ratio has declined from an average value of 16.6 per cent in the first decade to 10.3 per cent in the last, or nearly 40 per cent. Equally remarkable, the decline occurred in every one of the twenty-one countries (except for Portugal, that registered no change). What makes this development so extraordinary is that it has long been taken for granted that the saving rate would be a fairly stable number, over a limited span of years; certainly this belief is explicit in Keynes and implied in Smith's views. Even if one were prepared to believe that, during those years, in a particular country there might have been a serious weakening of virtues and a rise of profligacy – and this explanation has been advanced for many countries, including the US – one would find it hard to explain why the disease was contagious, spreading rapidly to the entire OECD. On the other hand, the LCH can account for this surprising development, in that, according to the LCH, some of the major variables that should affect the saving ratio did behave in parallel fashion for all or most countries and for understandable reasons.

The first variable is the growth rate, the crucial factor in the LCH. In the course of the 1970s, after the first oil crisis, productivity began a steep decline that continued into the 1980s. Between the 1960s and the 1980s, the annual growth rate of GNP fell (mostly reflecting slow productivity growth, but also inadequate demand) from a remarkable 4.9 per cent to 2.4 per cent – a decline of 50 per cent or of the same magnitude as saving. And the decline was fairly universal (the only exceptions are the UK and Norway which started with relatively low growth and had negligible increases). The causes of the generalized decline in productivity are still not well understood, but, in view of embodied technical progress, international transfer of technology and competition, it is not surprising that it took on the aspects of an epidemic.

A second important novelty in behaviour which characterizes this period is the deterioration in government finances. Everybody, these days, is acutely aware of the deterioration in the US budget. After adjusting the official estimates to exclude the government net invest- ment, the deficit rose by an impressive 5.5 per cent of GNP, of which 3 per cent occurred in the 1980s. But it is less known that this development was, by no means, unique to the US. In fact, in about two-thirds of the countries the deterioration was *more* serious than in the US, reaching nearly 10 per cent in Sweden. The average deteriora- tion was 5.8 per cent, worse than for the US.

These figures are not adjusted for the effect of inflation. Inflation may be expected to increase interest rates roughly one-for-one. It thereby increases interest payments and the overall deficit of the government. But that increase is, in reality, offset by the erosion in the purchasing power of the government debt. Thus to obtain the true interest cost one must subtract from interest paid, the gain to the government arising from the real depreciation of the debt. That gain is the debt multiplied by inflation. Because of rising inflation and because of rising debt–income ratios, the magnitude of that correction increased for almost every country, rising on average by nearly two percentage points, thereby reducing the deficit from an uncorrected 5.8 per cent to 3.8 per cent after correction.

Of course, the same correction, with opposite sign, should be applied to the private sector by reducing interest received as well as private income and saving. But even after correction, the figures indicate an impressive rise in deficits, though the causes why large increases occurred simultaneously in most countries are less obvious.

But what if the private sector fails, partially or totally, to understand that it should exclude from its income the correction? The effect of this 'inflation illusion' clearly must be to swell consumption and therefore to reduce saving. It follows that this type of inflation illusion could be among the possible explanations for the fall in saving during the last three decades, characterized almost everywhere by substantial inflation.

THE LIFE CYCLE HYPOTHESIS
AND THE DECLINE IN SAVING:
SOME EMPIRICAL EVIDENCE

The role of the variables described above was tested systematically through standard statistical techniques (regression over a cross-section of country averages for each decade and of countries' changes in the variables between decades). The results appear to support substantially the LCH. Growth turns out to be generally the most important explanatory variable with a coefficient typically between 1.4 and 1.5, broadly consistent with the LCH prediction. The effect of the deficit due to government expenditure, which should reduce saving very little in the Barro model and by some three-quarters of the deficit in the LCH, actually is found to reduce saving quite substantially, typically between 0.6 per cent and 0.7 per cent, though with some variation from sample to sample. Inflation illusion also appears to contribute to the reduction of national saving in this period. The estimated proportion of the inflation component of interest consumed is, generally, between 50 per cent and 70 per cent. Our tests also included some demographic variables suggested by the LCH. These variables are generally found to affect saving as expected.

Table 3.1 illustrates the above result by showing, for the average of all countries as well as country-by-country, how the movement of the relevant variables between the 1970s and 1980s contributed to the explanation of the movement of saving over that period. The effects are estimated by regression analysis. The equation used is shown at the top of the table. The variable we are trying to explain is the change in the average value of the national saving–income (mnp) ratio, between the decade of the 1970s and that of the 1980s (through 1987). Saving is corrected for inflation; dgrowth and dlag are the changes in the rate of growth between the 1970s and 1980s and between the 1960s and 1970s, respectively. dsurp is the change in the surplus of general government, corrected for inflation and for government investment; dtax is the change in taxes net of transfers; and ddebtad is the change in the inflation correction. The last three variables are expressed as a percentage of income (net national product).

The bottom row of the table shows the role of the (change) in each of the explanatory variables stated at the head of each column, in accounting for the change in the average saving ratio between the 1970s and 1980s, implied by the equation. From column (6) we see that the saving ratio declined by 5 percentage points, or one-third, between the 1970s and 1980s. And from Column (5), which shows the change as computed from the equation at the top, it is seen that the model accounts very well for the actual change. What are the forces accounting for the decline? The first, reported in Column (1), is income growth. To measure growth we use both the current and the lagged growth to allow for the fact that the response of saving to growth may be expected to occur gradually. From the last row of Column (1), it appears that the reduction in growth resulted in a major reduction in saving by 1.8 per cent, nearly 40 per cent of the total decline. The major remaining effect is that of the deficit: as the surplus decreased by three percentage points (from 4.3 to 1.3), national saving decreased by nearly as much (or 2.7 per cent). The increase in taxes was very small on average in the period, and had a negligible effect on saving. The same is true for the effect of inflation illusion, as on average the inflation adjustment rose negligibly in the period, less than 11 percentage points. But though these true effects tend to cancel out on average, they are of some importance for individual countries as can be seen in the remaining rows of the table, which relate to individual countries. Column (6) reports the actual change and confirms the epidemic nature of the decline in saving, which fell in all but two countries – Norway and Switzerland which registered relatively modest increases. From Column (1) it is seen that the negative effect of the slowdown in growth is nearly universal. Only the UK bucked the trend. The effect reaches −4 and −4.5 per cent for Japan and Greece, respectively, compared with the average of −2 per cent. Similarly, the surplus (Column (2)) decreased almost uniformly except for Norway) with peaking around −7 per cent for

Table 5.1 Factors accounting for changing saving behaviour (1970–80)

The role of major variables affecting the change in the savings rate, 1970–80 (based on regression equation).

dns = 0.93 × dgrowth + 0.64 × dlag + 0.90 × dsurp − 0.28 × dtax − 0.37 × ddebtad

Country	Growth[1]	Surplus	Net tax	Inflation Correction	Estimated Change	Actual Change	Difference
	%	%	%	%	%	%	%
(1)	(2)	(3)	(4)	(5)	(6)	(7)	(8)
Canada	−1.22	−4.02	0.31	−0.29	−5.22	−3.90	−1.32
US	−0.18	−3.31	0.29	0.25	−2.96	−5.00	2.04
Japan	−4.02	0.24	−0.33	−0.20	−4.31	−4.40	0.09
Australia	−1.17	−3.16	−0.44	0.29	−4.47	−7.60	3.13
Austria	−2.17	−3.49	−0.05	0.05	−5.66	−5.00	−0.66
Belgium	−2.46	−4.37	0.64	−0.71	−6.89	−7.40	0.51
Denmark	−1.20	−3.42	−0.77	−1.02	−6.41	−7.30	0.89
Finland	−1.22	−3.08	−0.57	−0.37	−5.24	−3.50	−1.74
France	−2.54	−1.94	−1.05	−0.18	−5.73	−8.25	2.53
Germany (West)	−1.94	−1.29	−0.38	−0.21	−3.82	−3.60	−0.22
Greece	−4.58	−6.96	0.24	−0.36	−11.67	−12.20	0.53
Iceland	−0.67	−7.41	−0.15	0.02	−8.20	−7.31	−0.89
Ireland	−2.00	−3.96	0.21	0.08	−5.67	−4.80	−0.87
Italy	−2.62	−2.17	−0.47	−0.33	−5.59	−5.80	0.21
Netherlands	−2.45	−2.93	1.06	0.34	−3.97	−3.10	−0.87
Norway	−0.21	4.33	0.78	−1.41	3.49	1.80	1.69
Portugal	−3.17	2.89	−1.38	−1.61	−3.27	−2.20	−1.07

Spain	-2.87	-2.14	-1.05	-0.49	-6.55	-7.10	0.55
Sweden	-1.06	-2.96	-1.29	-1.15	-6.45	-5.80	-0.65
Switzerland	-1.40	-0.29	-0.31	0.03	-1.97	0.80	-2.77
UK	0.83	-6.86	1.98	2.13	-1.92	-2.00	0.08
Average	**-1.82**	**-2.68**	**-0.13**	**-0.25**	**-4.88**	**-4.94**	**0.06**

Key
dns = change in inflation-adjusted national savings as a percentage of national income.
dgrowth = change in the growth rate from 1970s to 1980s.
dlag = change in the growth rate from 1960s to 1970s.
dsurp = change in inflation-adjusted general government surplus as a percentage of national income.
dtax = change in inflation-adjusted general government net taxes as a percentage of national income.
ddebtad = change in the inflation correction, calculated as: (net public debt/nnp)* (cpi).

[1]Sum of the effects of the change in current and lagged growth.

Greece, Ireland and the UK. The change in taxes, deficit constant, had a small effect in this period, the largest being 2 per cent for the UK. Finally, the effect of inflation illusion is quite variable because the size of the inflation adjustment rose only in thirteen countries out of twenty-one. Still it exceeds −1 per cent for three countries and 2 per cent for another.

The explanatory variables in the table do not include income, the central Keynesian variable. The reason is that we have tried this variable, and in several variants found consistently that it did not help to explain the saving ratio, a result implied by the LCH.

CONCLUSION

We have compared Smith's view of the determinant of saving with the Keynesian framework and that of the new theories of the consumption function, particularly the life cycle model. We have focused on the ability of the alternative theories to explain a major recent phenomenon, namely the deep and widespread fall of the national saving rate in the last three decades at least among the OECD countries. We have shown that the LCH can provide a fairly close account of what happened relying on the behaviour of two major variables: the rate of growth of the economy and the government deficit. In contrast, the two more traditional theories do not seem to provide a basis for understanding the current sharp fall in the saving ratio and its simultaneous occurrence in some twenty countries. Keynes's main explanatory variable, income, explains nothing of the observed movement of the saving ratio, while the real variables explain too much. Similarly the explanation of saving behaviour does not seem to be found in Smith's metaphor of a dramatic struggle between virtuous frugality, spurred by the instinct of self-improvement, and prodigality, pushed by the passion for present enjoyment; but rather in the old time slogan, 'Save for a rainy day', or 'Save when you need it least, have it when you need it most' (the slogan of the Wilkensberg Saving Bank, Pennsylvania), coupled with phenomena resulting from aggregation.

REFERENCES

Barro, R.J. (1974) 'Are Government Bonds Net Wealth?' *Journal of Political Economy*, 82.

Fisher, Irving (1930) *The Theory of Interest*, New York: Macmillan.

Friedman, Milton (1956) *A Theory of the Consumption Function*, Princeton: Princeton University Press.

Harrod, R.F. (1948) *Towards a Dynamic Economics*, London: Macmillan.

Keynes, J.M. (1936) *General Theory of Employment, Interest and Money*, New York: Harcourt, Brace.

Modigliani, Franco (1990) 'Perché è diminuito il saggio di risparmio in Italia?' in S. Biasco, A. Roncaglia and M. Salvati (eds) *Instituzioni e Mercato nello Sviluppo Economico*, Festschrift in honour of Paolo Sylos Labini, Rome: Gius. Laterza.

Modigliani, Franco and Brumberg, Richard (1954) 'Utility Analysis and the Consumption Function: An Interpretation of Cross-Section Data', in K.K. Kurihara (ed.) *Post-Keynesian Economics*, New Brunswick, NJ: Rutgers University Press. Reprinted in A. Abel (ed.) (1980) *The Collected Papers of Franco Modigliani*, vol. 2, Cambridge, Mass.: MIT Press.

Modigliani, Franco and Brumberg, Richard (1980) 'Utility Analysis and Aggregate Consumption Functions: An Attempt at Integration', in A. Abel (ed.) (1980) *The Collected Papers of Franco Modigliani*, vol. 2, Cambridge, Mass.: MIT Press.

Proctor, D. (1968) 'Survey of Changes in Family Finances', Board of Governors of the Federal Reserve System, November.

6

THE SUPPLY OF LABOUR AND THE EXTENT OF THE MARKET

James M. Buchanan

The greatest improvement in the productive powers of labour, and the greater part of the skill, dexterity, and judgment with which it is anywhere directed, or applied, seems to have been the effects of the division of labour.

(I, i, 1)

As it is the power of exchanging that gives occasion to the division of labour, so the extent of this division must always be limited by the extent of that power, or, in other words, by the extent of the market.

(I, iii, 1)

INTRODUCTION

As these early, and familiar, statements in *The Wealth of Nations* make clear, Adam Smith sought to ground his argument for widening the exchange nexus on the increase in the production of economic value that extended specialization makes possible. Smith's primary targets were the restrictions on voluntary exchanges imposed by ill-advised mercantilist policies. The elimination of restrictions on trade effectively extends the market, thereby allowing for the exploitation of previously unrealized gains from specialization. Smith did not, to my knowledge, attend to the prospect for extending the market along the internal work–leisure margins of individualized choice.[1] If, however, gains are there to be secured by the mere opening up of markets, there must also be gains to be realized from a generalized increase in the quantities of input, specifically labour input, supplied to the exchange or market nexus. By supplying more inputs to the market in

104

exchange for the increments in income that will, in turn, be expended on the goods and services generated in the market, individuals may, internally, extend the size of the network. An economy in which there are one million workers who supply, on average, forty hours of work per week, is twice the size of an economy, other things being equal, in which the same one million workers supply, on average, twenty hours of work per week.

In this paper, I shall concentrate on this internal means of extending the size of the market. I shall first defend the basic proposition that the size of the market can indeed be extended through such internal means. This defence will require a definition of the necessary conditions under which such extension in market size does generate the Smithian results. Under the existence of such conditions, independent individual choices between work effort supplied to the market and leisure need not generate Pareto optimal results, even when all of the standard requirements are met. Relevant external economies may remain in voluntaristic equilibrium. I shall argue that one means of internalizing these externalities is through the instillation and maintenance of a work ethic. By making work praiseworthy and leisure blameworthy, at least over some relevant ranges in labour supply, participants may effectively internalize the external economy that the Smithian theorem on the extent of the market implies.

Adam Smith would not quarrel with my argument here, nor indeed would most modern economists when they present the elementary principles of their discipline to general audiences in the very first chapters of their textbooks. On the other hand, and by contrast, many modern economists would find it difficult to reconcile these elementary Smithian principles with the centre notion of competitive equilibrium, a notion that occupies so much attention in later chapters of the self-same textbooks. The formal conditions required for competitive equilibrium must be adjusted, in some fashion, to accommodate the theorem that economic value increases with an extension of the market. The contradiction between two widely accepted principles necessarily comes into attention when internal rather than external increases in market size are examined at all closely.

'PRODUCTION' FOR OWN CONSUMPTION AS A NON-TRADEABLE GOOD

International trade theorists make a categorical distinction between goods (and services) that are tradeable across the boundaries of national economies and goods (and services) that are non-tradeable, with the latter being produced exclusively for domestic consumption or final end-use. To my knowledge the fully analogous distinction between tradeable and non-tradeable goods at the level of each individualized 'economy' has not been emphasized, at least not sufficiently that its implications for the extent of the market, and, hence, for potential gains from the division of labour, have been widely recognized. The international trade theorist would not question the proposition that a shift from the production of non-tradeables to the production of tradeables would facilitate an extension of the trading network among nations and that such an extension would make possible increased international specialization, with consequent aggregate increases in economic value. Indeed, Adam Smith's central message might well be interpreted as a variant of this proposition. To the extent that artificially maintained political restrictions reduce the effective set of potentially tradeable goods, a removal of such restrictions will enhance the wealth of citizens.

The analogous proposition seems, however, to be much less acceptable, or at least analytically more challenging, when applied to the 'economy' of each single owner of a potentially productive resource. The basic distinction between the utilization of a resource for trade, that is, for the production of goods or services entered into market exchange, and the utilization of a resource for own consumption, that is, for production of something that is internally used, may be made here. Owners of resources, or resource capacities, may (if they are free to choose) supply these resource units to the market, directly or indirectly, or they may withhold such units from the market, thereby 'producing' for own or internal consumption.

The implications of the distinction here may assume important practical relevance only for labour, where non-market utilization, at least over some ranges of potential supply, is presumed to produce 'goods' that are of positive value to the owner-supplier-chooser. The individual, as holder-owner of labour capacity, faces a choice between offering this capacity (or any part thereof) to the market, either by producing goods directly for sale to others, or by selling capacity, as such, to others (persons, firms) who combine such purchases of inputs to organize the production of goods finally offered for sale, and withholding this capacity, thereby 'producing' something that is of value internally, whether this be leisure in the sense of inactivity or the active pursuit of other preferred end-uses of effort.

The simple point to be made here is that the choices made by individuals along the work–leisure margin determine the extent of the market or exchange nexus, and, through this, the degree of specialization to be potentially exploited. That part of resource capacity that is withheld from the market for own use is non-tradeable and, therefore, places a limit on the overall size of the tradeables sector. The point becomes obvious when placed in an extreme setting. If all persons in a community should choose to become fully self-sufficient and, hence, to withhold all resource capacity from exchange, there could be no specialization at all.

WORK AND WELFARE

Note that, in the analytical construction suggested, leisure, inclusively defined as the non-supply of work to the market, remains a 'good' as a positively valued argument in the individual's utility function. But the choice made by the individual between this 'good' and other goods that are demanded indirectly through the supply of work effort to the market must exert an external effect on others through the impact on the extent of the market itself. Each supplier of work, at the margin, exerts an external economy on others in the economy. By supplying more hours, days, weeks, or years, to the market, the individual who so acts benefits others indirectly through the extension of the market that results from the expenditure of income incrementally earned on marketed goods and services, that is, on tradeables.

Further, the external economy may be Pareto relevant in that some generalized agreement among all input suppliers, and output demanders, may be worked out which will involve more input supply and which will generate results that benefit all parties. (I abstract here from all sectoral effects where differential relationships of complementarity and substitutability, that stem, in part, from non-homogeneity among inputs, may obscure the underlying effect that I want to emphasize. Ideally, appropriate compensations could always be worked out and implemented so as to insure that the beneficial effects from the extension in market size are enjoyed by every market participant.)

The claim here is that the market, even in competitive equilibrium, is not a 'moral free zone', to use David Gauthier's terminology (Gauthier, 1985). Choices made by individuals reciprocally exert an impact on each other. This result seems to contrast dramatically with that part of conventional competitive theory which concentrates on the demonstration of the Pareto optimality properties of the idealized competitive equilibrium, sustained by the voluntary choices of all participants. The optimality property stems, of course, from the idealized conditions imposed on the presumed interaction process, one of which must deny the applicability of the fundamental Smithian theorem concerning the effects of market extension. Among the idealized conditions for the optimality of competitive equilibrium, there is the requirement that all production takes place under constant returns.

Note that, under constant returns, a change in the size of the market, whether generated internally or externally, does not modify the price vector of inputs relative to outputs. There is no Pareto relevant external economy involved in a decision made by one person to supply more units of work input to the marketplace. In so doing, the person in question secures the *full* value of the increment of output that the action generates. There is no effect, positive or negative, on the economic position of anyone else in the exchange nexus. The market is, indeed, 'moral free' in this setting, and no one need express or feel concern as to the choices made by others along the work–leisure, or any other, margin.

The generation of this result, whether expressed in optimality-efficiency or in moral-free terms, must necessarily deny the existence of any overall increase in economic value associated with a generalized increase in the size of the market. The range of applicability for gains from the division of labour, from specialization, must be presumed to have been exhausted at some size of the economy smaller than that which operates to produce the idealized competitive equilibrium. But economists seem to have devoted little effort to any attempts to specify even some proximate sizes at which specialization ceases to generate gains, sizes that must, if indeed they should exist, depend critically on the state of technology and other socio-political variables.[2]

GENERALIZED INCREASING RETURNS

The minimal departure from the setting for competitive equilibrium that is required to accommodate the basic Smithian theorem on the extent of the market involves some allowance for increasing returns to the production of tradeable goods in the economy, but these increasing returns need not take the form that is most familiar to economists. And I should stipulate here that my interest lies exclusively in the minimally required departures from the conditions for idealized competitive equilibrium; the possible presence and extent of increasing returns of the garden-variety sort, as might be empirically observed, falls outside the area of interest of this paper.

We can approach the issues here initially by reference to Marshallian external economies in production, although, even here, the analogy is somewhat misleading. In the Marshallian setting, firms in an industry produce competitively without knowledge that their costs depend, inversely, on the size of industry output. Individual firms have, therefore, no incentive to expand particular output so as to capture industry-wide advantages of scale. The generalized increasing returns that will allow for the applicability of the Smithian theorem need not show up in any Marshallian sense, at least not *ex ante*. For the increase in the extent of the market, for all tradeable goods, to generate increases in economic value, properly measured, returns must be increasing (costs must decrease) *somewhere* in the economy, but the identification of the location of this source of gain may not be possible until *after* the expansion of demand that calls additional production (in such an industry and elsewhere) into being.

Consider the following scenario. Assume that, for any reason, there is a generalized increase in the supply of work effort; persons offer more hours of work at the going wages, and institutional barriers do not prevent their implementation of these choices. Persons in the economy, generally, are observed to work harder than before the change. But persons who have supplied the additional quantity of labour inputs to the market have presumably done so for the purpose of being able to purchase an increased quantity of output from the market. Suppliers are motivated by the prospect of becoming demanders. Say's law is surely valid at this juncture of the analysis. Supply emerges only because it enables its own demand to become possible.

The additional income secured from the sale of additional input returns to the market as additional demand for market-produced tradeable output. This extension in demand, which is matched by the initiating increase in supply that made it possible, will create the potential for the exploitation of further specialization, *in some production*, that remained just below the margin of economic variability in the pre-change equilibrium. The real cost of production in the affected industry falls (measured in minimally necessary quantities of inputs required to produce any given output). But the firms in the affected industry, or anywhere else in the economy, need not have been able to identify in advance which industry would experience the increasing returns. And, even if prior identification could have been

109

made, the full exploitation of the scale advantages would not have been possible without the increase in demand in the economy generally.[3]

My emphasis here is on the *demand-side* source of possible opportunity to exploit gains from specialization, a source that stems initially from the proceeds of the sale of additional inputs to the market. In his seminal paper on increasing returns, Allyn Young (1928) stressed that 'buying power' is what 'constitutes a large market'. My emphasis is exclusively microeconomic, but there are also analytical affinities between the argument sketched out and that developed by Martin Weitzman (1982), whose interests and emphases are exclusively macroeconomic. His argument suggests that generalized increasing returns can offer plausible microeconomic foundations for understanding the emergence of quasi-competitive unemployment equilibria. In particular, Weitzman notes the contradiction between the Smithian emphasis on the division of labour and the constant returns condition in standard competitive theory. Earlier, N. Kaldor (1972) stressed the same point in the context of a generalized critique of equilibrium theory.

CHARACTERISTICS OF THE WORK-SUPPLY EXTERNALITY

The particular characteristics of the work-supply externality analysed here warrant more detailed discussion. First, the externality need not be identified by any such attributes as location, occupation, or industry classification. The behavioural margin of relevance involves the supply of productive effort to the exchange nexus at any point and at any level of productivity, although, of course, the more productive the effort the larger the external economies. It is worth stressing, in particular, that the operating features of the industry within which the work–leisure choice is made are totally irrelevant. The external economy emerges from all work–leisure choice margins, whether in increasing, constant, or decreasing returns to industries. The increase in value to the overall nexus exerts its external effect only as and when the input supplier returns the added value to the market as a consumer-purchaser, generating thereby an increase in effective demand. If the extent of the market limits the potential for deriving the advantages of specialization, at least one industry in the totality that describes the production-exchange nexus must exhibit increasing returns of the sort indicated. And the direct or primary beneficiaries stemming from the increase in effective demand are those persons who include in their consumption portfolio the goods so produced.

The externality identified here differs from those that are more often treated in welfare economics in at least two basic characteristics. There need be no relation of contiguity, locational or otherwise, between the generator of the external effect and the recipients of the benefit (or harm). By comparison, consider a few familiar examples. The pollution of the river reduces the fishing and swimming opportunities for those who live downstream. The resident who maintains a fine flower garden increases the utility of the neighbours. Coasian cattle trample the crops of nearby wheatgrowers. Marshallian firms are in the same industry. On the other hand, the work-supply externality is potentially economy-wide. The individuals who supply additional work generate value to persons who may be 'far away' in all dimensions.

A second difference between the work-supply externality and others that are more familiar lies in the way in which the benefits (or harms) enter the utility functions of those who are externally affected. If the good, X_i, exhibits increasing returns, then, consequent on an increased production of X_i, the externality affects all purchasers of X_i through a reduction in the price, P_i. There is no effect directly on the utility function analogous to that generated by the addition of floral splendour by the neighbouring gardner or the production of honey by the nearby bees. The consumer-purchaser of X_i finds the budget constraint shifted by the change in price. And this price effect is not, in this case, offset by a compensating price shift elsewhere in the economy, as faced by this or any other purchaser. The effect emerges as a pure price change, in real terms, made possible by the increase in aggregate supply of valued productive capacity to the economic nexus. Here the analyst must resist the temptation to disregard the externality because it enters the utility function through price. In the traditional terminology, the externality is 'technological', and, hence, Pareto relevant, because it expands the choice set of some persons in the nexus, without fully offsetting restrictions in the choice sets of others.

Two emendations to the conventional externality logic can be helpful in facilitating an understanding of the work-supply effect. If we assume that consumption is generalized in the sense that all final goods are included in each participant's preferred consumption bundle, then everyone in the economic nexus, in the role of final user of the good produced under conditions of increasing returns, becomes a beneficiary of the increase in the supply of work effort on the part of any worker in the whole system. Or, if we introduce a model of household production, where Beckerian Z goods are 'produced' with an appropriate set of X goods directly purchased from the market, then any reduction in the price of an X good modifies the production function for some Z good, making the externality appear analogous to those that are more familiar with the orthodox analysis.

INTERNALIZATION THROUGH A WORK ETHIC

In a more extended treatment (Buchanan 1989), I have discussed in some detail the alternative means through which the work-supply externality might be internalized. In that discussion, I have suggested that none of three familiar institutional means of correction seem likely to prove effective, largely because of the economy-wide nature of the external effects. Coasian bargaining, politicized correction, and spontaneous institutional evolution – all of these avenues for possible internalization seem to be severely limited in application. We are left with a fourth choice, that which involves an internalization of the work-supply externality through the installation, maintenance and transmission of an ethical precept that will effectively modify the constraint set that describes individual choice between work and non-work.

It is difficult to introduce ethical or moral constraints into the analytical apparatus of the economic theory of choice (Levy 1988). The person who supplies work to the market appears simply to adjust quantities of supply to the parametric wage per time unit that is confronted. It is possible, however, to depict the effect of an ethical precept if we modify the constraint set appropriately as illustrated in Figure 6.1. The indifference contours represent the relative evaluation of the two arguments, leisure (non-work) and income (other goods purchasable from the market). The market wage to which the individual adjusts hours (days, weeks) of work supply is shown by the slope of the line BY. This line need not, however, represent the effective constraint set for the chooser if there exists an ethical norm which makes a sense of guilt emerge when work supply falls below certain minimal limits. The presence of a work ethic may modify the effective constraints for the person to produce the kinked frontier, YMR. Over the range, MR, the individual suffers an internalized psychic cost. In this setting, the individual attains his maximum utility at the corner solution, M. Given the ethical constraint that is

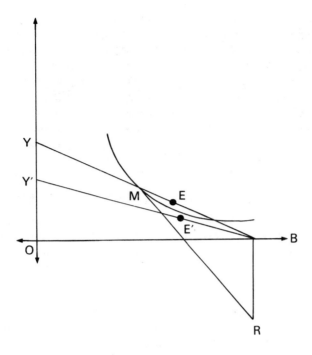

Figure 6.1 Effect of an ethical precept

presumed to be operative, the position E, which could seem to maximize utility, is simply unavailable.

If the individual could, in some fashion, escape from the binding constraint of the work ethic, and if this were possible *in isolation*, the preferred position at E might seem to be feasible. But note that, if *all* persons in the economy should similarly escape from the ethical constraint, E would no longer be available. As all persons reduce the supply of work as might be dictated by their pure naked preferences, the extent of the market would shrink, and, by the Smithian theorem, the exploitable range of specialization would be reduced. Wage rates would fall to some position such as that shown by the line BY'; individual equilibrium would be reached at E', which, by construction, lies on a preference contour lower than that which passes through M. If generalized over all work suppliers in the economy, the existence of the ethical constraint allows for at least some internalization of the externality.

I have, of course, deliberately constructed the figure to demonstrate the projected result. Clearly, as further geometric manipulation could show, the constraint that is exercised by a generalized work ethic might be so strong as to produce results less preferable than those attainable in total absence of such constraint, even given the extent of the market influence on resource productivity. The construction does suggest, however, that, so long as the Smithian theorem applies, the non-internalized voluntaristic equilibrium must remain non-optimal. From this result it follows that, within limits, the presence of some constraining influence of a work ethic must be deemed to be efficiency-enhancing.

WORK AS BENEVOLENT SELF-INTEREST

Perhaps the single most familiar statement in *The Wealth of Nations* is that which tells us that 'it is not from the benevolence of the butcher, the brewer, or the baker, that we expect our dinner, but from their regard to their own interest' (I, ii, 2). We understand Adam Smith's argument here, but if we take the conventional theory of distribution in the competitive economy seriously we immediately sense an apparent contradiction. If the butcher, and everyone else, takes from the economy precisely the equivalent of the value added to the economy by their efforts, how do we benefit from individuals' self-interested behaviour?

Suppose that the butcher decides to retire early and to go fishing, and that he does so out of strict self-interest. How will this change in his behaviour affect the rest of us? Not at all in the long-term sense if we accept the marginal productivity theory of distribution and assume that the economy is effectively competitive. The size of the market will become a mite smaller upon the butcher's retirement, but after other butchers expand their scales of operation, prices will return to the same levels that existed before the butcher ceased to butch.

I have argued that the conventional theory of competitive adjustment must surely be in error in this inference, and that we must look for ways to modify the conventional reasoning to allow for some accommodation of Smith's central theorem concerning the gains from trade that an extended division of labour facilitates. I have sought to show that, in order for the utilities of participants to be affected by a change in the size of the market, some relaxation of the constant returns condition for idealized competitive equilibrium must be effected. There must exist increasing returns in at least one industry in the all-inclusive exchange nexus.

Fortunately for my purposes, I am not required to enter directly into controversial areas of analysis involving the consistency between increasing returns and competitive equilibrium.[4] Nor is it necessary for me to specify, even conceptually, the relative share in total production that may emerge from increasing returns operation, or to identify those industries where increasing returns prevail.

I have suggested that the burden of internalization of the work-supply externality may rest with the embodiment of ethical norms in the work choice. To the extent that an ethic of work enters into the choice calculus of input suppliers, whether or not this be conscious, consumers somewhere in the economy secure spillover benefits. There is economic content in the ethic of work. And because there is economic content, there is some justification for both individualized and collective efforts to promulgate, maintain and transmit this ethic through the culture as well as intergenerationally.

The butcher's benevolent self-interest dictates that work does 'good' for others and this is lost when he goes fishing. The anti-work ethic of the 1960s summarized in the admonition 'take the time to smell the flowers' involves an explicit invitation to destroy economic value for others than the addressee. And, of course, the size of the external effects is directly related to the market value of the input potentially supplied. A radiologist who loafs around harms others more than the comparable behaviour of a McDonald's employee.

I have deliberately limited discussion in this paper to the work–leisure choice along the time unit dimension as the potential source of expansion or contraction in the size of the market. The analysis is obviously applicable to qualitative as well as quantitative dimensions, and to the choices of potential suppliers of resources other than work effort.

My suggestion that the work-supply externality is fully analogous to the 'trade extension' externality would not, as noted earlier, be surprising to trade theorists.[5] But the analysis has implications for many other policy areas such as population control, immigration, women's entry into the labour force, work requirements for welfare, and retirement programmes, along with evident inferences for tax institutions. My concern does not, however, extend to the derivation of implications for these policy questions. I limit emphasis here to the work supply externality, as such, motivated in large part by my initial query concerning the possible economic content in a work ethic. If my purpose must be generalized, it is to convince fellow economists that we remain ethically as well as economically interdependent, along the work–leisure choice margin as along so many others.

NOTES

1 Adam Smith did, of course, make the somewhat confused distinction between productive and unproductive labour, which may, in some stretch of imaginative generosity, be interpreted as a recognition of the relevance of the internal choice margin. For a fascinating treatment of the productive-unproductive distinction in the history of economics, see Helen Boss (1990).

2 In a curiously inconclusive paper, George Stigler (1951) fully appreciates the analytical dilemma here. But he seems to want to accept both the validity of Smith's theorem and the usefulness of the competitive equilibrium constructions. This stance is, perhaps, justified in part by Stigler's primary interest in the implications for the organization of industry.

3 Identification of the increasing-returns industry (or industries) would, of course, make possible efficiency-enhancing *shifts* in demand patterns, within an overall fixity in input utilization. But there would remain some remaining gains to be captured by expanded input supply.

4 A general summary of the whole set of increasing-returns controversies, along with appropriate references to the literature, is found in the Palgrave entry of Vassilakis (1987).

5 See W.J. Ethier (1982) for useful analysis that also contains references to the international trade literature.

REFERENCES

Boss, Helen (1990) *Theories of Surplus and Transfer: Parasites and Producers in Economic Thought*, Boston: Unwin and Hyman.

Buchanan, James M. (1989) 'Economic Interdependence and the Work Ethic', duplicated, Center for Study of Public Choice, George Mason University.

Ethier, W.J. (1982) 'National and International Returns to Scale in the Modern Theory of Institutional Trade', *American Economic Review*, 72, June, 389–405.

Gauthier, David (1985) *Morals by Agreement*, Oxford: Oxford University Press.

Kaldor, N. (1972) 'The Irrelevance of Equilibrium Economics', *Economic Journal*, 82, 1237–55.

Levy, David (1988) 'Utility Enhancing Consumption Constraints', *Economics and Philosophy*, 4, 69–88.

Stigler, George (1951) 'The Division of Labor Is Limited by the Extent of the Market', *Journal of Political Economy*, LIX, June, 185–93.

Vassilakis, S. (1987) 'Increasing Returns to Scale', in J. Eatwell, M. Milgate and P. Newman (eds) *The New Palgrave Dictionary of Economics*, vol. 2, London: Macmillan, 761–5.

Weitzman, Martin (1982) 'Increasing Returns and the Foundations of Unemployment Theory', *Economic Journal*, 92, December, 787–804.

Young, Allyn (1928) Increasing Returns and Economic Progress', *Economic Journal*, 38, 527–42.

7

THE INVISIBLE HAND IN MODERN MACROECONOMICS

James Tobin

THE INVISIBLE HAND AND THE KEYNESIAN DICHOTOMY

The 'invisible hand', one of the great ideas of history and one of the most influential, is Adam Smith's most important legacy to macroeconomics, as to all economics. It is particularly important today as the ultimate inspiration for the new classical macroeconomics and the real business cycle theory. These are intellectual movements that engage many of the best brains in the profession, especially among younger cohorts and especially in the United States. They dominate the agenda even of theorists and econometricians who are sceptical or hostile to their methods and conclusions.

These movements are revolutions counter to Keynesian economics, itself a revolution against invisible hand orthodoxy. Keynes claimed to have detected a massive market failure. Workers were involuntarily unemployed; workers who were willing to work at real wages not exceeding their marginal productivities. Employers did not hire them because of insufficient *effective* demand for what they would produce. The employment and output of the idle workers would enhance social welfare. Yet the market mechanism could neither prevent this failure nor correct it – could not correct it, that is, in good time and without government assistance. Keynes alleged this market failure to be an endemic flaw in capitalism.

The Great Depression lent credibility to Keynesian theory. So did the postwar prosperity of the advanced capitalist economies, which was widely attributed to the use of Keynesian stabilization policies. In the profession something of a reconciliation was achieved between Keynesian macroeconomics and classical or neoclassical microeconomics. Paul Samuelson called it the 'neoclassical synthesis'. At least it was coexistence, with each tradition assigned its domain, its text-book chapters, and its semester of the introductory course. The new terms with prefixes micro and macro signalled the division of the subject. Here is the Keynesian dichotomy in Keynes's own words:

> I see no reason to suppose that the existing system seriously misemploys the factors of production which are in use.... It is in determining the volume, not the direction, of actual employment that the existing system has broken down.... Thus I agree with [Silvio] Gesell that the result of filling in the gaps in the classical theory is not to dispose of the 'Manchester System', but to indicate the nature of the environment which the free play of economic forces requires if it is to realise the full potentialities of production.
>
> (Keynes 1936: 379)

In other words, the invisible hand does just fine, with one giant exception. Once this failing is remedied, once full employment is restored and maintained, classical economics comes into its own, telling how resources are allocated, how relative prices are determined, and how private and social utilities are maximized. And Keynesian economics tells how to restore and maintain full employment.

Keynes, it is true, was also critical of the inequalities of income and wealth generated by free market capitalism. In this, however, he was not out of the mainstream of his classical opponents, notably including Professor A.C. Pigou. Moreover, Keynes asserted that the high propensity of wealthy countries to save, which might be a source of unemployment and stagnation if left to itself, could if channelled into accumulation of capital so reduce its rate of return as to bring about 'the euthanasia of the rentier'.

As the domain of economics was divided, business fluctuations or 'cycles' were macro phenomena, to be understood by theories of aggregate demand set forth by Keynes and his successors. This was also initially the viewpoint of monetarists like Milton Friedman, who differed from Keynesians with regard to the determinants of aggregate demand, the sources of disturbances in it, and the proper instruments and strategies of stabilization of demand. Aggregate demand theories were, and still are, the rationales of the equations of most econometric models – academic, proprietary and governmental.

THE CLASSICAL COUNTER-REVOLUTION

There were always true believers in the invisible hand who were uncomfortable with the macro/micro partition and with the rationale for it offered by the neoclassical synthesis. Many of them were general equilibrium theorists, or at any rate economists who took seriously its market-clearing paradigm. They balked at describing as 'equilibrium' any situation with excess supplies or demands in any markets, let alone in whole economies. Direct or indirect disciples of Adam Smith, they believed that movements of prices – including wages and interest rates – would quickly or instantaneously eliminate excess supplies or demands. They understood how governmental or monopolistic restrictions of competition might delay or prevent market clearings. If so, the remedies would be removal of the restrictions; in any case Keynesian fiscal and monetary operations would be futile or worse. They saw Keynesian macroeconomic theory as dependent on an arbitrary and gratuitous assumption, endogenous inflexibility of money wage rates, which apparently attributed irrationality, even 'money illusion', to private agents.

In the 1970s unrest of this kind exploded into outright rebellion. There were reasons for this explosion outside of the profession, as there always are for major developments in economics, as there were in the times of Smith and Ricardo and Marx as well as those of Keynes. Just as the Great Depression of the 1930s was an environment favourable to the Keynesian revolution, the Great Stagflation of the 1970s inclined both economists and the general public to welcome the counter-revolution. The sociology of our discipline is fascinating, but I am concerned here rather with its internal dialectics.

The new classical economics is, as the name applies, a revival of the major macroeconomic propositions of Smith, Say, Ricardo and Mill.[1] These propositions were less explicit and conscious in Smith than in his followers, but they were there none the less and served to inspire Say and other successors. They are implications of his central anti-mercantilist themes: that national wealth consists in the capacity to produce useful commodities, or goods that can be traded for them, rather than in the accumulation of gold and silver money, and that free competitive markets yield optimal results while government regulations are counter-productive. The two main macroeconomic propositions are Say's law, i.e. the impossibility of generalized excess supply, and the neutrality of money, that 'veil' that obscures the true and real economic phenomena to near-sighted observers.[2]

119

Real business cycle theory is a logical spin-off of new classical macroeconomics.[3] The business fluctuations we observe, this theory alleges, are sequential equilibria moving in response to basic exogenous shocks. These shocks are changes in tastes (as among work and leisure, consumption now and consumption later), in technology and productivity, in resource availabilities, and in external supplies, demands and prices. There can be no Keynesian shocks to effective aggregate demand, because markets clear so that there are never any excess supplies or demands. That disposes of the 'Keynesian dichotomy', the view that business cycles are disequilibrium phenomena, fluctuations of demand around a fairly smoothly growing capacity to produce. Real buisiness cycle theory erases the common distinction between long-term growth trends and short-period cycles. They are one and the same. Supply and demand move together, not necessarily smoothly. All the shocks, all the outcomes that matter, are real. Nominal prices, money supplies, indeed all variables measured in the monetary unit of account, are irrelevant sideshows. Money is neutral not just in the long run but in the short run too. (Of course, gold and silver and other commodities of intrinsic non-monetary value may double as money. Changes in their supplies and demands and values in terms of labour and other goods and services will have real consequences.)

MACROECONOMICS IN *THE WEALTH OF NATIONS*

Adam Smith would feel at home with most of the content of his self-anointed modern disciples, if not with their language, style and methodology. His theory of economic progress in Book III focused on the growth of 'stock', accumulated savings as purchasing power over labour, at the disposition of business entrepreneurs. Continuously oriented to the most profitable uses and embodied in the most productive forms, stock is deployed to exploit opportunities for applying new technologies and for extending the division of labour. Smith emphasized stock as circulating capital. He appears to have assumed a one-period lag between inputs of labour and materials and outputs of saleable goods, in the manner of Piero Sraffa's twentieth-century classical model of production and prices. This assumption enabled Smith to speak of profits on stock interchangeably as mark-ups and as rates of return over time (I, vi, 6).

Smith would not be surprised that rates of growth fluctuate and are sometimes negative. He never found reason for such fluctuations in generalized shortages or excesses of demand. Nor did he find them in monetary expansions and contractions, even of gold and silver, nor in the commodity export or import surpluses that bring money into the nation or drive it out. In contrast, Hume expected monetary expansions and contractions to have at least temporary real effects, which indeed are part of the classical specie flow mechanisms of balance of payments adjustment (Dillard 1988: 303; II, ii, 96).

Smith said little about the determinants of saving and of the size and pace of accumulations of stock, but he regarded these as constraints on growth. He correctly saw holdings of gold and silver as diverting stock from productive employment, and therefore he welcomed prudent substitution of paper money for these precious metals. He was talking of banknotes, in modern terms 'inside money', liabilities that enable banks to make productive business loans, real bills. He seemed unworried about possible inflationary dangers of this process, expecting rather that over-issue would depress the exchange values of the notes of errant banks (II, ii, 48–59).

Smith evidently believed in purchasing power parity for tradeable goods, even in the short run. He anticipated a theory that returned to fashion about twenty years ago as 'the monetary theory of the balance of payments', (Smith 1776: 284–8, 308–9, 403–6; Kindleberger 1984: 8; Frenkel and Johnson 1975). It concerns a system of fixed exchange rates, for example the gold standard. According to this model, the stock of money in any one country is just what is needed and desired to handle the economy's real transactions at given international nominal prices. The country is presumed to be too small to affect those prices by itself. Anything that creates in the one country an excess demand for real money balances, e.g. productivity gains that increase output and transactions at existing prices, will suck gold into the country, entailing temporarily an export surplus. And vice versa, an expansion in domestic credit and banknote issue could create an excess supply of money. It would be worked off by export of gold (or by incurring gold debt to foreigners) and import of goods. The worldwide aggregate of nominal money supplies determines worldwide nominal prices.

Adam Smith's specific macroeconomic ideas are not an important part of his legacy to modern 'new classicals'. The invisible hand is their true inspiration. They reject the Keynesian dichotomy and expect competitive markets to transmute self-interest into public interest in macroeconomic as well as microeconomic outcomes. I turn now to an examination of the legitimacy of this application of Smith's great idea.

THE INVISIBLE HAND AND GENERAL EQUILIBRIUM THEORY

In *The Wealth of Nations* the invisible hand is a conjecture, an audacious and powerful idea to be sure, but an unproved assertion. It is a long way and almost two centuries from Smith to Arrow–Debreu, from the invisible hand to the twin fundamental theorems of welfare eonomics (Arrow 1953; Debreu 1959). These maintain that (1) a competitive equilibrium is Pareto-optimal; and (2) any Pareto-optimal allocation is a competitive equilibrium for some distribution of endowments. Of course, Pareto-optimality is a very weak criterion. Smith (IV, ii, 9) identifies 'public interest' with maximum 'annual revenue of the society', which I take to be real net national income. Two roads were travelled: the Anglo-Saxon line of economic theory through Marshall and Pigou; and the continental European road via Léon Walras, Vilfredo Pareto and Maurice Allais. Thanks to Irving Fisher, John R. Hicks and Paul Samuelson, the two strands came together earlier in this century.

Smith's conjecture was eventually rigorously proved by Arrow and Debreu, but at considerable cost to its generality. Let me remind you of some of the possible violations of the restrictive but necessary assumptions, stressing particularly those of macroeconomic significance.

Non-convexities

The fundamental theorems cannot survive non-convexities in tastes or technology. Smith himself eloquently and realistically stressed specialization and division of labour as sources of efficiency and progress. But general equilibrium theory cannot cope with economies of scale and scope. For one thing, if these non-convexities can be internalized in single firms, they are inconsistent with perfect competition.

Imperfect competition

The fundamental theorems require that all agents treat market prices as parameters beyond their control. This is the meaning of perfect competition. However, because of non-convexities or other factors many prices are not impersonal data but decisions of firms and individuals or outcomes of negotiations. Smith was, understandably, imprecise on this point. The 'market' was a vague metaphor for many varieties of institutions for the purchase and sale of commodities, not a rigorous concept. The same is true for many uses of the term today, indeed for almost all lay discussions.

Externalities

Third-party effects not considered by firms and households are a well-known source of market failures. Deals among the parties, even if conceivable, entail transactions costs. Competitive markets do not naturally exist for by-product goods and bads. Externalities are often treated as exceptional *curiosa* (orchards and beehives) in older welfare economics literature. But the spate of environmental hazards now tells us that externalities are no joke.

Time and uncertainty

Saving, investment and other intertemporal choices are not easy to introduce into general equilibrium models. Choices involving uncertainty are harder still. Irving Fisher and J.R. Hicks made important contributions. Arrow and Debreu 'solved' these problems simply by multiplying the list of commodities and distinguishing them by the time and 'state of nature' prescribed for delivery. The states of nature exhaust all possible contingencies. Competitive markets determine simultaneously prices for all these commodities. The market opens only once; the rest of economic history is just the deliveries then contracted. Lo and behold the fundamental theorems apply! One difficulty is that the number of 'commodities' would be so numerous relative to the number of transactors that competitive markets could not exist for most commodities. This is true even though it suffices to have a number of markets equal to the sum of the number of states of nature and the number of basic goods and services rather than to their product.

'Sequence economies' and incomplete markets

In actual economies spot markets are open continuously or repeatedly, few futures contracts are traded and few contingencies are insurable. As a result, there are plenty of opportunities for market failures. Rational expectations methodology, the theoretical rage of the last twenty years, can be seen as an attempt to compensate for missing markets. It attributes to agents a great deal of global knowledge of the structures of the economies and markets in which they are operating. However, it has not been shown how agents can acquire this knowledge from sequential observations generated by incompletely informed market participants. Those observations are distorted by the misinformations that guided the agents. Note, by the way, that Smith's invisible hand alleged that every individual need responds only to local information and incentive. That conjecture certainly remains unproved.

Instabilities

Prices set in multiple interrelated markets might not clear all the markets of excess supplies and demands all the time. 'False' trading may occur at wrong prices. Presumably prices and quantities will then move in response to excess supplies and demands. Will these movements converge to the equilibrium? It is not sure without additional restrictive assumptions, for example that traded commodities are 'gross substitutes' in collective excess demand functions. A particular example of instability, related to the incompleteness of markets and the difficulty of forming rational expectations, concerns the responses of competitors to a profitable opportunity for investment. If a margin of price above cost opens up, the opportunity for each firm appears large, maybe indefinitely large if constant returns to scale apply. Each firm knows the market will absorb only a finite expansion of capacity in aggregate, but is ignorant of its competitors' plans. This situation can lead to overbuilding and to cobweb cycles, familiar in office space and ships.

Money

There is no room for money, especially paper money but also the fiat component of commodity money, in these general equilibrium models. Attempts to introduce it have foundered on the economies of scale and externalities that are intrinsic virtues of money. In consequence of these virtues, markets – whether perfectly or imperfectly competitive – generate prices in money rather than in Smith's labour hours or any other commodity numeraire. Since money useful as a means of exchange is necessarily also a store of value, decisions to hold it over time are intertwined with other saving and investment decisions and are not necessarily neutral.

KEYNES'S REVOLT AGAINST THE PREMISES OF CLASSICAL MACROECONOMICS

Keynes was quite clear about the theoretical foundations of his rebellion against classical – he could have said neoclassical – macroeconomics. Markets or other processes set nominal wages, not real wages, and nominal prices, not relative prices. These nominal wages and prices are sticky, if only because there is not continuous and instantaneous market clearing. Perceiving, as did Smith, that money is a store of value competitive in savers' portfolios with other assets, including real capital, Keynes rejected, as Smith did not, money neutrality.

Shocks to aggregate real demand frequently occur, possibly because business firms change their views of the future profitability of capital investments and of the acceptability of the risks, possibly because consumers decide to shift consumption between present and future. Keynes was quite explicit about missing markets, particularly the absence of futures markets. When a consumer decides not to eat lunch today, he conveys a negative demand signal to his customary restaurant but no signal of when in the future and where he intends to spend the amount saved. No investment is undertaken to prepare for his future demands (Keynes 1936: 210–13). Absent of such signals or Arrow–Debreu contracts, businesses and other investors who buy long-lived durable assets are exposing themselves to incalculable risks (Keynes 1936: Chapter 12). Keynes also envisaged monetary shocks, changes in money supplies or velocities, which may become real demand shocks because nominal prices are sticky. But it is a vulgar fallacy, all too epidemic nowadays, to describe these as the only sources of Keynesian aggregate demand fluctuations.

Keynes questioned the capacity of the economy, once displaced from full employment equilibrium, to return to that equilibrium on its own. The normal price responses to excess supply would not, he said, be reliable adjustment mechanisms for nominal wages and prices all over the economy. He did not believe that increased flexibility of nominal wages and prices would reduce the volatility of real output and employment in response to real demand or monetary shocks. Price reductions would not occur instantaneously, fast enough to forestall even temporary declines in output and employment. Price reductions would take real time. The process of deflation itself – the argument also applies to disinflation – would discourage demand, quite possibly aggravating the disequilibrium instead of correcting it (Keynes 1936: Chapter 19, especially p. 265).

Keynes's multiplier comes on stage as soon as it is admitted that even part of the adjustment to changes in aggregate demand takes place in quantities. The multiplier reinforces the changes in quantities. This is an implication of the point that Keynes regarded as his most important innovation, the principle of effective demand. Agents' purchases are constrained by the amounts they actually realize from selling their endowments (of labour, for example), regardless of how much they would buy if they could sell all they want to sell at prevailing prices. This point was rediscovered by the mathematically formal 'general disequilibrium theory' of recent years (Barro and Grossman 1976; Malinvaud 1977).

In situations of excess supply of labour and of capital capacity, there are positive 'multiplier' externalities to individual increases in expenditure on goods and services, for example business capital investments. These give the government a role in economic stabilization, not only via expenditures, taxes and monetary measures but possibly also via indicative planning in the style of Jean Monnet.

Keynes's departures from the assumptions of general equilibrium theory are all, I submit, legitimate and reasonable. They do not reflect vulgar ignorance or casual neglect of the standard paradigm of economic theory, but rather a recognition of its shortcomings in application to real-world macroeconomics. Neither Keynes nor the architects of the subsequent 'neoclassical synthesis' solved all the theoretical problems involved, including the specification of suitable equations for macroeconometric models. Younger generations of theorists will find a challenging and fruitful agenda here if they overcome the temptations of the new classicals.

ROBINSON CRUSOE MACROECONOMICS

New classical macroeconomics begins with the position that the invisible hand, in the form of modern general equilibrium theory, deserves the benefit of the doubt. That is, the burden of proof is on anyone who contends that market failures occur and that there is room or need for government macroeconomic policy. Of course, these latter-day disciples of Adam Smith know that today's economies are not like those described in *The Wealth of Nations*, much less like those described in Arrow–Debreu. Following Milton Friedman's 'methodology of positive economics', they hypothesize that actual economies function 'as if' the general equilibrium model applied.

Real business cycle models simulate a simple economy with classical properties, subjected to a random process of technological shocks, and compare the variances and covariances of the simulations with those from actual economies. The tests have little power. If the hypothesis that they are the same cannot be rejected by the comparisons, it is accepted, even though simulations of many other models could survive similar comparisons.

Even weak tests reject new classical explanations of cyclical fluctuations of employment and unemployment as voluntary intertemporal choices. According to these explanations, periods of high unemployment reflect choices of leisure now in anticipation that work will yield higher real wages later. No reasonable empirical estimates of responses of leisure–work–consumption choices to real wages are anywhere near large enough to explain fluctuations of the magnitude of postwar business cycles, let alone those of the 1930s. Moreover, the unemployed themselves say they are searching for work and are not out of the labour force. In times of high unemployment, disproportionately large numbers of unemployed result from lay-offs rather than voluntary quits. The Keynesian story fits the facts much better.

Real business cycle models concern Robinson Crusoe economies. A single representative individual is making choices for the whole economy. This simplification enables the model-builder to derive behaviour explicitly from rational optimization subject only to constraints of resource availabilities and technology. Obviously this is not a money economy. It is not even the barter economy Smith and the classicals perceived through the veil of money. It is not even a market economy, because no transactions need occur. Any prices generated are just the shadow prices of the optimal allocations chosen by Robinson Crusoe.

In Keynes's view the essential task of macroeconomics was to explain how markets do and do not coordinate the behaviours of diverse agents: households and firms, savers and investors, workers and employers, creditors and debtors, bulls and bears, citizens and governments. To assume away this diversity is to default the responsibilities of the profession to maintain seriousness and relevance.

Adam Smith is not responsible for excesses committed in his name. His main purpose was to oppose protectionism and other regulations favouring special interests at the expense of the general public. His important message was that the accumulation of precious metals by contriving foreign trade surpluses was contrary to the national interest, for the true wealth of a nation lay in its capacity to deliver useful goods and services to its citizens. Modern macroeconomists of all shades could agree, and usually do.

Who knows what Smith would have thought of Walras, Arrow and Debreu, or of Lucas, Sargent and Barro? *The Wealth of Nations* is a very down-to-earth book, with a simple thematic moral, a rudimentary theoretical model, an imaginative intuition, a vast collection of historical and institutional material, and a great deal of wisdom and common sense. Perhaps looser claims for the invisible hand, less sweeping, less rigorous and less abstract than general equilibrium models, would be more congenial to Smith. Second-best claims that admit market failures but say governments are worse? Schumpeter's argument for the substantial but uneven progress due to the innovations of temporary monopolies? Perhaps Smith would not be altogether unfriendly to Keynes's activism against mass unemployment and to Keyne's contention that such macroeconomic activism would enable the principles of the 'Manchester School' to achieve their full potential.

NOTES

1   The major figures are Robert Lucas, Thomas Sargent and Robert Barro. See Lucas 1981, Sargent 1976, Lucas and Sargent 1978, Barro 1974. 'Rational expectations' is the important theoretical and methodological innovation. But the neoclassical assumption of market-clearing is essential for the strong macroeconomic propositions.

2   Dillard (1988) refers to the 'veil' proposition as the 'barter illusion' of classical economists, who of course scorned vulgar 'money illusion'. Like Keynes, Dillard contests the view that a money economy is a supremely efficient system of multilateral barter. The efficiencies of money as a medium of exchange come at a cost, namely that Say's law is not assured.

3   For exposition of this theory of business cycles see Plosser 1989.

REFERENCES

Arrow, Kenneth (1953) 'Le Rôle de Valeurs Boursieres pour la Repartition la Meilleure des Risques', *Econométrie*, Paris: Centre National de la Recherche Scientifique, 41–8.

Barro, Robert (1974) 'Are Government Bonds Net Wealth?', *Journal of Political Economy*, 82, November–December, 1095–117.

Barro, Robert and Herschel Grossman (1976) *Money, Employment and Inflation*, Cambridge: Cambridge University Press.

Debreu, Gerard (1959) *Theory of Value*, New York: Wiley.

Dillard, Dudley (1988) 'The Barter Illusion in Classical and Neoclassical Economics', *Eastern Economic Journal*, XIV (4), October–December, 299–318.

Frenkel, Jacob and Harry G. Johnson (1975) *The Monetary Approach to the Balance of Payments*, London: George Allen & Unwin.

Keynes, John Maynard (1936) *The General Theory of Employment, Interest, and Money*, New York: Harcourt Brace & Co.

Kindleberger, Charles P. (1984) 'Was Adam Smith a Monetarist or a Keynesian?', *Business Economics*, January, 5–12.

Lucas, Robert E. Jr (1981) *Studies in Business Cycle Theory*, Cambridge, Mass.: Massachusetts Institute of Technology Press.

Lucas, Robert E. Jr and Thomas J. Sargent (1978) 'After Keynesian Macroeconomics', in *After the Phillips Curve*, Conference Series no. 19, Boston: Federal Reserve Bank, 49–72.

Malinvaud, Edmond (1977) *The Theory of Unemployment Reconsidered*, Oxford: Basil Blackwell.

Plosser, Charles I. (1989) 'Understanding Real Business Cycles', *Journal of Economic Perspectives*, 3, Summer, 51–77.

Sargent, Thomas J. (1976) 'A Classical Macroeconomic Model for the United States', *Journal of Political Economy*, 84, April, 207–38.

8

ADAM SMITH AND HUMAN CAPITAL

Theodore W. Schultz

I begin this paper with a discussion of Adam Smith's concept of the useful abilities acquired through education, study or apprenticeship, always at a real expense, which consists of capital fixed in people. Investment in this form of capital is motivated by the expected rate of return. I then consider the implications of the lack of a theory of the extension of markets. A compelling theory is still an unfinished part of economics. Lastly I turn to human capital in the modernizing economy with its proliferation of human capital, vast specialization and its increases in the value of human time and advances in useful knowledge.

The significance of human capital is receiving increasing analytical attention, especially so since the Second World War. However, an awareness of the existence of this form of capital has a long history. It is clearly evident in many parts of *The Wealth of Nations*. Adam Smith boldly included all of the acquired useful abilities of the inhabitants and members of the society as capital. Smith reckoned that the acquisition of this class of capital by a person through

> education, study, or apprenticeship, always costs a real expense, which is a capital fixed and realized, as it were, in his person. . . . The improved dexterity of a workman may be considered in the same light as a machine or instrument of trade which facilitates and abridges labour, and which, though it costs a certain expense, repays that expense with a profit. (II, i, 17)

Smith treats the incentives to invest in this class of human capital in much detail along with many historical accounts of such investment processes. Ponder, however, Smith's jaundiced views of the value of public education for women and of the diligence of public teachers being corrupted by the endowments of schools and colleges.

A great deal of economics is condensed by Smith in the following paragraph (V, i, b, 8).

When any expensive machine is erected, the extraordinary work to be performed by it before it is worn out, it must be expected, will replace the capital laid out upon it, with at least the ordinary profits. A man educated at the expense of much labour and time to any of those employments which require extraordinary dexterity and skill, may be compared to one of those expensive machines. The work which he learns to perform, it must be expected, over and above the usual wages of common labour, will replace to him the whole expense of his education, with at least the ordinary profits of an equally valuable capital. It must do this too in a reasonable time, regard being had to the very uncertain duration of human life, in the same manner as to the more certain duration of the machine. (I, x, b, 6)

What has been ignored in much of economics is the simple truth that people invest in themselves and that these investments are very large in modern high-income countries. Although economists are seldom timid in entering upon abstract analysis, some are even proud of being impractical, they have not been bold in coming to grips with investment in human beings. It is as if when they come even close, they proceed gingerly, afraid that they are stepping into deep water. No doubt there are reasons for being wary.

In my American Economic Association presidential address, 'Investment in Human Capital', I noted some deep-seated moral and philosophical issues.[1] Free men are first and foremost the end to be served by the economy; they are not property, nor are they marketable assets. The mere thought of treating human beings as investment objects is offensive. Our values and beliefs inhibit us from thinking of human beings as capital goods, except in slavery, and this we abhor. We are ever mindful of the long struggle to rid society of indentured servitude and slavery and to evolve political and legal institutions to keep men free of bondage. Hence, to treat a human being as capital could appear to reduce man, once again, to a mere material component, as if he were a piece of physical property.

No less a person than J.S. Mill at one time insisted that the people of a country should not be looked upon as wealth because wealth existed only for the sake of people. But surely Mill was wrong; there is nothing in the concept of human wealth and for that matter in human capital contrary to his idea that it exists only for the advantage of people. By investing in themselves, people can enlarge their economic opportunities. It is one way free human beings can enhance their welfare.

131

EXTENSIONS OF MARKET CAPITAL

Smith's famous theorem is that the division of labour depends on the extent of the market. In today's economic language, this means that the real gains in the productivity of labour, including 'the greater part of the skill, dexterity, and judgment with which it is anywhere directed, or applied' (I, i, 1), are the consequences of the division of labour. Various components of human capital are specified by Smith. But the conditions and the analytics to explain the extensions of the market, their origins, and the increases in income derived from such extensions were not resolved by Smith.

Smith does appeal to various historical extensions of markets that had their origins in developments that reduced the costs of transportation. The long standing effects of great rivers and of inland navigation are featured. 'It is remarkable that neither the ancient Egyptians, nor the Indians, nor the Chinese, encouraged foreign commerce, but seem all ot have derived their opulence from this inland navigation' (I, iii, 7). Explaining extensions of the market is at best a weak part of the division of labour analysis.

Smith could not have anticipated the vast increases in specialized human capital and the large increases in personal income derived from human capital. Ever more specialization is clearly evident in countries that are successful in the modernization of their economy. Not knowing the economics of extensions of markets, how useful it is to hold fast to Smith's theorem that the division of labour is limited by the extent of the market? Vast increases in specialized human capital imply that the extent of the division of labour and the extent of the market must have increased greatly. I doubt that our knowledge about economic changes over time is sufficient to explain the sources of these vast extensions of the market. When it comes to explaining this source of the increases in income, it continues to receive a low priority from economists.

Allyn Young is a notable exception.[2] He perceived that there are latent implications in Smith's theorem that provide clues to explanations. Young began his classic paper, 'Increasing Returns and Economic Progress', with these words, 'My subject may appear alarmingly formidable, but I did not intend it to be so.' The formidable analytical task was to explain the origins of the changes in the economy that account for the large observed increases in income. There were and still are many unsolved issues: (1) measured output exceeding measured inputs; (2) unexplained long-term increases in per capita income;

(3) decline in the economic importance of farm land; (4) increase in the value of time; and (5) the proliferation of human capital in the modernizing economy.

Young turned to latent implications in Smith's theorem. Young reasoned that there exists an economic process in which the interactions between particular extensions of the market and of specific types of extensions in the division of labour explain increasing returns and economic progress.

The pursuit of investing in specialized human capital to attain increasing returns is not a venture guided by wishful thinking.[3] There are classes of private and public investments that have been and continue to be made guided by expectations of attaining increasing returns. Highly skilled geneticists and biologists, who specialize in their research on food producing plants and animals, have made advances in knowledge that make the recent extraordinary increases in food production possible. Ponder the explanation of the Golden Age of agricultural research that occurred beginning in the 1950s and on into the 1980s. All-in-all, the world population doubled. World food production more than doubled. Real expenditures worldwide on agricultural research have increased more than sevenfold since 1950. These large increases in investment in research were made and continue to be made in response to the perceived high returns from this class of investments. So too are the sizable investments in research in the case of the remarkable event of the origins, productivity and profitability of the computer. There is one element that all such events have in common; they are all cost saving and income increasing.

Advances in knowledge are a decisive factor in economic progress. The increases in the quality of both physical and human capital originate primarily out of the advances in knowledge. The value of the acquired abilities of human beings are in large measure revealed in wages, salaries, self-employed earnings and entrepreneurial rewards. Engineers who graduate currently will have learned many new elements in their specialization that were not known and therefore not taught to engineers who graduated several decades ago. This is also the case for scientists, medical personnel, technicians of various sorts, and economists. Moreover, the stock of human capital, which consists of a large array of components, has been increasing at a higher rate than that of physical capital.[4]

Smith was not overly occupied with diminishing or increasing returns. That his division of labour entails specialization was not belaboured. That the cost of an education is a form of fixed capital was not treated as an indivisibility to ascertain its effects on returns. That market expansion, division of labour, advances in technology, specialization and increasing returns go hand in hand in achieving economic progress is implied, but was not featured by Smith.

The private and public investments in the development of highly skilled geneticists and biologists, who in my example become highly specialized in their research on food producing crops and animals, give rise to patterns of returns that are consequences of the indivisibilities that are specific to the human capital of geneticists and biologists.

Sherwin Rosen is both cogent and concise on specialization.

> Incentives for specialization, trade, and the production of comparative advantage through investment are shown to arise from increasing returns to utilization. Hence, the rate of return is increasing in utilization and is maximized by utilizing specialized skills as intensively as possible. Identically endowed individuals have incentives to specialize their investments in skills and trade with each other for this reason, even if production technology exhibits constant returns to scale. The enormous productivity and complexity of modern economies are in good measure attributable to specialization.[5]

Hindsight has some advantages. We now know that advances in technology are endogenous events. These advances are man-made. They originate from within the economy. They are made by people who possess in their person special skills consisting of components of human capital. It is increasingly so in this age of high technology. We may be well advised to concentrate our analytical work on the following interacting income increasing sources: advances in technology, proliferation of human capital and the increases in specialization.

We need a theory to analyse the interactions of physical and human capital accumulations that induce investment in specialized human capital. We need to identify the specific external effects of human capital postulated by Robert Lucas.[6] These effects are viewed as a spillover from one person to another. The implication is that people at each skill level are more productive in high than in low human capital environments. Human capital enhances the productivity of both labour and physical capital. Lucas sees 'human capital accumulation as a social activity, involving groups of people, in a way that has no counterpart in the accumulation of physical capital'.

Given our academic vested interest, dare we ask, does the economics of specialization apply to the professions? Machlup's studies show that a great deal of specialization prevails and that the exent and complexity of our knowledge producing professions bespeak human capital specialization and that it accounts for much of the realized productivity.[7]

When early English economists observed the high rates of increases in production in various manufacturing industries, they attributed a part of the additional income to increases in returns. Favourable changes in economic conditions in manufacturing, transportation and trade in their day came to be known as the Industrial Revolution. As an economic process it had much in common with what is now referred to as the Green Revolution in agriculture.

Specialization driven by the proliferation of capital and by advances in technology, innovations and discoveries are income increasing economic events.[8] Most of them are small, micro events, as in the case of a farmer's increase in corn yields made possible by hybrid seed. Such events can, as a rule, be identified and measured. Their economic effects are in general ascertainable. But when increases in income are attributed to large, 'macro events' – the Industrial Revolution, for example – the specific sources of the increases in incomes are difficult to isolate and measure.

Nature, as Marshall had perceived it, is a minor source of these income increasing events. For most analytical purposes they are consequences of the activities of human beings. They may have their origin either from within or outside of the economic system. Those that originate from within would be included in Schumpeter's theory of economic development. These income increasing events have become important sources of additional income streams. They spawn related income increasing events. The economy of many countries has a built-in capacity to create income increasing entities, notably by means of organized research, including R & D, university-based science research, and investment in education as well as in the distribution of knowledge.

ANALYTIC LEVERAGE OF HUMAN CAPITAL

To gauge the relative strength of the leverage of human capital, requires an all-inclusive concept of capital. From Fisher we have the required concept, but it has seldom been used to gauge the economic importance of human capital.[9] The economic effects of various institutions on human capital are rarely on the research agenda of economists. We do have Common's *Legal Foundations of Capitalism*.[10] Would that economics could have been blessed by a marriage of Fisher's all-inclusive concept of capital and Common's legal foundations of Fisher's capital. Presently, however, economists who specialize in growth models seldom mention institutions. There is no hiding the fact that our new analytical cupboards are bare on thinking by economists about institutions.

Marshall's economic perceptions pertaining to knowledge, property rights and organization remain cogent.

> Capital consists in a great part of knowledge and organization: and of this some part is private property and the other part is not. Knowledge is our most powerful engine of production.... Organization aids knowledge.... The distinction between public and private property in knowledge and organization is of great and growing importance; in some respects of more importance than that between public and private property in material things.[11]

Marshall's perceptions are being strongly supported by the large body of human capital research of the last three decades.

There are significant differences in the nature of property rights between human and non-human capital. Rosen is succinct in his account of the main ideas in human capital.[12] On the issue of the difference in property rights he states, 'Ownership of human capital in a free society is restricted to the person in whom it is embodied.... A person cannot, even voluntarily, sell a legally binding claim on future earning power.' It follows that a person cannot sell asset claims on himself.

> The legal system places many fewer restrictions on the sale and voluntary transfer of title of nonhuman capital.... The institution of slavery was the primary example of a transferable property right in human capital. To be sure, the involuntary elements of slavery are essential, but even voluntary systems have not been unknown. Similarly, indentured servitude was an example of a legally enforceable long-term contractual claim on the human capital services of others.

But keep in mind that there are countries that impose severe political and legal restrictions on transfers of title to non-human capital: the chief example is collective and state ownership of non-human capital in planned economies.

Thus, at the extreme, people who are bound by the institution of slavery, have no property rights in their human capital. Poor people who are free in general have property rights in the small amount of human capital that is a part of their person. In my *Restoring Economic Equilibrium: Human Capital in the Modernizing Economy*, I argue the case for extending property rights in human capital. I concentrated on high income societies where investments in human capital have been large, and where the rise in the value of human time has been pronounced, and where the property rights of people in their human capital have been enlarged and protected.

In societies where wages, self-employment earnings, salaries, and earnings of entrepreneurs account for three-quarters, or a greater share of personal income, important institutional changes in favour of human capital property rights have occurred during recent decades. The political and legal origins of these changes appear to be fairly easy to document.

There is much to be said for undertaking research using the logic of Yoram Barzel in his *Economic Analysis of Property Rights* to analyse the various origins of changes in property rights.[13] Self-interest should motivate scholars and scientists, including economists, to determine the effects on incentives of extending property rights in human capital that go beyond existing patents and copyrights, that increase safety in the workplace, safety in travel and safety where one lives. The effects of tenure rights on incentives are unresolved. To what extent are honours weak substitutes for additional financial rewards for various unprotected intellectual and other human capital components?

The notable advances in human capital theory and in the wide array of supporting empirical studies are evaluated with authority by Rosen in his essay on *Human Capital*.[14] The increasing economic importance of human capital in the modernizing economy is not in doubt. The economic leverage of human capital exceeds that of non-human capital in high income countries where it accounts for most of the personal income of people.

The basic element in my approach to human capital is in the linkage of the rate of return to the investment in human capital. This linkage is evident in Smith's explanation of the relative earnings of physicians and other professional workers. The compensatory nature of earnings on prior investments points to opportunities forgone, which is a fundamental cost of undertaking the investment.

Rosen correctly credits Gary Becker for having developed

The fundamental conceptual framework of analysis for virtually all subsequent work in this area. Following Schultz's lead, Becker organized his theoretical development around the rate of return on investment, as calculated by comparing the earnings streams in discounted present value to alternative courses of actions. Rational agents pursue investments up to the point where the marginal rate of return equals the opportunity cost of funds.[15]

We have a theory of supply of human capital that gives us empirically refutable restrictions on intertemporal and interpersonal differences in the patterns of earnings and other aspects of productivity. In focusing on the development of a person's skills and earning capacity over the life cycle, human capital theory has evolved as a theory of 'permanent income' and wealth.

The best studies to date pertain to education as a form of human capital. Moreover, education is the most important component of human capital. In this area Jacob Mincer and Zvi Griliches have made outstanding contributions. An issue of special interest to me is entrepreneurial ability. The advances in the modernization of agriculture have led to many studies of the entrepreneurship of farmers. The results are that there are few economic regularities that are as valid empirically as the proposition that the entrepreneurial abilities of farmers are enhanced by their education.

Dale Jorgenson has devoted a great deal of his research over several years to establish the economic value of education. I draw on an updating of that research by Jorgenson jointly with Barbara Fraument.[16] Their results are based on education in the United States. They reckon

the lengthy gestation period between the application of educational inputs ... and the emergence of human capital embodied in the graduates of educational institutions. Furthermore, some of the benefits of investing in education, such as greater earning power, are recorded in transactions in the labor market, while others – better parenting or more rewarding employment of leisure – remain unrecorded.

The value of the time spent working has expanded very rapidly in postwar United States. The increases in this value have been greater for women than for men at all levels of educational attainment, which reflects the more rapid increases in labour force participation of women. The proportional increase in the value of market labour time has been greatest for college-educated men and women.

The total value of market activities for all educational attainments in the United States, adjusted for the increase of the price level between

138

1948 and 1984, rose by a factor of 3.3; for males who attained a college education it increased by a factor of 6.6; and for females by a factor of 12.9. The Jorgenson–Fraumeni estimates of the value of non-market activities, which rest on a critical assumption, exceeded the value of market activities. Investments in formal education in 1982–4 dollars increased from 184 to 772 billion dollars, by a factor of 4.2. Investments in college education of males and females combined increased from 36.3 to 523 billion, an increase by a factor of 14.5.

CLOSING COMMENT

At the beginning of this paper I cited Adam Smith to show that Smith clearly perceived that the critical economic connection is the rate of return to investment in 'education, study, or apprenticeship ... which is a capital fixed and realized, as it were, in his person.' On the basic properties of human capital, Adam Smith stands high, as he does on the division of labour, limited by the extent of the market. But we still do not have a compelling theory of market extensions. Smith presented many particular cases. So do economists now. Smith could not have anticipated the extrordinary rise in the economic importance of human capital.

In retrospect it has been the increasing economic importance of human capital, consisting of the acquired abilities of people – their education, work experience, skills and health – that explains most of modern economic progress. It is 'human capital' not space, cropland, energy, or other physical properties of the earth, that is decisive in improving the income and welfare of people in the modernizing economy. A critical view would stress that in making investments land is overrated, whereas effort made to increase the quality of human agents is underrated.[17]

NOTES

I am indebted to John Letiche for useful suggestions and to Margaret Schultz for her library search.

1   Presented 28 December 1960, published in *The American Economic Review*, LI, March 1961, pp. 1–17.
2   Allyn A. Young (1928) 'Increasing Returns and Economic Progress', *The Economic Journal*, December, 527–42.
3   Theodore W. Schultz (1988) 'On Investing in Specialized Human Capital to Attain Increasing Returns', in Gustav Ranis and T. Paul Schultz (eds)

The State of Development Economics, New York: Basil Blackwell.

4 I draw here on a part of Chapter 14, in Theodore W. Schultz (1990) *Restoring Economic Equilibrium: Human Capital in the Modernizing Economy*, New York: Basil Blackwell.

5 Sherwin Rosen (1976) 'Substitution and Division of Labor', *Econometrica*, 45 (1), 861–8. Also, (1983) 'Specialization and Human Capital', *Journal of Labor Economics*, 1, 43–9.

6 Robert E. Lucas, Jr 'On the Mechanics of Economic Development', his Marshall Lecture, May 1985, published in *Journal of Monetary Economics*, 22, 1988, 3–42.

7 Fritz Machlup (1962) *The Production and Distribution of Knowledge in the United States*, Princeton, NJ: Princeton University Press and his (1980) *Knowledge: Its Creation, Distribution, and Economic Significance. Knowledge and Knowledge Productivity*, Princeton, NJ: Princeton University Press; (1982) *The Branches of Learning*, Princeton, NJ: Princeton University Press; and his last (1984) *The Economics of Information and Human Capital*, Princeton, NJ: Princeton University Press.

8 Based on a part of chapter 17 of my *Restoring Economic Equilibrium* (see note 9 above).

9 Irving Fisher (1906) *The Nature of Capital and Income*, New York: Macmillan and Co.

10 John R. Commons (1924) *Legal Foundations of Capitalism*, New York: Macmillan and Co.

11 Alfred Marshall (1930) *Principles of Economics*, 8th edn, Book IV, Ch. 1, London Macmillan and Co., 138–9.

12 Sherwin Rosen (1987) 'Human Capital' in John Eatwell, Murray Milgrate and Peter Newman (eds) *The New Palgrave: A Dictionary of Economics*, London: Macmillan.

13 Yoram Barzel (1989) *Economic Analysis of Property Rights*, Cambridge: Cambridge University Press, 1–121.

14 Rosen, op. cit.

15 ibid.

16 Dale W. Jorgenson and Barbara M. Fraumeni, 'Investment in Education and US Economic Growth', presented at a NBER Conference, 4–5 May 1990.

17 The basis for this assessment is set forth in my (1981) *Investing in People: The Economics of Population Quality*, Berkeley, CA: University of California Press.

9

THE PRESENT STATE OF ECONOMIC SCIENCE

Wassily Leontief

At the time of Adam Smith's death economics was in a splendid state: *The Wealth of Nations* presented a perfect, systematic synthesis of the contributions of his distinguished predecessors. His detailed, often eloquent factual descriptions of the economic structure – not only of the contemporary but also of many of the older societies – provided a solid basis for a convincing theoretical explanation of their day-to-day operations. Moreover, the long and broad historical perspective characteristic of an eighteenth-century philosopher enabled Adam Smith to trace the subtle interdependence between the structural and the corresponding functional changes that marked the development of the budding capitalistic system on the eve of its explosive growth. In reading *The Wealth of Nations* one is struck by concrete descriptions of the ongoing technological change and theoretical emphasis on the role it was bound to play in economic growth and the concomitant rise of private and public welfare. This was the time when the great French *Encyclopedia*, as well as the early volumes of the newly established US Census of Manufacturers, contained detailed, richly illustrated descriptions of various newly improved processes of production. Far from being dismal, economics was at that time a very fashionable discipline. Alexander Pushkin made the hero of his Byronic poem, Eugen Onegin, read *The Wealth of Nations* and discuss knowledgeably the balance of trade.

Two hundred years passed. The recent quarterly issue of the *Journal of Economic Literature* records the titles of some 450 books and 2,800 articles presumably deserving serious professional attention. It lists moreover the titles of some twenty new economic journals that have been launched in a single year. In spite of this extensive output, in the judgement of most outsiders and many inside observers, economics as a scientific discipline does not now seem to be in a very healthy state.

141

How else could one interpret the fact that a well-attended conference was recently held under the auspices of the American National Science Foundation with the specific purpose of redefining economics as a special field of 'rhetoric'?

To the extent that much of the writing on that subject deals with questions of practical policies, advocacy has naturally to play an important role in it. Rhetoric has, however, to be put aside when it comes to the pragmatic task of finding the means that have to be used to attain a given final goal. Between the means and the ends of causes and effects embedded in the intricate fabric of the economic system's processes, the description of its structure and its operational properties has still to be recognized as the most significant, if not the only, object of economics as an empirical science.

Why has economics as an empirical discipline advanced so slowly in recent years despite the high level of activities referred to above? Has it entered an era of diminishing returns? In natural sciences measuring and counting are introduced from the outside by the investigator. For an economist observing production and consumption, selling and buying, measuring and counting constitute a tangible part of the reality that he observes and sets out to explain. Despite, or possibly because of that, systematic use of formal mathematical language was in our discipline rather slow to come.

Re-reading in the early parts of *The Wealth of Nations* the detailed description of price formation through the process of mutual adjustment between supply and demand of various goods and services and the sophisticated tracing of indirect effects of technological changes, one is tempted to translate Adam Smith's verbal arguments into the mathematical language of a modern economics textbook. This is what to some extent Alfred Marshall did in relegating in his *Principles* a concise presentation of his verbal arguments to the mathematical appendices. In modern theoretical writing the emphasis usually seems to be reversed: mathematical equations constitute the centrepiece while the explanation of their relations to the observed or at least observable reality is relegated to brief introductory remarks and statistical appendices.

Assuming that the algebra is correct, the practical implications of a purely formal argument depend on the validity of the factual premises with which it starts and the empirical implications of the formal conclusions to which it leads. Hence the usefulness of a model-building enterprise depends critically on the empirical interpretation of mathematical symbols employed in it.

The task of the economist should be facilitated by the fact that the activities and transactions that he sets out to describe are objects of practical concern to those who are actually engaged in them. Anyone who has tried to explain to a Soviet citizen the functioning of a free competitive economy can appreciate the advantage of having immediate, direct access to such a natural, personal source of factual information. Moreover, from time immemorial governments for their own practical purposes compiled population, foreign trade and what we would now call real estate statistics and economists made ample use of these data. But as the problems that they wanted to address became more and more complex, economists seemed to become satisfied with doing their theoretical modelling in more and more general hypothetical terms. Demand curves were supposed to be downward sloping and supply curves upward sloping. The indifference curve had to be concave and the isoquant convex. Mathematical formulation permits theoretical model-builders to secure the internal logical consistency of their constructs but leaves the question of their factual relevance entirely open.

In the 1920s and the early 1930s the exploitation of formal implications of maximizing behaviour permitted the theorists to demonstrate the power and empirical relevance of purely deductive reasoning by explaining the implications of so-called second-order conditions of such behaviour. The assumption of so-called dynamic stability made it possible to stretch even further the claim of realistic relevance for very general formal reasoning in the study of economic changes although the recent admission of the possibility of 'chaotic' behaviour might weaken this claim. It is the translation of directly observable reality into international terms at one end of a mathematical argument and the translation of the mathematical symbols into observable facts at the other end that really counts. And such translation can be given only in ordinary non-mathematical language.

Early attempts at derivation of 'statistical' demand and supply curves paved the way for the development of more and more sophisticated uses of indirect statistical inference, now employed in economics more routinely than in many other fields. Paradoxically, the very ease with which a theoretical model can now be fitted with the help of powerful electronic computers, purely automatically, to any given set of data has led to trivialization of the critically important problem of the proper relationship between abstract model-building and systematic fact finding in economic research.

Last year Professor Trigve Havelmo was awarded a Nobel Prize for having demonstrated forty years ago that because of the close mutual interdependence among all the different sectors of an economic system the curve fitting computation, if carried out separately for each of its component parts, is bound to yield biased estimates of all parameters. In principle at least it has to be carried out in the form of one large single operation. As the system becomes bigger and bigger indirect statistical estimation of the numerical magnitudes of all parameters of the given theoretical model becomes impractical. To simplify their task the builders of econometric models follow the example of pure theorists and resort to aggregation.

The structure and the operation of the entire national economy is typically described by a relatively small number of aggregative variables (and a correspondingly small number of indirectly estimated, aggregative structural parameters). Actual measurement of such variables as 'total GNP', the level of total employment, the price levels of all consumers' and producers' goods, that is, the computation of appropriate aggregative index numbers, is usually delegated to hard working economic statisticians.

It is a rather thankless task. The long history of search for an ideal index number formula has only demonstrated that aggregation is inevitably bound to yield a blurred picture of observable reality. It also frequently conceals the lack of detailed factual information. Under such conditions, even in the long run no effective process of natural selection among competing theories can take place. As a result of this, the pages of professional journals become over-populated. The flow of complicated theoretical models, the empirical validity of which can be neither proved nor disproved by conventional methods of indirect statistical evidence, continues.

Compared with the tremendous pressure that physicists, biologists, and other natural scientists exert on governments to provide them with the costly equipment needed for their research, professional and in particular academic economists do not seem to feel an urgent need for compilation of databases that would enable them to implement empirically their theoretical constructs. This is particularly true when it comes to realistic analysis of technological changes. The practical knowledge possessed by the engineering community has been hardly tapped by general model-builders in that field. Only governments possess the legal authority and sufficiently large financial resources to organize comprehensive and detailed databases needed for serious empirical implementation of theoretical models of national economics which tend rapidly to emerge into a single world economy.

Economists played admittedly a leading role in building up the truly comprehensive system of national and international accounts. Accounting can, however, contribute to the explanation of an economic system as much, but not more than corporate accounting can contribute to the analysis of operation of a private company just as a flat, two-dimensional shadow of a three-dimensional edifice does not provide enough information to understand a multidimensional structure. Modern social and economic statistics fall very short of what would be needed to implement a realistic, working model of a complex modern economy.

While fundamental economic research seems to be stagnating, promising developments take place on its periphery in various applied fields. For instance in energy modelling, in modelling of the role played by production and utilization of agricultural products within the frame-work of all other parts of a particular national economy, or in modelling of a national transportation system, very far reaching degrees of disaggregation permit close cooperation with experts who possess practical operational knowledge of the particular field and even of only a small part of it.

10

ECONOMICS: RECENT PERFORMANCE AND FUTURE TRENDS

Jan Tinbergen

Adam Smith, to whom the 1990 conference was dedicated, is rightly considered as the founder of economic science. So one of the ways in which we may honour him is to describe and evaluate the development of economic science. This is, by its nature, a very subjective undertaking. I, for one, have a limited knowledge of the tree we call economic science and know that I can only deal with some branches and their leaves. My evaluation is bound to differ from that of most of my colleagues. However, our contributions together may show enough harmony to contribute to the celebration of Adam Smith's bicentenary.

What I propose to do is, first, to try to locate our science in the universe of all sciences; second, to paint sketchily our tree by a sample of recent results of economic thinking; and third, to speculate about desirable further blossoming of that discipline. These three sections will be increasingly subjective, but let us enjoy diversity instead of being irritated by it – a device I also recommend to nations with different social systems.

ECONOMICS IN THE UNIVERSE OF ALL SCIENCES

At two centuries old, economics is rather young, surrounded by an impressive forest of many much older sciences. Switching to scientific terminology I shall call the forest the 'universe of sciences' and make an attempt to sketch it with the aid of a multidimensional space. My attempt – presented recently on the occasion of the 375th anniversary of the University of Groningen – made me believe that a sketch requires a six-dimensional space as a minimum. Let me indicate briefly which characteristics of the existing sciences I think determine their location in the universe. The six characteristics are

146

(i) Whether the science considered is a methodological or an object science.
(ii) Whether it deals with living or dead objects.
(iii) If with living objects, what is the position in which the living objects stand to each other.
(iv) If with living objects, whether mental or corporeal activities are studied.
(v) What time period is dealt with.
(vi) Whether the science considered is pure or applied.

A few examples may clarify these characteristics. Physics is an object science, whereas mathematics is a methodological science. Biology clearly deals with living objects, for instance animals, and the position in which animals stand to each other may be that of competing for the same food. Sciences dealing with human beings may deal with the position of teacher to pupil, e.g. pedagogics. Archaeology deals with objects of centuries ago, whereas modern history deals with objects of only a few centuries ago. Biology as a rule is a pure science, but medicine is an applied science.

Using a geometrical way of describing the universe of sciences – which we do when speaking of a (six-dimensional) space, each characteristic may be called a coordinate. Some coordinates can only assume three values: the fourth coordinate, for instance, may be mental, corporeal or neither mental nor corporeal. The latter applies to all sciences dealing with dead objects. Other coordinates may assume many, even an infinity of values, such as time. As noted, the number of dimensions may be more than six. Thus, the third co-ordinate, the position in which the objects studied stand to each other, may be more complicated than one-dimensional. Or, a seventh coordinate may be the degree of determinism (or, inversely, of stochastism) and an eighth coordinate may be the age of a science.

What, now, is the position of economic science in this universe of sciences? To me it seems that economics is a rather young science, dealing with human beings, in a position of competing for scarce resources and using mental activities. If we also want to use the seventh coordinate, we may add that the degree of determinism is much lower than that of astronomy a few centuries ago, and probably higher than that of sociology. Another additional remark about the nature of economics may be that it often participates in interdisciplinary research, in contrast to, say, astronomy.

DEVELOPMENTS IN ECONOMIC THOUGHT

I turn now to the presentation of some examples of recent development of economic science. By 'recent' I mean the last half century. The examples are selected from my own works and from related works by other economists. The subjective character of such a selection has already been noted. The first example is one of a qualitative nature, the distinction between collective and individual goods and services. As is well-known, collective goods can be consumed by one individual without affecting the possibility of their being consumed by other individuals.

The concept of collective goods and services has been enriched in the last two decades by the introduction of three more particular types of collective goods (in what follows goods also cover services): semi-collective, quasi-collective and part-collective goods. Semi-collective goods were introduced by Dreze (1974) of which an interesting example is a collective good that is only available in a restricted geographical area. Quasi-collective goods were introduced by Brown and Jackson (1978), Goedhart (1975), Wolfson (1979) and others. By these goods they mean goods made available by public authorities at a price below costs and with a private component. An example is schooling. My contribution is the concept of part-collective goods (Tinbergen 1984). This is a category that constitutes a continuum between private and purely collective goods. Examples are highways in periods of congestion or the police at times when demand for their services is unusually high due to some particular event. Demand may then surpass capacity.

A second recent development of economic science has been the study of a number of problems in dynamic mathematical economics which deal with the problems of business cycles and, later, economic development. Interest in business cycles was stimulated very much by the Great Depression of the 1930s. Since cycles are movements around a trend, cycles cannot be studied in vacuo, but as a supplement also need theories of long-term movements. After the Second World War the problem of underdeveloped countries needed studies of long-term movements for its own sake. Later still the developed countries discovered that their own long-term economic movements deserved study because of structural problems and the theory of long waves attracted the interest of several authors.

The study of economic cycles started with studies of agricultural products. The first was about the cycles in pig and pork prices and production, pioneered by Hanau (1930). As a consequence of a lag T between prices and quantities supplied, endogenous cycles can be generated, also called cobweb cycles, because of the shape of the graphical presentation. An initial deviation from the equilibrium price may start such a cycle: a higher-than-equilibrium price causes a higher supply after T time units and this will cause a lower-than-equilibrium price. Another T time units later, supply will be higher-than-equilibrium and one cycle has been completed. Its period P equals twice the time lag T. Amplitudes may be constant, decreasing or increasing. This depends on the relative absolute slopes of the demand curve and the supply curve around their point of intersection. Constant amplitudes occur if the absolute slopes are equal, decreasing amplitudes if the absolute slope of the demand curve is larger than that of the supply curve and increasing amplitudes if the absolute slope of the demand curve is smaller than that of the supply curve.

Similarly to the pork market, the coffee market also showed, during the period of non-intervention, cycles due to the lag between price changes and changes in supply. Here the lag is around seven years and, accordingly, the period of the cycles about fifteen years. In the cases of pork and coffee, which are consumer goods, the mechanism is simpler than in the case of means of production. In the latter case we have to deal with two markets: the market for the total quantity of capital goods (for example the total tonnage of ships) available and the market for new capital goods (new ships) to be built. The relationship between the two is that the latter supply is the differential of the supply on the former market. The interconnecton was studied in my article (Tinbergen 1931) and the main result of that study was that cycles appear for which the period P is four times the time lag T. Other results are that the latter relation is only exact if at the same time the cycles show constant amplitudes. Increasing amplitudes are accompanied by shorter periods and decreasing amplitudes by longer periods, depending on the slopes of the (demand and supply) reaction curves, in contrast to the situation found for consumer goods.

The cycles so far discussed may be called 'lag cycles'. Another type is 'life-time cycles'. The well-known example here is of replacement investments of capital goods. In their pure form they appear if all capital goods of a certain type have exactly the same duration of life T. If, by accident, at time $t = 0$ an additional investment in that type had taken place, there will be a replacement at time $t = T$ and, if nothing in the rest of the economy changes, at times $t = 2T$, $t = 3T$, etc. This theory is also known as the 'echo theory'.

Around 1929 a discussion developed as to whether general business cycles should be considered as lag cycles or as life-time cycles. S. de Wolff, a Dutch Marxist economist, published a theory (de Wolff 1929) according to which the 'juglar' cycles of about eight years and the 'long' cycles (known as 'Kondratiefs' by those who did not know Van Gelderen, another Dutch economist), were both life-time cycles for machines and infrastructural capital goods respectively. The main point of the discussion was whether or not the spread in life time would very soon spread the replacement investments. As I showed in 1959 the amplitude of the life-time cycle could very well remain constant if re-investment depended not only on life time, but also on the cyclical position (or 'phase' of the cycle) of the economy.

Another topic of mathematical economics is the acceleration principle. This states that the fluctuations in the production of a good are much less outspoken than the fluctuations in the production of the capital goods required for the production of the good considered. A simple example would arise if one shoe machine were needed to produce one shoe. The output of new shoe machines would have to be 3 if the output of shoes was to rise from 100 to 103, but would fall dramatically to 1 if the output of shoes then rose only from 103 to 104, and would collapse to zero if the output of shoes then remained consistent at 104.

The acceleration theory is based on the assumption that producers always use the full capacity of their equipment. Upon statistical testing I found (Tinbergen 1938) that the production of capital goods in some industries for which data are available could not be explained very well with the aid of the acceleration principle. Profits appeared to be a determinant of more importance. In all probability the assumption that shoe factories always use their full capacity is not realistic. The principle appears to be more successful when applied to the particular type of capital constituted of commodity stocks or inventories. It can be shown (Tinbergen 1942) that the acceleration principle then fits the facts fairly well and that a short cycle with a period of two to three years results from it. This cycle can be observed in raw material imports when compared to consumption.

A topic related to the phenomenon of cycles is the distinction made between types of equilibrium. In the simplest case dealt with, that of the cobweb theorem, the equilibrium of demand and supply is stable, if the slope of the demand curve is steeper than that of the supply curve. Any disruption of a market equilibrium caused by an exogenous force will be brought back to that equilibrium by the operation of the market forces of demand and supply. If, however, the slope of the demand curve is less steep than that of the supply curve, the equilibrium is unstable: prices and quantities traded will deviate increasingly from the equilibrium position.

More complicated forms of either demand or supply curves may lead to interesting and more complicated types of equilibrium. A famous example was introduced by Kaldor (1940) in which demand for all products together will depend on income in such a way that with low income it will be inelastic: a minimum has to be maintained for both consumer and producer goods. With high total income demand will also show an inelastic character (the phenomenon of satiation may occur, or total production capacity may limit demand satisfied). For a middle range of total income demand will be more elastic. Such a demand curve may bring about three equilibria: the upper and the lower equilibrium stable and the middle equilibrium unstable. Exogenous shocks of sufficient strength may move the system from one to the other stable equilibrium, where it may stay for some time. The wave-like movements do not have an endogenous periodical character. This theory adds an interesting possibility to the explanation for the usually long duration of low production and employment during the Great Depression.

As I have already explained, research on cyclical movements requires a complement of research on long-term economic development. The latter also became interesting in its own right when policies to develop the underdeveloped countries were needed. Although economic science from its start showed interest in a theory of long-term movements, a quantitative approach started much later. Lack of statistical data probably is the main reason for this late start. Among the authors who specialized on this subject S. Kuznets should be mentioned first. He devoted a large part of his research to the careful collection of statistical evidence and integrated this material in his contribution to the series 'Studies in Comparative Economics' (Kuznets 1966).

My own contribution (Tinbergen 1942, 1959) consists of attempts to build a mathematical model of trend movements. The purpose of the study was twofold. First, to estimate the time shape of the trend of total production; and second, to estimate the growth rates of production, employment and capital as functions of savings, technological development, population and wage norms. The answer to the first problem I found was that a much more complex time dependency is apparent than in the usual statistical trend determination. The answer to the second problem is also complex and is summarized in Table 10.1. The Cobb–Douglas production function chosen was the one with exponent 1/4 for capital and 3/4 for labour. In the publication quoted a number of conclusions were drawn to which the reader may be referred. They are numerous and illustrate the complexity of the problem. They also show the desirability (at the moment of publication) of more knowledge on λ', the flexibility of wages and salaries. A similar model was presented, without knowledge of mine (which was written in German), by Solow (1956).

In 1930 the Econometric Society was established. Econometrics was defined as the testing of economic theories by the use of statistical information. For such testing economic theories had to be formulated mathematically. Econometrics could also be considered as the cooperation of mathematical economics and mathematical statistics. Essentially therefore the birth of econometrics meant the transformation of economics into a mature science. For lack of qualitative information this coming of age took a long time: a century and a half, or a century, if we take A.A. Cournot (1839), the first mathematical economist, as the starting point. Econometrics introduced the standard scientific process into economics. In order to explain observed facts and figures a hypothesis is formulated and tested by requiring sufficient similarity between observations and the theory. If the similarity is not sufficient – acording to the scientist's norm – another theory is chosen and tested. This process of adapting theory to observations is continued until the norm of similarity is attained. The process may also be called 'learning from errors' (cf. Tinbergen 1987) and is as old as science – hence, much older than economics. In this connection it is useful to remind econometrists of the existence of a method known as 'path analysis', used by sociologists and psychologists and almost identical to econometrics, but some twenty years older.

Econometrics can be used in two ways, briefly to be called forecasting and planning. Forecasting consists of the estimation of the values of variables in the future, assuming that the interrelations between these variables will not change. Planning consists of determining the values of instrument variables so as to maximize social welfare; social welfare being expressed in terms of target variables. Forecasting is much less reliable than planning, because it depends on unknown components of future variables on which assumptions must be made. Forecasting also depends on variables dealt with by other sciences (cf. Tinbergen 1989).

A list of interrelations between a number of variables which characterize one economy, when satisfying some conditions, is called a model. The number of unknown variables appearing in the list must be equal to the number of equations and each equation must represent a structural relation. Structural relations may be definitions, technological

Table 10.1 Growth rates for capital quantity, employment and production for the middle of the period and for different values of λ'

$\lambda' =$	0	1/2	∞	-1
$\overset{\bullet}{K} =$	χ	χ	χ	χ
$\overset{\bullet}{u} =$	$\chi + 4\varepsilon' - 3\lambda'_0$	$\dfrac{\chi}{2} + \dfrac{\beta'}{2} + 2\varepsilon' - \lambda'_0$	$\dfrac{1}{4}\chi + \dfrac{3}{4}\beta' + \varepsilon'$	$\beta' + \lambda'_0$
$\overset{\bullet}{a} =$	$\chi + 4\varepsilon' - 4\lambda'_0$	$\dfrac{\chi}{3} + \dfrac{2}{3}\beta' + \dfrac{4}{3}\varepsilon' - \dfrac{4}{3}\lambda'_0$	β'	$-\dfrac{\chi}{3} + \dfrac{4}{3}\beta' - \dfrac{4}{3}\varepsilon' + \dfrac{4}{3}\lambda'_0$

relations, or behavioural relations. Definitions may reflect the relationship between the price of a commodity, the quantity traded and the value traded. A definition may also be the definition of profits as the difference between receipts and expenditures; and so on. A technological relation may be a production function or some tax revenue in its dependence on the tax base.

The model may be formulated as a theory, with coefficients as well as variables written as symbols (e.g. Latin letters for variables and Greek letters for coefficients). The model may also be formulated, after econometric testing, with numerical values for the coefficients, as an empirically tested model. The first of these was a simple twenty-two equation model for the Dutch economy 1923–35 (Tinbergen 1936, 1959). This model was to be used to a policy to be followed by the Dutch government after 1936 and various alternative policies were compared, such as devaluation, reduction of wages, the execution of public works, protection, all numerically specified, and a few more. Among the instruments chosen that of devaluation appeared to me most effective in creating employment.

Soon, other models were built, especially for the United States by Tinbergen, Klein and Goldberger, followed later by the Brookings Institution (Duesenberry, Fromm, Klein and Kuh, 1965), and Eckstein (1983). For an increasing number of countries econometric models were built; for the United Kingdom by Stone (1981), for Norway by Faaland, for France by the Commissariat du Plan, etc. Economic policies started to become supranational with the foundation of the European Community and that policy was analysed in particular by Kirschen (1964). Some types of policies required worldwide models of which examples are those built by Polak (1953), Leontief (1977) and others, a subject to which I will refer later.

Discussion on the building and application of economic models has contributed considerably to a better understanding of many problems connected with economic policy. The most important institution where the subject has been discussed from a variety of viewpoints is the Cowles Commission, where the world's foremost economists contributed to a series of studies, many of which have been published in the Cowles Commission monograph series.

One example of a better understanding of the interrelationships between the economic variables describing an economy is that, in contrast to what some politicians think, there is no one-by-one correspondence between targets and instruments. This view implies that, for instance, employment equilibrium depends on the wage rate, balance of payments equilibrium on the exchange rate, equilibrium of commodity markets on commodity prices, and so on. The normal situation is, however, that the set of targets depends on the set of instruments. Another example of a well-known misunderstanding is the view that in order to cure a certain undesirable situation the causes of that situation have to be known. If, for instance, there is too little food per capita, the cause may be too high an increase in population. The remedy is not to eliminate the cause, that is, to kill some of the new-born babies, but to make available, as the cure, more food.

A long-standing debate among econometricians has been whether it is possible to measure the level of welfare of individuals. The word often used instead of welfare is utility; another term used is ophelimity (Pareto) and still another, satisfaction. These will be used as synonyms. Welfare is one of the central concepts of economics, of which the task could be described as maximizing welfare. In the past a considerable number of economists argued as if that concept is measurable (or 'cardinal'). Pareto, and many other economists agreed with him, considered ophelimity as an 'ordinal' concept: a higher consumption causes more satisfaction, but how much more we do not know. For the theory of demand and supply and the ensuing price formation it is not necessary to know much more. Recently, the number of economists adhering to the measurability of satisfaction has been increasing again. For an enumeration of economists who have been actively engaged in such measurement I may refer to Tinbergen (1985). It seems valuable to stress that empirical research by Levy and Guttman (1975) shows that in the case they studied economic determinants explained less than half of the variance in observed welfare.

In today's world economic policy is, to a very large extent, implemented by national authorities. International policies as a rule are the subject of cooperation between national governments, a cooperation preceded by negotiations between sovereign states. Although in Western Europe preparations are being made for an integration, supranational decisions as yet are limited. The first supranational authority was the High Authority of the European Coal and Steel Community, which is empowered to impose certain measures directly upon the coal, steel and some steel product-producing enterprises.

International economic problems and policies are as old as – in fact older than – economic science. Problems of international trade and capital movements had to be solved long before the existence of the Roman Empire. Adam Smith's contributions to economic thinking as a matter of course also applied to these problems and the general philosophy of *laisser-faire* found its counterpaert in free-trade doctrines, which played a large role in the nineteenth century, the only completed century in which economic science has existed. In particular after the Second World War the structure of the world economy went through a process of great change, the number of sovereign nations almost trebled and levels of prosperity became much more widespread. The under-developed economies became the new actors, determining many new problem types, often in the framework of the United Nations. Strong impulses towards the need for new developments also originated from more recent problems of which the problem of the pollution of the environment is the best-known example. I will deal with the most important of today's world problems when I come to discuss the desirable future developments of economic science.

Among the recent developments of economics in the field of international problems it seems worthwhile to discuss another example, because it leads to an elegant extension of the Keynesian models of income formation. The starting point is that a distinction is made between two types of goods and services: those which can and those which cannot be traded internationally, to be called international and national goods and services. (We shall use the word goods to cover both goods and services.) Examples of non-tradeable goods ('non-tradeables') are buildings and some other very heavy goods, and services to be rendered on the spot (many consumer services) or within some country, such as those rendered by civil servants. Sometimes the frontier between national and international goods cannot be drawn very precisely, but in other cases there is a sharp frontier. Thus, civil servants and teachers may be foreigners, but for the overwhelming part they are nationals of the country considered. Also, the dividing line between heavy and light goods is not easy to draw, but most building inputs are of the heavy type. Attempts to estimate the portion of national product that consists of non-tradeables show that that portion is close to one half, and, remarkably, does not depend very much on the size of the country. This is remarkable, because for the world as a whole all goods are national goods and for a small island state with only one product practically all goods are international. Evidently this is valid only for very small countries.

In Tinbergen (1965) the simplest possible model is presented of the introduction of tradeables and non-tradeables into a Keynesian model. It presents formulae which show the different effects in such an economy of different policies on the country's total income and total domestic expenditure.

X total national expenditures
X_N total national expenditures on national goods (non-tradeables)
X_I total national expenditures on international goods (tradeables)
Y national income
Y_N income from the production of non-tradeables
Y_I income from the production of tradeables
E exports (tradeables by definition)
M imports (also tradeables only)
D initial deficit on trade balance

We slightly changed the notation, in order to avoid some misunderstandings that may be caused by the original notation.

The following equations connect these variables:

$$X = Y - D \tag{1}$$
$$X = X_N + X_I \tag{2}$$
$$Y = Y_N + Y_I \tag{3}$$
$$Y_N = (1 - \mu_N) X_N \tag{4}$$
$$Y = X + E - M \tag{5}$$
$$X_N = \xi_N X \tag{6}$$
$$M = \mu Y \tag{7}$$

Equation (1) is either the definition of D or, in two policy problems to be discussed, the value to be given to X in order to attain trade balance equilibrium. Equations (2) and (3) are balance equations. Equations (4) and (6) determine income from producing non-tradeables and the quantity of non-tradeables produced. Equation (5) defines national income as the difference between gross product $X + E$ and imports M and Equation (7) fixes imports. The coefficients used are:

μ_N imports needed to produce a unit of non-tradeables;
ξ_N portion of expenditures spent on non-tradeables; and
μ ratio of imports to national income.

Realistic values of these coefficients are $\xi_N = 0.5$ and $\mu_N = \mu = 0.2$. These will be used in the numerical illustrations.

Two problems will be considered and solved. In Problem (i) the trade balance deficit D will be eliminated by a deflationary policy and an additional production of tradeables, Y_I will be produced in an attempt to reduce the unfavourable consequences of the deflation policy. In Problem (ii) the trade balance deficit will again be eliminated, but it will be assumed that developed countries will assist the given country, supposed to be underdeveloped, by opening their markets, for instance by reduction of import duties or quantitative import restrictions.

In Problem (i) the given variables are D and Y_I; the other variables can be expressed as functions of these data. We are interested mainly in X, Y, E and M and find:

$$Y = \frac{-\xi_N(1 - \mu_N)D + Y_I}{1 - \xi_N(1 - \mu_N)} \tag{8}$$

$$X = \frac{-D + Y_I}{1 - \xi_N(1 - \mu_N)} \tag{9}$$

$$E = \frac{D\{1 - (1 + \mu)(1 - \mu_N)\xi_N\} + \mu Y_I}{1 - \xi_N(1 - \mu_N)} \tag{10}$$

$$M = \mu Y \tag{11}$$

With the numerical values of the coefficients we obtain:

$$Y = -0.67\,D + 1.67\,Y_I \tag{8'}$$
$$X = -1.67\,D + 1.67\,Y_I \tag{9'}$$
$$E = 0.87\,D + 0.33\,Y_I \tag{10'}$$
$$M = -0.13\,D + 0.33\,Y_I \tag{11'}$$

From it we see that the lower the national income and especially expenditures, the larger the balance of trade deficit.

In Problem (ii) the data are D and E and the solutions:

$$Y = \frac{1}{\mu}(-D + E) \tag{12}$$

$$X = -(1 + \frac{1}{\mu})D + \frac{E}{\mu} \tag{13}$$

$$M = -D + E \tag{14}$$

$$Y_I = \{-\frac{1}{\mu} + (1 - \mu_N)(1 + \frac{1}{\mu})\xi_N\}D + \frac{E}{\mu}\{1 - (1 - \mu_N)\xi_N\} \tag{15}$$

(In the original text the μ in the coefficient of E was erroneously omitted).

With the numerical values of the coefficients we get:

$$Y = -5 D + 5 E \tag{12'}$$
$$X = -6 D + E \tag{13'}$$
$$M = -D + E \tag{14'}$$
$$Y_1 = -2.6 D + 3 E \tag{15'}$$

In this case the deflationary policy is much worse than in Problem (i), but opening the markets of developed countries is a powerful policy instrument in favour of national income and, less so, of national expenditure.

The model is a useful instrument in analysing the consequences of the existence of non-tradeables. This also applies to another well-known method of analysis, input–output analysis, pioneered by W.W. Leontief. Introducing in it the existence of non-tradeables leads to an alternative method which I have named semi-input output analysis.

I turn now to a discussion of different social and economic orders. Human history and geography show a great variety of such orders. They change over time from very primitive to complicated systems: from tribal orders in small isolated areas, such as small islands, to orders as they now prevail in technically highly developed countries. But also simultaneously we find very different systems. Still there are tribal orders, and highly developed systems which differ from almost-capitalist to almost-communist systems.

In the two centuries in which economic science has existed the most intensive discussions about what is the 'best' order were those between capitalism and socialism. Adam Smith is considered not only the father of economic science, but also of the 'free society' or the system of *laissez faire*. His most important critic was Karl Marx (1818–83), who coined the term 'capitalism' for that order and considered as its important characteristic that the means of production or capital goods are owned privately. The system of socialism which he thought to be preferable would be characterized by public ownership of the means of production. Also the markets, regulating the production and distribution of goods and services under capitalism would be replaced by a system of central planning. Marx's theory of the development of society was that capitalism, as the consequence of the forces at work in it, would automatically change into socialism through the socialist revolution.

Around 1850, when Marx lived and wrote about this process capitalism was the social order in Britain, from where it spread to the European continent and to the other developed countries. It seems preferable to stick to this definition, and not to call present-day developed countries capitalist, since they already contain important deviations which started in Britain around 1850. Legislation introduced elements of social security and transformed these countries into mixed systems. Similarly, the only example of pure socialism was the system that prevailed briefly after the Russian Revolution of October 1917. In the meantime the Soviet Union has also introduced capitalist elements, such as managers, private plots of land, and some personal services. Strictly speaking today's communist-ruled countries also are mixed systems.

The socialist movement created by Marx started as a homogeneous set of national parties, cooperating in the ('First') International. Around 1900 a split developed into a more radical and a more moderate direction. The more moderate socialists' opinions were, among many other issues, that democratic methods of decision making are preferable to authoritarian ones and that small enterprises could be better left private. When the democratic socialists in the German parliament voted in favour of the war budget, they certainly made a tremendous mistake, which hardened relations with the communists. Also the democratic socialists' participation in the postwar German government intensified the conflict, since they countered the attempt to seize power made by communist groups. For a long time the communists in all European countries considered the social democrats as their worst enemies, almost worse than the 'bourgeois' parties.

Scientific socialists also held different opinions, but their differences were less outspoken and less vehement. The well-known Polish economist Oskar Lange defended a 'market socialism' and the less-known American socialist James A. Yunker a 'pragmatic market socialism'. My own attempt to find a scientific base for a socialist order took welfare economics as its starting point. The best social order is, according to this view, the one that maximizes total welfare of the country's population. This approach has the advantage that it supplies a common starting point for capitalism and socialism and shows that the former neglects one of the maximum conditions, namely the condition that the marginal utilities of income must be equal for all individuals (Tinbergen 1959, 1965).

In the relationship between communists and democratic socialists a fundamental change has taken place as a consequence of the statement by the Secretary-General of the Soviet Union Communist Party, Mikhail Gorbachev, that the productivity of the communist system is considerably lower than that of the mixed economies of Western Europe and the United States or Japan. Politically this means that the split in the socialist movement and the bitter internal struggle has been unnecessary; an enormous loss in energy and time. It also opens up perspectives for a safer world with less conflict and quicker development.

FUTURE DEVELOPMENTS IN ECONOMIC SCIENCE

Finally, let me review briefly the main requirements for the future development of economic science. As noted earlier in this lecture, the subject of economic science implies the probability of its being involved in many types of interdisciplinary research. Welfare, the central concept of economics, does not only depend on economic determinants, but also on many others, which even explain a larger part of welfare changes than the economic variables noted by Levy and Guttman (1975), as observed earlier. For the future of economics there are good reasons for this feature to continue and even grow. This will become clear in what follows. Political science is one of the important disciplines with which cooperation will be intensified; demography also will have to be taken into account and technological sciences – both pure and applied – will be desperately needed.

The importance of demography springs from the ever more threatening overpopulation with which the world is faced. Even India, so much aware of the necessity of family planning, still grows to such an extent that soon after the year 2000 it will have a billion inhabitants. Ironically Europeans think that they are threatened by a reduction in population; in fact they are yielding a service to the world at large, especially if they help to school and train people of other continents. The importance of the technological sciences hardly needs emphasis, if we think of the environmental policies or of the problems involved in leaving a sufficient quantity of natural resources for the coming generations.

What then will have to be the most desirable future developments of economic science? The subjective character of this topic has already been mentioned. To me it seems that the aim in which economic science has to assist is, above all, that of an optimal international development. Step-by-step the world has become involved in four great problems, the solutions to which require decision making at world level. These tasks are so grave that all available forces have to be utilized and economic science can – and so must – be an important coordinator of the policies involved. The problems I have in mind are

(i) Security, i.e. the prevention of war.
(ii) Cleaning the environment and keeping it clean.

161

(iii) Improving (which means making less unequal) the world income distribution, which is terribly unequal.

(iv) Ensuring that enough natural resources remain available for the infinity of later generations to whom we should permit a life at least as happy as that of our generation.

This last is perhaps the most difficult of all. Since for a considerable part of the present generation life is not satisfactory at all, a happier life indeed is what we should aim at, which illustrates the difficulty of this fourth task. What contribution should eonomic science be making to these tasks?

The problem of maintaining security, that is preventing war, has become a problem that must be solved, especially in the nuclear era, as every serious citizen or statesman now knows. That solution is largely political, but economics is basic to it because peace is an all-important determinant of welfare, the central concept of economics and also because economics teaches us what the favourable effect on the economies of the world is and how that effect can be used so as best to serve mankind's welfare. Again, the problem of how to prevent war is to a large extent an interdisciplinary problem. Knowledge of weapons systems or of treaties concluded in the past are examples of supplementary, or rather fundamental, knowledge from other disciplines. In the last few years the likelihood that results will be attained has increased considerably as a consequence of President Gorbachev's initiatives and the reactions of US Presidents Reagan and Bush.

An important contribution by economic science is the solution for the problem of how to avoid the unemploymeent caused by armament reduction. How can the savings on armament production be used and what employment effects will this different use create? A preliminary estimate of the increase in optimal development assistance seems to show that the amount is of the same order of magnitude as the targeted reduction in armament expenditure. It would be important to refine the calculations of optimal development assistance and of armament reduction in order to find, for instance, whether additional amounts will become available for spending in the developed countries, for urgent purposes in those nations.

Environmental policies receive increasing support from the general public and politicians. The increasing emphasis by economists on the necessity to spend more on pollution abatement has persuaded many that more must be spent. The economists' contribution to the problem was a negative one in the sense that they showed that this cannot be implemented by single countries, as it would reduce the countries' competitive situation in the world market. The economic question which arises is what level of decision making is optimal for environmental policies. A distinction must be made between various types of environment and their pollution. In all probability, ocean and atmospheric pollution must be abated by worldwide measures. This would clearly be a task of the United Nations Environment Programme. Soil and river pollution probably do not require such a high level of decision making and more accurate economic research in this field is urgent. Another example of economic research to be recommended concerns the types of pollution which can be anticipated for the future and when new production processes will be applied. Still another example is more accurate research of the cause of forest quality decline or a more precise policy programme of optimal transportation systems.

I have already stated that world income distribution is 'terribly unequal'. We may add that distribution did not change very much between 1950 and 1980 (cf. Summers *et al.* 1984). During that period the amount of development assistance provided by the industrial countries was about half of the 0.7 per cent of their gross national product that had been recommended in 1969 by the Pearson Commission, though a few individual countries behaved as recommended. One means by which economic science could contribute to the urgent need for the formulation of a better policy of development cooperation would be to find a better criterion than that of the Pearson Commission. An example of such a criterion would be to raise the income of developing countries to twice the present income (in relation to the income of the developed countries) in a period after which a considerable portion of the present population of the poor countries would still be alive (say around twenty years). The economists in charge of such research should estimate how much development assistance would be needed to meet that aim. A provisional estimation supplied a figure of some 2 or 3 per cent of GNP. Research of this type could contribute simultaneously to the problems already discussed in connection with disarmament. The order of magnitude matches the results obtained by Yunker (1988).

As I have already mentioned, the most difficult problem the world faces may be the problem of how to leave enough of the world's natural resources for future generations. In order to illustrate this problem in the simplest possible way let us choose as a preliminary target the aim that the population and the annual quantity of consumer goods should both be kept constant. Further let us assume that the total volume of natural resources available is already known. Deviations from that simple set-up may – and must – be discussed afterwards. The main difficulty of the problem is to find ways and means to 'feed' an infinite number of future generations from an existing finite quantity of natural resources. The main answer is to follow a policy of ongoing technological progress enabling a given world population to produce a constant annual quantity of consumer goods with the aid of a regularly diminishing quantity of these finite natural resources. This leaves unanswered the following questions:

1 What to do if population does not remain constant?
2 What to do if technological development does not continue as assumed?
3 What to do if the initial estimate of the stock of finite resources turns out to be inaccurate?

It would be a useful contribution by economic science if it gave the answers to these questions, cooperating with demography, technology and, for instance, geology and agronomy.

I have formulated a number of future tasks for economic science. In my opinion these tasks deserve priority, but that opinion reflects the subjective character of our discipline – which I admitted from the start.

REFERENCES

Brown, C.V. and P.M. Jackson (1978) *Public Sector Economics*, Oxford: Martin Robertson.

De Wolff, S. (1929) *Het Economisch Getijd* (*The Economic Tide*), Amsterdam: J. Emmering.

Dreze, J.H. (1974) *Investment under Private Ownership: Optimality, Equilibrium and Stability*, Core reprint, Louvain-la-Neuve.

Duensenberry, J.S., G. Fromm, L.R. Klein and E. Kuh (1965) *The Brookings Quarterly Econometric Model of the United States*, Amsterdam: North Holland.

Eckstein, O. (1983) *The DRI Model of the US Economy*, New York: McGraw Hill.

Goedhart, C. (1975) *Hoofdlijnen van de leer der openbare financien*, Leiden.

Hanau, A. (1930) 'Die Prognose der Schweinepreise', Sonderheft 18 der Vierteljahreshefte der Konjunkturforschung, Institut für Konjunkturforschung, Berlin.

Kaldor, N. (1940) 'A Model of the Trade Cycle', *Economic Journal*, L, 78–92.

Kirschen, E.S. (1964) *Economic Policy in our Time*, Amsterdam; North Holland.

Kuznets, S. (1966) *Modern Economic Growth*, New Haven and London: Yale University Press.

Leontief, W.W. *et al.* (1977) *The Future of the World Economy*, New York and Oxford: Oxford University Press.

Levy, S. and L. Guttman (1965) 'On the Multivariate Structure of Wellbeing', *Social Indicators Research*, 2, 361–88.

Polak, J.J. (1953) *An International System*, Chicago: University of Chicago Press.

Solow, R.M. (1956) 'A Contribution to the Theory of Economic Growth', *Quarterly Journal of Economics*, LXX, 65–94.

Stone, R. (1951) *Aspects of Economic and Social Modelling*, Geneve: Droz.

Summers, R. *et al.* (1984) 'Changes in the World Income Distribution', *Journal of Policy Modeling*, 6, 237–70.

Tinbergen, J. (1931) 'Ein Schiffbauzyklus?' *Weltwirtschaftliches Archiv*, 34, pp. 152–64. ('A Shipbuilding Cycle?'; also in L.H. Klaassen, L.M. Koyck and H.J. Witteveen (eds) *Jan Tinbergen Selected Papers*, 1–14.)

Tinbergen, J. (1936, 1959) 'An Economic Policy for 1936'; also in *Selected Papers*, 37–84.

Tinbergen, J. (1938) 'Statistical Evidence on the Acceleration Principle', *Economica*, May, 164–76.

Tinbergen, J. (1942) 'An Acceleration Principle for Commodity Stockholding and a Short Cycle Resulting From It' in O. Lange, F.M. McIntyre and Th. O. Yntema (eds), *Studies in Mathematical Economics and Econometrics*, Chicago: University of Chicago Press, 255–67.

Tinbergen, J. (1959) 'Lag Cycles and Life Cycles' in L.H. Klaassen, L.M. Koyck and H.J. Witteveen (eds), *Jan Tinbergen Selected Papers*, Amsterdam: North Holland, 85–92.

Tinbergen, J. (1965) 'Spardefizit und Handelsdefizit' (Savings Gap and Trade Gap), *Weltwirtschaftliches Archiv*, 95, 89–101.

Tinbergen, J. (1984) 'On Collective and Part-collective Goods', *De Economist*, 132, 171–82.

Tinbergen, J. (1985) 'Measuring of Utility (or Welfare)', *De Economist*, 133, 411–14.

Tinbergen, J. (1987) 'Measuring Welfare of Productive Consumers', *De Economist*, 135, 231–6.

Tinbergen, J. (1989) 'The Impact of the Forecasting Capacity of one Science on that of other Sciences', *International Journal of Forecasting*, 5, 3–5.

Van Herwaarden, F.G. and A. Kapteyn (1971) 'Empirical Comparison of the Shape of Welfare Functions, *European Economic Review*, 15, 261–86.

Yunker, J.A. (1988) 'A World Economic Equalization Program', *World Development*, 16, 921–33.

Wolfson, D.J. (1979) *Public Finance and Development Structure*, Baltimore and London: The Johns Hopkins University Press.

APPENDIX TO CHAPTER 3

Maurice Allais

I ILLUSTRATION OF THE THEORETICAL THOUGHT OF ADAM SMITH, HIS PREDECESSORS AND HIS CONTEMPORARIES

The two central ideas of the fundamental economic analysis of the eighteenth century are as follows:

- The search for, realization of and distribution of surpluses, the essential motors of the functioning of an economy of markets.
- The existence of an underlying order in the functioning of an economy of markets.

These ideas can be illustrated by some particularly significant quotations from Adam Smith, from his predecessors and from Condillac. These quotations are all the more signficant when compared with one another. Comparison here is facilitated by grouping comparable quotations together. In view of the special importance of Condillac's work *Le Commerce et le Gouvernement,* which was published in the same year, 1776, as Adam Smith's *The Wealth of Nations,* the quotations from Condillac are presented separately.

Adam Smith: *The Wealth of Nations,* 1776

The generation of surpluses[1]

'This division of labour, from which so many advantages are derived, is not originally the effect of any human wisdom, which foresees and intends that general opulence to which it gives occasion. It is the necessary, though very slow and gradual consequence of a certain propensity in human nature which has in view no such extensive utility: propensity to truck, barter, and exchange one thing for another ...

'Whoever offers to another a bargain of any kind, proposes to do this.

166

Give me that which I want, and you shall have this which you want, is the meaning of every such offer; and it is in this manner that we obtain from one another the far greater part of those good offices which we stand in need of. It is not from the benevolence of the butcher, the brewer, or the baker that we expect our dinner, but from their regard to their own interest. We address ourselves, not to their humanity but to their self-love, and never talk to them of our own necessities but of their advantages ...

'As it is by treaty, by barter, and by purchase, that we obtain from one another the greater part of these mutual good offices which we stand in need of, so it is the same trucking of disposition which originally gives occasion to the division of labour.'

'When the quantity brought to market is just sufficient to supply the effectual demand and no more, the market price naturally comes to be exactly, or as nearly as can be judged of, the same with the natural price. The whole quantity upon hand can be disposed of for this price, and cannot be disposed of for more. The competition of the different dealers obliges them all to accept of this price, but does not oblige them all to accept of less ...

'The whole quantity of industry annually employed in order to bring any commodity to market naturally suits itself in this manner to the effectual demand. It naturally aims at bringing always that precise quantity thither which may be sufficient to supply, and no more than supply, that demand.'

'The whole of the advantages and disadvantages of the different employments of labour and stock must, in the same neighbourhood, be either perfectly equal or continually tending to equality. If in the same neighbourhood, there was any employment evidently either or less advantageous than the rest, so many people would crowd into it in the one case, and so many could desert it in the other, that its advantages would soon return to the level of other employments.'

The underlying order in the functioning of an economy of markets[2]

'Every individual is continually exerting himself to find out the most advantageous employment for whatever capital he can command. It is his own advantage indeed, and not that of the society, which he has in view. But the study of his own advantage naturally, or rather necessarily leads him to prefer that employment which is most advantageous to the society ...

'It is only for the sake of profit that any man employs a capital in the support of industry; and he will always, therefore, endeavour to employ it in the support of that industry of which the produce is likely to be of the greatest value . . .

'He generally, indeed, neither intends to promote the publick interest, nor knows how much he is promoting it. By preferring the support of domestick to that of foreign industry he intends only his own security; and by directing this industry in such a manner as its produce may be of the greatest value, he intends only his own gain, and he is in this, as in many other cases, led by an *invisible hand* to promote an end which was no part of his intention . . .

'Nor is it always the worse for the society that it was no part of it. By pursuing his own interest he frequently promotes that of the society more effectually than when he really intends to promote it . . .

'The statesman, who should attempt to direct private people in what manner they ought to employ their capitals, would not only load himself with a most unnecessary attention, but assume an authority which could safely be trusted, not only to no single person, but to no council or senate whatever, and which would nowhere be so dangerous as in the hands of a man who had folly and presumption enough to fancy himself fit to exercise it.'

'It is thus that every system which endeavours, either, by extraordinary encouragements, to draw towards a particular species of industry a greater share of the capital of the society than what would naturally go to it; or, by extraordinary restraints, to force from a particular species of industry some share of the capital which would otherwise be employed in it; is in reality subversive of the great purpose which it means to promote. It retards, instead of accelerating, the progress of the society towards real wealth and greatness; and diminishes, instead of increasing, the real value of the annual produce of its land and labour.

'All systems either of preference or of restraint, therefore, being thus completely taken away, the obvious and simple system of natural liberty establishes itself of its own accord. Every man, as long as he does not violate the laws of justice, is left perfectly free to pursue his own way, and to bring both his industry and capital into competition with those of any other man, or order of men. The sovereign is completely discharged from a duty, in the attempting to perform which he must always be exposed to innumerable delusions, and for the proper performance of which no human wisdom or knowledge could ever be sufficient; the duty of superintending the industry of private people, and directing it towards the employments most suitable to the interest of the society.'

Predecessors of Adam Smith

The generation of surpluses

Pierre de Boisguilbert (1704)[3]

'Commerce only arises from reciprocal utility, and each of the parties, the buyers as much as the sellers, must have an equal interest in selling or buying and an equal need to do so.'

Robert Turgot (1766–9)[4]

'Reciprocal need has brought about the exchange of what one has for what one has not ... it is natural for each party to it to want to take the most that he can and to give the least that he can. And, being both equally masters of what they bring to the exchange, it is for each of them to weigh his attachment to the commodity he gives against his desire for the commodity he wants to take, and consequently to fix the quantity of all the things to be exchanged. If they don't agree, they will have to come nearer, giving a little on either side, offering more and contenting themselves with less.'

'This superiority in estimated value, attributed by the acquirer to the thing acquired over the thing yielded, is essential to the exchange, indeed its sole motive. Everybody would stay as he was if he could not find an interest, a personal profit, in exchanging; if, in relation to himself, he did not think he was taking more than he was giving.'

'The value of wheat and of wine is by no means the result of haggling between two individuals in relation to their reciprocal needs and abilities; it is fixed by the balance of the needs and abilities of the totality of sellers of wheat against those of the totality of sellers of wine.'

The underlying order of the functioning of an economy of markets

Pierre de Boisguilbert (1704)[5]

'As long as things remain in this state of equilibrium, nobody has the resources to enrich himself, whatever his condition, except by forcing his work and skill on his neighbour.'

'Equilibrium among all commodities is the sole means of conserving general affluence.'

169

Mercier de La Rivière (1767)[6]

'It is of the essence of order that an individual's particular interest should never be separated from the common interest of everybody; we find a most convincing proof of that in the effects naturally and necessarily produced by the fullness of freedom which ought to reign in commerce . . .

'Personal interest, fostered by the fullness of this freedom, palpably and perpetually presses each particular man to perfect and multiply the things he can sell, thus to enlarge the quantum of enjoyment he can procure to other men in order to augment by this means the quantum of enjoyment that other men can procure by exchange with him. *That is the way the world goes round* . . .

'The desire for enjoyment transmits motion to society, a motion eternally tending towards the best possible state of affairs . . .

'With property and liberty upheld, the most perfect order reigns without the help of any other law . . .

'Stop and wonder how each man is the instrument of happiness in other men, and how the happiness of an individual seems to be transmitted like the motion.'

Robert Turgot (1770)[7]

'The market value of commodities, the revenue, the prices, the salaries, the population, are things which are linked to one another by mutual dependence and which find by themselves their equilibrium according to a natural proportion; and this proportion will always be maintained so long as commerce and competition are entirely free.'

Condillac: *Le Commerce et le Gouvernement*, 1776

The generation of surpluses[8]

'It is wrong to say that, in exchanges, equal value is given for equal value. On the contrary, each of the parties always gives something less for something more.

'A woman I know bought a piece of land, then counted out the money to pay for it and said: Nevertheless *I'm really very happy to get a piece of land just for that.* There is sound reasoning underneath her naivety. We can see that she did not much value the money she kept in her coffer; so that she was giving something less for something more. On the other hand, the man who sold the land felt the same, and said: *I made a good sale there.* So he also thought he had given something less for something more. That is the way of things among people who make exchanges.

'As a matter of fact, if equal value was always exchanged for equal value, neither of the parties could gain. But each of them does gain, or ought to. Why? Because things have a value only relative to our needs: what is more to one is less to another, and vice versa.'

'When commerce arises from the exchange of things of which there is an excess, everyone gives something which has no value for himself, because he cannot use it, and takes something which does have a value, because he can use it. So everyone gives something less for something more.

'I have too much wheat, and not enough wine: it is the reverse with you, too much wine, and not enough wheat. So you need my useless excess of wheat; and I need your useless excess of wine. We therefore consider an exchange: I offer you wheat for wine, and you offer me wine for wheat.

'If my excess is what you need to consume, and the other way about, we can make a mutually advantageous exchange, because we are both giving away something useless for something necessary to us. Then I reckon that my wheat is worth to you what your wine is worth to me and you reckon that your wine is worth to me what my wheat is worth to you . . .

'As we bargain, you offer me the least wine you can for so much wheat; while I offer you the least wheat I can for so much wine.

'But necessity will compel us to stop haggling: for you must have wheat, and I must have wine.

'So since you will not and cannot give me all the wine I need, I decide to consume less of it; and you on your side also opt to cut down the consumption of wheat you had in mind. So we move towards one another. I offer you a little more wheat, you offer me a little more wine; and, after several offers have gone back and forth, we strike a deal. We agree, for example, to exchange a cask of wine for a bushel of wheat.'

'If what I offer you was worth the same to you as what you offer me (or in other words possessed equal utility); and if what you offer me was worth the same to me as what I offer you, we would both keep what we had and make no exchange. When we do, we must both judge that we are each taking more than we are giving, or that we are giving something less for something more.'

'The true price must be equally advantageous for everyone.'

'In this state of affairs, the trade in goods produced will not enrich some at the expense of others, because nobody will gain too much, and all will gain something.'

'Only competition among the largest possible number of buyers and sellers can put the right price on things, that is to say, the price which, being equally advantageous for all nations, stops anything becoming too dear or too cheap.'

'What has produced commerce, and maintains it, is the fact that the customs and opinions of different peoples make values unequal; that is what ensures, in exchanges, that everybody has the advantage of giving something less for something more.'

'Out to hurt one another, each of the nations wants to enjoy exclusive advantages from commerce; each in its exchanges wants the benefits just for itself. They do not see that, by the nature of exchanges, there are necessarily benefits on both sides, because both sides are giving something less for something more.'

The underlying order of the functioning of an economy of markets[2]

'The general character of men is that they want to take advantage of those who depend on them, and all would be despots if they could. But when, in different respects, the dependence is mutual, all are forced to yield to one another, and none can abuse the need that others have of him. So interests converge; they merge – and though all men appear dependent, in fact they are all independent. This is order: it is born out of the joint and several interests of all the citizens.'

'The need of citizens for one another places them all in mutual dependence.'

'Thus there will be a continual balancing of wealth and population among the provinces. This balancing will be maintained by industry and competition and, without arriving at a permanent equilibrium, will always seem to tend that situation and will always be very near it.'

'Because everyone can choose his occupation, and enjoys full freedom, the labour of one does not harm the labour of another. Competition, which distributes jobs, puts everyone in his place.'

'Only competition among all traders can make commerce flourish to the advantage of each country. "Faire" and "Laisser faire" should be the motto of every nation. Only trade which is always open and always free can contribute to the happiness of all together and of each one separately.'

'Here is the main advantage of free trade. It multiplies the number of traders; it widens competition as far as possible; it distributes wealth with less inequality; and it puts the right price on everything.'

Notes

1   Adam Smith (1776) *An Inquiry into the Nature and Causes of the Wealth of Nations*, R.H. Campbell and A.S. Skinner (eds), Oxford: Clarendon Press, 1976, 24–7, 74, 75, 16. To Adam Smith the division of labour is the simple consequence of the generation of surpluses realized in each exchange.

2   Adam Smith, ibid., 454, 455, 456, 687. The existence of an underlying order in the functioning of an economy of markets is the guiding, intuitive idea which dominates the whole of Adam Smith's work. It is constantly found in one form or another in every chapter of every book. To Smith there is no contradiction between the fact that consumers and enterprises act in their own interest and the fact that individual decisions lead to an overall situation characterized by an underlying order. Everything happens as if an 'invisible hand' led each one to take decisions appropriate to the overall result.

3   Pierre de Boisguilbert (1704) *Traité de la Nature*, reproduced in *Pierre de Boisguilbert ou la naissance de l'économie*, Paris: Institut National d'Etudes Démographique, 1966, 876. Boisguilbert has been more or less neglected by economic historians. Now that he has been rediscovered, it is clear how far ahead of his time he was. One must subscribe to the judgement of Roger Dehem (1978) *Précis d'histoire de la théorie économique*: 11:

> Boisguilbert was not an explicit theoretician, but he had the genius of perceiving the economic order underlying the social reality and the political system. The depth of thought, as well as some difficulty in the expression, go some way to explaining why this author of genius has not received the recognition he deserves.

4   Robert Turgot (1766) 'Réflexions sur la Formation et la Distribution des Richesses', *Oeuvres*, II, 552; *Oeuvres*, III, 1769, 91; *Oeuvres*, II, 553. Turgot was at once a practitioner and a theoretician. His writings are by any standards of exceptional interest and Turgot is certainly an unknown genius. Schumpeter stresses 'Turgot's brilliant achievements, his unchallenged place in the history of our science, and his evident title to membership in the triumvirate in which Beccaria and A Smith are his

173

colleagues', and in commenting on Turgot's 'Reflections' he writes:

> Such as it is, Turgot's theoretical skeleton is, even irrespective of its priority, distinctly superior to the theoretical skeleton of the *Wealth of Nations*.... It is not too much to say that analytic economics took a century to get where it could have got in twenty years after the publication of Turgot's treatise had its content been properly understood and absorbed by an alert profession. As it was, even J.B. Say – the most important link between Turgot and Walras – did not know how to exploit it fully.
>
> ((1954) *History of Economic Analysis*, New York: Oxford University Press, 248–9)

Turgot was far from satisfied with his work, despite the praise it received (see *Oeuvres*, II, 533, note a).

5   Pierre de Boisguilbert (1704) *Dissertation sur la Nature des Richesses*, in *Pierre de Boisguilbert ...*, op. cit., 986–7 and 995. The first quote from Bosguilbert, corresponds, more than a century in advance, to Pareto's definition of situations of maximal efficiency.

6   Mercier de La Rivière (1767) *Ordre Naturel et Essential des Sociétés Politiques*, II, in *Collection des Principaux Economistes*, Paris: Guillaumin, 444. This quote from Mercier de La Riviere more than prefigures Adam Smith's term 'the invisible hand'.

7   Robert Turgot, *Oeuvres*, op. cit., III, 334.

8   Etienne Bonnot de Condillac (1776) *Le Commerce et le Gouvernement considérés relativement l'un à l'autre*, in *Mélanges d'Economie Politique*, Paris: Guillaumin, 1847, 267, 290–1, 255–6, 292, 325, 377, 328, 292–3, 363; and 338, 337, 381–2, 349 and 443. By its clarity, penetration and range, Condillac's work is certainly of exceptional interest. Three quarters of a century before Gossen, Jevron and Walras, Condillac founded the modern theory of ability and value. On this analysis he developed, much ahead of his time, a general theory of the generation of surpluses, of general economic equilibrium and of maximal efficiency. On this level his work is much superior to Adam Smith's. We can do justice to this book, little known and never translated into English, by repeating Jevon's judgement on Cournot and Gossen: 'The story of these neglected books is truly strange and discouraging; but the day will come when the eyes of those who see not will be opened' ((1871) *The Theory of Political Economy*, Preface to the second edition: 36).

APPENDIX

II THE GENERAL THEORY OF SURPLUSES, FUNDAMENTAL CONCEPTS AND THEOREMS

The general case

To simplify the exposition, it is assumed that one good (U) enters all preference and production functions, and that its quantity can vary continuously. Except for the hypothesis of continuity with respect to this good (U), the discussion in this first part is free of any restrictive hypothesis of continuity, differentiability or convexity for the goods $(V) \ldots (W)$ considered, preference indexes and production functions[1].

Structural conditions

The needs of every unit of consumption, individual or collective can be entirely defined by considering a preference index

$$I_i = f_i(U_i, V_i, \ldots, W_i) \tag{1}$$

increasing as it passes from a given situation to one it finds preferable. Every quantity V_i is counted *positively* if it refers to a consumption, *negatively* if it refers to a service supplied.

The set of feasible techniques for a unit of production j can be represented by a condition of the form

$$f_j(U_j, V_j, \ldots, W_j) \geqslant 0 \tag{2}$$

where every quantity V_j is considered as representing a consumption or an output depending on whether it is positive or negative. The extreme points corresponding to the boundary between possible and impossible situations represent states of maximum efficiency for the production unit considered. They may be represented by the condition

$$f_j(U_j, V_j, \ldots, W_j) = 0 \tag{3}$$

The function f_j may be called the production function. It is defined up to any transformation which leaves its sign unchanged.

Distributable surplus corresponding to a given modification of the economy

The distributable surplus $\delta\sigma_u$ relative to a good (U) and to a realizable modification of the economy which leaves all preference indexes unchanged is defined as the quantity of that good which can be released following this shift.[2]

175

Let us consider an initial state (ξ_1) characterized by consumption values U_i, V_i, ..., W_i and U_j, V_j, ..., W_j (positive or negative) of the different units of consumption and production. We have

$$\sum_i U_i + \sum_j U_j = U_0; \quad \sum_i V_i + \sum_j V_j = V_0, \ldots,$$

$$\sum_i W_i + \sum_j W_j = W_0 \tag{4}$$

where U_0, V_0, ..., W_0 designate available resources. Let $(\delta\xi_1)$ be a feasible modification of (ξ_1) characterized by finite variations δU_i, δV_i, ..., δW_i, δU_j, δV_j, ..., δW_j, and let

$$(\xi_2) = (\xi_1) + \delta(\xi_1) \tag{5}$$

represent the new state.

According to (4) we naturally have

$$\sum_i \delta V_i + \sum_j \delta V_j = 0 \tag{6}$$

for every good (U), (V), ..., (W). From (3) we also have for every unit of production j

$$f_j(U_j + \delta U_j, V_j + \delta V_j, \ldots, W_j + \delta W_j) = 0 \tag{7}$$

According to (1) the preference indexes become

$$I_i + \delta I_i = f_i(U_i + \delta U_i, V_i + \delta V_i, \ldots, W_i + \delta W_i) \tag{8}$$

The δI_i can be positive, zero, or negative.

Let us now define a third state (ξ_3) by the condition that by the modification $-\delta\sigma_{ui}$ of just the quantities $U_i + \delta U_i$ all the preference indexes return to their initial values. We then have the conditions

$$f_i(U_i + \delta U_i - \delta\sigma_{ui}, V_i + \delta V_i, \ldots, W_i + \delta W_i)$$
$$= f_i(U_i, V_i, \ldots, W_i) \tag{9}$$

The state (ξ_3) can be termed 'isohedonous' with the state (ξ_1). In passing from (ξ_1) to (ξ_3) the quantity

$$\delta\sigma_u = \sum_i \delta\sigma_{ui} \tag{10}$$

of the good (U) is released, as all the units of consumption find themselves again in situations which they consider equivalent, since their preference indexes return to the same values.[3]

The surplus $\delta\sigma_u$ has been released during the passage from (ξ_1) to

(ξ_3). It may then be considered that in the situation (ξ_1) this surplus was both realizable and distributable. It may further be considered that in passing from (ξ_1) to (ξ_2), it has in effect been distributed.

The distributable surplus thus defined covers the whole economy, but this definition can be used for any group of agents. It is necessary only to consider the functions f_i and f_j and the resources relating to this group in the preceding relations.

Any exchange system, with the corresponding production operations it implies, is deemed advantageous when a distributable surplus is achieved and distributed, so that the preference index of any consumption unit concerned increases. If an exchange and production system is advantageous, there must be at least one system of prices which allows it, the prices used by each pair of agents being specific to them. The distribution of the realized surplus between agents is determined by the system of prices used in the exchanges between them.

Conditions of equilibrium and maximum efficiency (theorems of equivalence)

In essence all economic operations of whatever type may be reduced to the search for, the achievement of, and the distribution of surpluses. Thus stable general economic equilibrium exists if, and only if, in the situation under consideration, there is no realizable surplus, which means

$$\delta\sigma_u \leqslant 0 \tag{11}$$

for all feasible modifications of the economy.[4] In such a situation the distributable surplus is zero or negative for all possible modifications of the economy compatible with its structural relations, and it is impossible to find any set of prices that would permit effective bilateral or multilateral exchanges (accompanied by the implied production operations) which are advantageous to all the agents concerned.

A situation of maximum efficiency can be defined as a situation in which it is impossible to improve the situation of some people without undermining that of others, i.e. to increase certain preference indices without decreasing others. The set of states of maximum efficiency represents the boundary between the possible and the impossible (see Figure A.1). From those definitions of the situation of maximum efficiency and stable general economic equilibrium, it

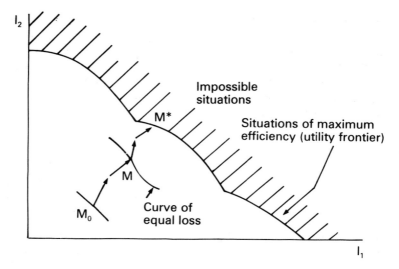

Figure A.1 The process of dynamic evolution

follows, with the greatest generality and without any restrictive hypothesis of continuity, differentiability or convexity, except for the common good (U), that:

- Any state of stable general economic equilibrium is one of maximum efficiency (first theorem of equivalence).
- Any state of maximum efficiency is one of stable general economic equilibrium (second theorem of equivalence).

Since there can be no stable general economic equilibrium if there is any distributable surplus, every state of stable general economic equilibrium is a state of maximum efficiency. Conversely, if there is maximum efficiency, there is no realizable surplus which could be used to increase at least one preference index without decreasing the others, and consequently, every state of maximum efficiency is a state of stable general economic equilibrium.

The dynamic process of the economy: decentralized search for surpluses and the economy of markets (third fundamental theorem)

In their essence all economic operations, whatever they may be, can be reduced to the pursuit, realization and allotment of distributable

178

surpluses. The corresponding model is the Allais model of the economy of markets (1967),[5] defined by the fundamental rule that every agent tries to find one or several other agents ready to accept at specific prices a bilateral or multilateral exchange (accompanied by corresponding production decisions) which will release a positive surplus that can be shared out, and which is realized and distributed once discovered. Thus the evolution of the markets economy is characterized by the condition.

$$\delta I_i \geqslant 0 \qquad (12)$$

for every consumption unit.[6]

Since in the evolution of an economy of markets, surpluses are constantly being realized and allotted, the preference indexes of the consumption units are never decreasing, at the same time as some are increasing. This means that for a given structure, that is to say, for given psychologies, resources and technical know-how, the working of an economy of markets tends to bring it nearer and nearer to a state of stable general economic equilibrium, hence a state of maximum efficiency (see Figure A.1), which is the third fundamental theorem.[7]

Economic loss

The loss σ_u^* which is associated with a given situation is defined as the greatest quantity of the good (U) which can be released in a transformation of the economy for which all the preference indexes remain unchanged (see Figure A.1).[8] It is a well determined function

$$\sigma_u^* = F[I_i, I_i, \ldots, I_n, U_0, V_0, \ldots, W_0] \qquad (13)$$

of the preference indexes I_i and of the resources V_0 which characterize this situation. The loss σ_u^* is an indicator of inefficiency, and $-\sigma_u^*$ an indicator of the efficiency of the economy as a whole.

The loss is minimum and nil in every state of maximum efficiency, and positive in every feasible situation which is not a state of maximum efficiency. It decreases in any modification of the economy, whereby some preference indexes increase, others remaining unchanged, or whereby some surpluses are released with no decline in some preference indexes.[9]

Paths to states of economic equilibrium and maximum efficiency

Since the preference indices I_i are continuous functions of the quantities

179

U_i of the common good (U), the boundary between the possible and the impossible situations in the hyperspace of preference indexes is constituted by a continuous surface. On this surface the loss σ_u^* is nil. This representation allows an immediate demonstration by simple topological considerations of propositions whose proof would otherwise by very difficult.

For every feasible situation which is not a state of maximum efficiency, represented by a point such as M_0, there are an infinity of realisable displacements M_0M enabling a situation of maximum efficiency M to be approached, such that all the preference indexes have greater values than in the initial situation M_0.[11]

Figure A.1 presents an illustration on a particular case[12] of the process of dynamic evolution by releasing and sharing out of surpluses during which the loss σ_u^* is constantly decreasing.

The fourth fundamental theorem

The fourth fundamental theorem results from the foregoing discussion and the consideration of Figure A.1. To any given initial situation whatsoever, assumed not to be a situation of equilibrium, there corresponds an infinite number of possible situations of equilibrium and maximum efficiency, each corresponding to a particular path and each satisfying the general condition that no index of preference should take on a lower value than in the initial situation.

General comment

An economy of markets can be defined as one in which the agents – consumption, production, and arbitrage units – coexist and are free to undertake any exchange transaction or production operation which can result in rendering some distributable surplus available. The principle of the markets economy is that any surplus realized is shared among all the operators involved. How the surpluses achieved are shared out depends on the specific systems of prices used in the exchanges between the agents concerned. The prices used are always specific to the exchange and production operations considered and there is never a unique system of prices used in common by all the agents.

Diagrammatic representation like that of Figure A.1 reveals clearly four basic facts:

(i) There is an infinity of situations of maximum efficiency corresponding to a given initial situation characterized by some distribution of property.

(ii) To each situation of maximum efficiency then corresponds a final distribution of property.

(iii) This final distribution depends on the initial situation and the distribution of surpluses in the course of the transition.

(iv) In any situation which is not a situation of maximum efficiency there exists an infinity of modifications of this situation leading to a situation of maximum efficiency and such as the situation of every one improves.

Thus there is a very strong interdependence between the point of view of efficiency corresponding to the discovery and realization of surpluses and the ethical point of view corresponding to their sharing.[13] In any event, since only what is produced can be shared, the incentive stemming from the partial or total appropriation of the surpluses by the various agents appears as a fundamental factor for the functioning of the economy of markets.[14]

Generation of surpluses in the differential case

Continuity and differentiability

The preceding definitions and theorems are very general and do not make any hypothesis of continuity, derivability or convexity, except the hypothesis of continuity for the common good (U). We now assume in addition that all the quantities and functions considered are continuous and that all functions have first and second order derivatives, the following developments being totally independent of any hypothesis of general convexity.[15]

Generation of distributable surplus

Consider any economic state (ξ) and a realizable modification $(\delta\xi)$ such that all the preference indexes I_i remain constant (isohedonous modification). Let the conditions of constancy of these indexes and the conditions corresponding to the production functions be written in the same general form

$$g_k(U_k, V_k, \ldots, W_k) = 0 \qquad (14)$$

where $U_k, V_k, \ldots, W_k$ represent the consumption of both consumption and production units. By convention, any quantity V_k, if positive, represents consumption, either by a consumption or a production unit. For any production or consumption unit, any parameter V_k, if negative, represents production of a good or a service.

Let dU_k, dV_k, $\ldots$, dW_k, be the first order differentials of the variations δU_k, δV_k, $\ldots$, δW_k of consumptions U_k, V_k, $\ldots$, W_k in the displacement $(\delta\xi)$. From (14), we have

$$g'_{ku} \, dU_k + g'_{hv} \, dV_k + \ldots + g'_{kw} \, dW_k = 0 \tag{15}$$

Let δV_{kl} be the quantity of (V) received by the consumption or the production unit k from the consumption or production unit l. By definition, we have

$$\delta V_k = \sum_{k \neq l} \delta V_{kl} \tag{16}$$

$$\delta V_{lk} = -\delta V_{kl} \tag{17}$$

Assuming that the displacement $(\delta\xi)$ is such that

$$\sum_k \delta V_k = 0, \ldots, \sum_k \delta W_k = 0 \tag{18}$$

Let

$$\varepsilon^k_{v,u} = g'_{kv} / g'_{ku} \tag{19}$$

The ratio $\varepsilon^k_{v,u}$ is the coefficient of marginal equivalence (or marginal rate of substitution) of goods (V) and (U) for agent k.[16] From (15) and (19) we have the relation

$$dU_k = - [\varepsilon^k_{vu} \, dV_k + \ldots + \varepsilon^k_{wu} \, dW_k] \tag{20}$$

between the first order differential dU_k, dV_k, $\ldots$, dW_k. If dU_k is positive, agent k receives a quantity dU_k to within the second order. If dU_k is negative, agent k supplies a quantity $-dU_k$ to within the second order.

From the condition (18), it follows that the displacement considered releases a global distributable surplus

$$d\sigma_u = -\sum_k \delta U_k \tag{21}$$

representing the excess of the quantities supplied over the quantities received of good (U) whose first order differential is

$$d\sigma_u = -\sum_k dU_k \tag{22}$$

From (16) and (20)

$$dU_k = - \sum_v^w \left[\varepsilon_{vu}^k \sum_{\substack{k,l \\ k<l}} dV_{kl} \right] \tag{23}$$

and from (17), we have

$$d\sigma_u = \sum_v^w \sum_{\substack{k,l \\ k<l}} (\varepsilon_{vu}^k - \varepsilon_{vu}^l) \, dV_{kl} \tag{24}$$

According to definitions (9) and (10) $d\sigma_u$ is the first differential of the global distributable surplus $\delta\sigma_u$ released in the displacement considered. For all economic agents the unit of value is defined by condition $u_k = u = 1$. The marginal values $v_k \dots w_k$ of goods $(V) \dots (W)$ for unit k are defined with respect to the u_k by the relations

$$\frac{g'_{ku}}{u_k} = \frac{g'_{kv}}{v_k} = \dots = \frac{g'_{kw}}{w_k} \tag{25}$$

$$u_k = u = 1 \tag{26}$$

Under the adopted sign convention, all the v_k are positive. We have from (19) and (26)

$$\varepsilon_{vu}^k = v_k \tag{27}$$

and relation (24) is written

$$d\sigma_u = \sum_v^w \sum_{\substack{k,l \\ k<l}} (v_k - v_l) \, dV_{kl} \tag{28}$$

where v_k and v_l are the marginal values of good (V) for units k and l. This summation covers all agents, both consumption and production units. It can thus be seen that all the differences between the marginal values in the situation (ξ) can give rise to the release of potential surpluses which can be released and distributed.[17]

The meaning of relation (28) is immediate. Thus if $v_k > v_l$ the relative value of good (V) is higher for agent k than for agent l. The transfer of a positive quantity dV_{kl} of good (V) from agent l to agent k therefore creates an additional positive value

$$d\sigma_{ukl} = (v_k - v_l) \, dV_{kl} \tag{29}$$

If in this 'isohedone' transformation a positive surplus $d\sigma_u$ (defined by relation (28)) is released, it can be distributed in such a way as to increase all preference indexes. In such a modification of the economy, the maximum distributable surplus diminishes, and the point representing the economic situation considered moves closer to the surface of maximum efficiency in the hyperspace of preference indexes. Naturally, for this condition to obtain, the corresponding exchanges and the changes of the consumptions and productions they imply in the production system, must effectively occur.

Conditions of stable general economic equilibrium and maximum efficiency of the economy

From condition (11) it follows that the necessary and sufficient condition for a situation (ξ) to be of stable equilibrium and maximum efficiency is that the distributable surplus $\delta\sigma_u$ defined by (9) and (10) be negative or zero for every feasible modification ($\delta\xi$), i.e. every modification that is compatible with the constraint conditions, i.e. the structural relations of the economy (3) and (4) above.

Condition (11) implies the two conditions

$$d\sigma_u = 0 \qquad \text{(first order condition)} \qquad (30)$$

$$d^2\sigma_u \leqslant 0 \qquad \text{(second order condition)} \qquad (31)$$

for any realizable and reversible modification ($\delta\xi$) in which the expressions of $d\sigma_u$ and $d^2\sigma_u$ represent the first and second differential of $\delta\sigma_u$.[18] Thus we have according to (30) using the above notations

$$d\sigma_u = \sum_i d\sigma_{ui} = \sum_i dI_{iv}/I'_{iv} = 0 \qquad (32)$$

Actually, and according to relation (28), the first-order condition (32) implies that when the quantities V_k are not nil, all the marginal values v_k are equal to a same value v and a same system of prices $u, v, \ldots, w$ then exists for all agents k concerned, such that

$$\frac{g'_{ku}}{u} = \frac{g'_{kv}}{v} = \ldots = \frac{g'_{kw}}{w} \qquad (33)$$

These equalities condense the general equimarginal principle into a single formulation. They express the fact that in a situation of equilibrium and maximum efficiency, the psychological (or objective) value v_k of the last dollar is the same for any agent (consumption or production unit) whatever use it is put to. Conditions (33) show the total symmetry of the implications of the psychological and technical structures of the economy.

Approximate value of the economic loss corresponding to the non-equality of marginal values in the neighbourhood of a situation of maximum efficiency

The integration of equation (28) along a path leading to a state of maximum efficiency leads to the following approximate estimate to within third order accuracy of the global loss involved in the initial situation (relation 13)

$$\sigma_u^* \sim \frac{1}{2_u} \sum_v \sum_{\substack{k,l \\ k<l}} (v_k - v_l)\, \delta V_{kl}^* \tag{34}$$

In this relation, the quantities $v_k - v_l$ represent the differences of marginal values in the initial state considered, and the δV_{kl}^* are the quantities of the good (V) received by operator k from operator l in the transition from the initial to the final state. Relation (34) is of the broadest generality, and holds whatever the initial state.[19] Its simplicity is really extraordinary in view of the complexity of the concept it represents, namely the maximum of the distributable surplus for all the modifications which the economy can undergo while leaving the preference indexes unchanged.

Generation of surpluses and marginal analysis

As a matter of fact a single relation, the relation (28) (or the equivalent relation (24)), condenses the whole generation of surpluses and marginal approach as they have developed, implicitly or explicitly, for over two centuries in the differential case. Subject only to the hypotheses of continuity and derivability implied by any marginal theory, it applies in all cases, and its simplicity is really extraordinary. It also shows the equilibrium and maximum efficiency can obtain only when all marginal values are equal, which is the equimarginal principle. This principle corresponds to the outcome of the dynamic process of the economy induced by differences in marginal equivalences and the realization of surpluses.[20]

From the foregoing discussion a double conclusion emerges: The theory of the dynamic generation of surpluses, on which the works of Adam Smith, his predecessors and his followers rely, implicitly or explicitly, is essential to an understanding of the underlying nature of all economic phenomena. The general theory of surpluses of which the classical theory since Adam Smith is only a special case, allows us to extend all its propositions to the most general case of discrete variations and indivisibilities.[21]

Notes

1 On the general theory of surpluses see: Allais (1943) *A la Recherche d'une Discipline Economique*, pp. 112–77, 181–211, 606–49; (1967) *Les Conditions de l'Efficacité dans l'Economie*; (1968a) *Les Fondements du Calcul Economique*, vol. II; (1968b) *The Conditions of Efficiency in the Economy*; (1971) *Les Théories de l'Equilibre Economique Général et de l'Efficacité Maximale*; (1974a) *Theories of General Economic Equilibrium and Maximum Efficiency*; (1981) *La Théorie Générale des Surplus*; (1986) *The Concepts of Surplus and Loss and the Reformulation of the Theories of Stable General Economic Equilibrium and Maximum Efficiency*; (1987) *The Equimarginal Principle, Meaning, Limits, and Generalisations*. See also the very abridged version published in the *New Palgrave*: Allais (1986) *Economic Surplus and the Equimarginal Principle*.

2 Allais (1943) ibid., pp. 610–16. The surplus considered here differs essentially from the concepts of 'consumer surplus' as usually considered in the literature (see Allais (1985) *The Concepts of Surplus and Loss and the Reformulation of the Theories of Stable General Economic Equilibrium*, pp. 149–51 and the corresponding notes 7 to 21, pp. 166–9).

3 Allais (1943) ibid., pp. 637–8.

4 ibid., pp. 606–12.

5 Allais (1967) *Les Conditions de l'Efficacité dans l'Economie*.

6 This condition is also satisfied by the market economy model in a situation of general economic equilibrium as a consequence of the postulate of general convexity, and by the Edgeworth model of recontract (see Allais (1981) op. cit., 560, pp. 356–9; (1987) op. cit., pp. 732–3). See also p. 46 above.

7 Naturally such evolution takes place only if sufficient information exists about the actual possibilities of realizing surpluses.

8 Allais (1943) op. cit., pp. 638–49.

9 This definition of the economic loss can be extended for any group of operators as follows. The maximum distributable surplus σ_u^* for any group of operators is defined as being equal to the maximum of the distributable surplus σ_u for this group, when one considers all the modifications of the economy which are compatible with the constraints.

10 The paternity of this representation has been unduly attributed to P. Samuelson (1950) whereas it was published for the first time in Allais, (1943) op. cit., n. 258–93, pp. 604–82 and systematically used by Allais in the following years; see Allais (1971) op. cit., n. 11, p. 385; and (1974a) op. cit., n. 18, pp. 176–7).

11 The basic fact for any economic policy is the existence, in any situation which is not one of maximum efficiency, of changes which can improve the situation of all people (see fourth fundamental theorem p. 180).

12 Allais (1974b) *Les Implications de Rendements Croissants et Décroissants*

sur les Conditions de l'Equilibre Economique Général et d'une Efficacité Maximale, p. 644.

13   The final situation of maximum efficiency to which the economy will be brought closer, will basically depend on the distribution of surpluses, which will be obtained by all those who find and release them. It is mainly this sharing of surpluses in the course of an operation which determines, more often than the initial state, the final situation which the economy will approach (see Figure A.1 p. 178).

The literature was continually influenced, implicitly or explicitly, by normative conceptions more or less identifying a state of maximum efficiency as an ethically optimum one. A good illustration is provided by the rather ill-chosen Anglo-Saxon term 'optimum allocation of resources' used to describe the equilibrium state of a market economy corresponding to a given initial situation, whereas the initial situation cannot in general be thought of as ethically optimal – or, for that matter, the path leading from it to the associated state of equilibrium (see Allais (1968b) 'The Conditions of Efficiency in the Economy', p. 6.

14   As a matter of fact, any criticism that might be made of the theory of markets economy also applies to the other theories, but the opposite is not true (see for instance, Allais (1987) op. cit., p. 739–40).

15   On the second order developments and their interpretations see Allais (1985) op. cit., pp. 162–3; (1986) op. cit., pp. 700–2 and 707; (1987) op. cit., pp. 65–6. For a thorough analysis see Allais (1981) op. cit., pp. 49–156 and 435–619.

16   Allais (1943) op. cit., pp. 609–10 and 617–21.

17   Allais (1968a) op. cit., p. 174; (1971) op. cit., n. 8, pp. 383–4; (1974a) op. cit., n. 15, pp. 174–5; (1986) op. cit., p. 704; and (1987) op. cit., p. 66. For a thorough analysis see Allais (1981) op. cit., pp. 86–90.

18   For the expression of $d^2\sigma_u$ see Allais (1968a) op. cit., pp. 196–9; (1971) op. cit., n. 8, p. 384; (1974a) op. cit., n. 15, p. 174; (1986) op. cit., p. 707; and (1987) op. cit., p. 66. For a thorough analysis see Allais (1981) op. cit., pp. 49–156.

19   See Allais (1952b) *L'Extension des Théories de l'Equilibre Economique Général et du Rendement Social au cas du Risque*, n. 8, pp. 31–2; (1968a) op. cit., p. 207; (1971) op. cit., n. 9, pp. 384–5; (1974a) op. cit., n. 16, pp. 175–6; (1986) op. cit., pp. 708–9; and (1987) op. cit., p. 67. For a thorough analysis see Allais (1981) op. cit., pp. 103–46.

20   The history of the progressive development of the dynamic theory of marginal equivalences and its generalizations goes back to the eighteenth century, and its guiding principles are present more or less clearly in such authors as Boisguilbert (1695–1705), Turgot (1766), Condillac (1776) and Adam Smith (1776).

As a matter of fact, and despite some too frequent beliefs to the contrary, there has never been a 'marginal revolution'. As of the eighteenth century, all the materials for the building of the equimarginal theory were present in embryo form and ready for implementation.

21   For an overall view on the general theory of surpluses and maximum efficiency and on the theory of general economic equilibrium and their extensions, see Allais (1985) op. cit., Appendix III, pp. 164–5.

III BIBLIOGRAPHY

For clarity the references are presented in seven sections, and in each section the references are presented in chronological order of their publication.

Adam Smith's works

Smith, Adam (1759) *The Theory of Moral Sentiments.*
—— (before 1759) *Essays on Philosophical Subjects by the Late Adam Smith*, 1793, Black and Hutton.
—— (1776) *An Inquiry into the Nature and Causes of the Wealth of Nations*, first edn London, 2 vols, 7 March 1776; second edn 1778; third edn, 1784, 3 vols, with important additions, and a long index; fourth and fifth edns 1786 and 1789.
—— (1828) MacCulloch's edition with annotations.
—— (1869) Thorold Rogers' edition, Oxford: Clarendon Press.
—— (1884) Nicholson's edition.
—— (1904) Edwin Cannan's edition, with an introduction and many annotations, 2 vols, London: Methuen.
—— (1970) Andrew Skinner's edition, with an introduction by Skinner, Harmondsworth: Penguin. Unfortunately this edition is limited to the Books I–III of *The Wealth of Nations.*
—— (1976) R.H. Campbell's and A.S. Skinner's edition with an introduction, 2 vols, Oxford: Clarendon Press.

French translations: Recherches sur la Nature et les Causes de la Richesse des Nations

—— (1781) Blavet's translation.
—— (1794) J.A. Roucher's translation, 5 vols, Paris: Buisson.
—— (1802) Germain Garnier's translation, 5 vols, Paris: Agasse. Reproduced in the *Collection des Principaux Economistes*, Paris; Guillaumin, 1843.
—— (1950) Translation of the Cannan edition, Paris: Alfred Costes.

Predecessors and contemporaries of Adam Smith

Boisguilbert, Pierre de (1695) *Le Détail de la France.* Reproduced in *Pierre de Boisguilbert ou la naissance de l'économie politique*, with general comments by Alfred Sauvy. Joseph J. Spengler, J.H. Best, Louis Salleron, Jean Fery, Akitern Kobota, Jean Molinier, Stephen L. McDonald (pp. 1–119), Paris: Institut National d'Etudes Démographique, 1966, 581–662.
—— (1704) *Traité de la Nature*, ibid., 827–78.
—— (1704) *Dissertation sur la Nature des Richesses*, ibid., 973–1012.
—— (1705) *Factum de la France*, ibid., 741–56.

Mandeville, Bernard (1705–14) *The Fable of the Bees: Or Private Vices, Publick Benefits.*

Cantillon, Richard (1725) *Essay on the Nature of Commerce,* 1755. First published in French, 1752, *Essai sur la Nature du Commerce en Général.* Reproduced, 1952, Paris: Institut National d'Etudes Démographiques.

Hume, David (1741–2), *Essays Moral and Political,* 2 vols. French translation, *Essais sur le Commerce, le Luxe, l'Argent, l'Intérêt de l'Argent, les Impôts, le Crédit Public,* etc., Paris: Guillaumin. *Mélanges d'Economie Politique,* with an introduction by G. de Molinari, 1847, 1–162.

Quesnay, François (1758–68) *Oeuvres,* reproduced in *Collection des Principaux Economistes,* II, with an introduction by Eugène Daire, Paris: Guillaumin, 1846. See also *François Quesnay et la physiocratie,* Paris: Institut National Démographique, 1958, 2 vols.

Turgot, Robert (1761–74) *Oeuvres,* with an introduction by G. Schelle, 5 vols, Paris: Librairie Félix Alcan, 1913–23. The famous essay by Turgot (1766) *Reflexions sur la Formation et la Distribution des Richesses,* is reproduced in vol. II, 533–601.

Mercier de la Rivière (1767) *Ordre Naturel et Essentiel des Sociétés Politiques,* second edn, 1846, with an introduction by Eugène Daire, *Collection des Principaux Economistes,* II, Paris: Guillaumin, 1846.

Steuart, James Durham (1767) *An Inquiry into the Principles of Political Oeconomy being an Essay on the Science of Domestic Policy in Free Nations,* 2 vols, London.

Necker (1770) *Sur la Législation et le Commerce des Grains,* reproduced in *Mélanges d'Economie Politique,* with an introduction by Gustave de Molinari, Paris: Guillaumin, 1848, 202–361.

Galiani (1770) *Dialogues sur le Commerce des Blés,* reproduced in *Mélanges d'Economie Politique* with an introduction by Gustave de Molinari, Paris: Guillaumin, 1848, 1–202.

Condorcet (1772–86) *Oeuvres,* reproduced in *Mélanges d'Economie Politique,* with an introduction by Eugène Daire, Paris: Guillaumin, 1847, 451–572.

Condillac, Etienne Bonnot de (1776) *Le Commerce et le Gouvernement considérés relativement l'un à l'autre,* reproduced in *Mélanges d'Economie Politique,* with an introduction by Eugéne Daire, Paris: Guillaumin, 1847, 243–471.

Bentham, Jeremy (1787) *Defence of Usury, showing the Impolicy of the Present Legal Restraints on Pecuniary Bargains,* published in French in *Mélanges d'Economie Politique,* with an introduction by Gustave de Molinari, Paris: Guillaumin, 1848.

On Adam Smith, his predecessors and his contemporaries

Say, Jean-Baptiste (1819) *Traité d'Economie Politique,* Discours préliminaire, XLVII–LX.

—— (1829) *Cours Complet d'Economie Politique Pratique,* II, 558–6.

Daire, Eugène (1847) 'Notice sur Condillac', in *Mélanges d'Economie Politique,* Paris: Guillaumin.

Baudrillart, H. (1853) 'Condillac (Etienne Bonnot de)', *Dictionnaire de l'Economie Politique,* I, Bruxelles: Meline, 502.

—— (1853) 'Condorcet (Marie-Jean-Antoine-Nicolas Caritat)', *Dictionnaire de l'Economie Politique*, I, Bruxelles: Meline, 503–5.

Garnier, Joseph (1853) 'Hume (David)', *Dictionnaire de l'Economie Politique*, I, Bruxelles: Meline, 972–3.

—— (1854) 'Mercier-Larivière', *Dictionnaire de l'Economie Politique*, I, Bruxelles, Meline, 171–3.

—— (1854) 'Montchrétien (Antoine de)', *Dictionnaire de l'Economie Politique*, II, Bruxelles: Meline, 248–9.

—— (1854) 'Quesnay (François)', *Dictionnaire de l'Economie Politique*, II, Bruxelles: Meline, 535–40.

Clément, Ambroise (1854) 'Say (Jean-Baptiste)', *Dictionnaire de l'Economie Politique*, II, Bruxelles: Meline, 649–55.

Coquelin et Guillaume (1854) 'Steuart (Jacques)', *Dictionnaire de l'Economie Politique*, II, Bruxelles: Meline, 732.

Monjean, M. (1854) 'Smith (Adam)', *Dictionnaire de l'Economie Politique*, II, Bruxelles: Meline, 683–90.

—— (1854) 'Turgot (Anne-Robert-Jacques)', *Dictionnaire de l'Economie Politique*, II, Bruxelles, Meline, 853–64.

Courcelle-Seneuil (1888) 'Notice sur la Vie et l'Oeuvre d'Adam Smith', *Oeuvres choisies d'Adam Smith*, Paris: Guillaumin.

Courtois, A. Jr (1894) 'Condillac (Etienne Bonnot de)' in Inglis Palgrave (ed.) *Dictionary of Political Economy*, second edn, 1987, I, 385.

Ashley, W.J. (1896) 'Montchrétien (Antoyne de)' in Inglis Palgrave (ed.) *Dictionary of Political Economy*, second edn, 1987, II, 808–9.

Courtois, A. Jr (1896) 'Mercier (alias Lemercier) de la Rivière, (Paul Pierre)' in Inglis Palgrave (ed.) *Dictionary of Political Economy*, second edn, 1987, II, 34–5.

Egerton, Hugh E. (1896) 'Hume (David)' in Inglis Palgrave (ed.) *Dictionary of Political Economy*, second edn, 1987, II, 340–3.

—— (1896) 'Mandeville (Bernard de)' in Inglis Palgrave (ed.) *Dictionary of Political Economy*, second edn, 1987, II, 682–3.

Bonar, J. (1899) 'Smith (Adam)' in Inglis Palgrave (ed.) *Dictionary of Political Economy*, second edn, 1987, III, 412–24.

Higgs, Henry (1899) 'Turgot (Anne-Robert-Jacques Turgot, Baron de l'Aulne)' in Inglis Palgrave (ed.) *Dictionary of Political Economy*, second edn, 1987, III, 590–4.

Ingram, J.K. (1899) 'Steuart (Sir James)' in Inglis Palgrave (ed.) *Dictionary of Political Economy*, second edn, 1987, III, 475–6.

Cannan, Edwin (1904) 'Introduction' in Adam Smith *The Wealth of Nations*, 2 vols, London: Methuen. French translation, 1950, Paris: Alfred Coste.

Schelle, G. (1913) *Introduction aux Oeuvres de Turgot et Documents le concernant*, I, 1913–23, 5 vols, Paris: Alcan.

Gonnard, René (1921) *Histoire des Doctrines Economiques*, third edn, 1941, Paris: Librairie Générale de Droit et de Jurisprudence.

Gide, Charles, and Rist, Charles (1926) *Histoire des Doctrines Economiques*, fifth edn, Paris: Recueil Sirey.

Rist, Charles (1926) 'Adam Smith', in Gide and Rist, *Histoire des Doctrines Economiques*, Paris: Recueil Sirey, 59–137.

Bousquet, G.-H. (1927) *Essai sur l'Evolution de la Pensée Economique*, Paris: Rivière.

Gemähling, Paul (1933) 'Adam Smith' in *Les Grands Economistes*, Paris: Recueil Sirey, 93–134.

Brehier, Emile (1938) *Histoire de la Philosophie*, II, La Philosophie Moderne, fourth edn, 1938, Paris: Félix Alcan.

Schumpeter, J. (1954) *History of Economic Analysis*, New York: Oxford University Press.

Lekachman, Robert (1959) *A History of Economic Ideas*, New York: Harper and Row, French translation, *Histoire des Doctrines Economiques*, 1960, Paris: Payot,

Faure, Edgar (1961) *La Disgrâce de Turgot*, Gallimard.

Blaug, M. (1962) *Economic Theory in Retrospect*, fourth edn, 1985, London: Heinemann Educational Books.

Leduc, Gaston (1968) 'Say (Jean-Baptiste)', *International Encyclopedia of the Social Sciences*, 14, New York, 23–5.

Mauro, Frédéric (1968) 'Mercier de La Rivière', *International Encyclopedia of the Social Sciences*, 10, New York, 248.

Rotwein, Eugène (1968) 'Hume (David)', *International Encyclopedia of Social Sciences*, 3, New York, 211–13.

Spengler, Joseph J. (1968) 'Condillac (Etienne Bonnot de)', *International Encyclopedia of the Social Sciences*, 3, New York, 211–13.

Stark, Werner (1968) 'Turgot (Anne-Robert-Jacques)', *International Encyclopedia of the Social Sciences*, 16, New York, 167–8.

Viner, Jacob (1968) 'Smith (Adam)', *International Encyclopedia of the Social Sciences*, 14, New York, 322–9.

Skinner, Andrew (1970) 'Introduction' to *The Wealth of Nations*, Harmondsworth: Penguin.

Bourcier de Carbon, Luc (1971) *Histoire de la Pensée et des Doctrines Economiques, I: De Montchrétien à Karl Marx*, Paris: Montchrestien.

Campbell, R.H. and Skinner, A.S. (1976) 'Introduction' to *The Wealth of Nations*, Oxford: Clarendon Press.

Dehem, R. (1984) *Histoire de la Pensée Economique*, Dunod: Les Presses de l'Université Laval.

Eltis, Walter (1987) 'Steuart (Sir James)', *The New Palgrave, A Dictionary of Economics*, 4, London: Macmillan, 494–7.

Groenewegen, Peter (1987) 'Condillac (Bonnot de)', *The New Palgrave, A Dictionary of Economics*, 1, London: Macmillan, 564–5.

—— (1987) 'Mercier de la Rivière (Pierre-Paul Mercier or Lemercier)', *The New Palgrave, A Dictionary of Economics*, 3, London: Macmillan, 449–50.

—— (1987) 'Turgot (Anne-Robert-Jacques, Baron de l'Aulne)', *The New Palgrave, A Dictionary of Economics*, 4, London: Macmillan, 707–12.

Rosenberg, N. (1987) 'Mandeville (Bernard)', *The New Palgrave, A Dictionary of Economics*, 3, London: Macmillan, 296–7.

Rotwein, Eugène (1987) 'Hume (David)', *The New Palgrave, A Dictionary of Economics*, 2, London: Macmillan, 692–5.

Badinter, Elisabeth and Robert (1988) *Condorcet*, Paris: Fayard.

The decentralized search for surpluses from J.B. Say to Léon Walras

Say, Jean-Baptiste (1819) *Traité d'Economie Politique* (A Treatise on Political Economy), fourth edn, 2 vols, Paris: Deterville; Calmann-Levy, 1972.

—— (1828–9) *Cours Complet d'Economie Politique Pratique*, third edn, 1852, 2 vols with notes by Horace Say, Paris: Guillaumin.

Ricardo, D. (1817) *On the Principles of Political Economy and Taxation*, 1 in Piero Straffa (ed.) (1951–5) Works and Correspondence, Cambridge: Cambridge University Press. French translation, *Principes de l'Economie Politique et de l'Impôt*, 1933–4, 2 vols, Paris: Alfred Costes.

Gossen, H.H. von (1854) *Entwickelung der Gesetze des menschlichen Verkehrs und der daraus fliessender Regeln für menschliches Handeln*, third edn, 1927, introduction by Friedrich Hayek, Berlin: Präger.

Jevons, W.S. (1871) *The Theory of Political Economy*, fifth edn, 1957, New York: Kelly. French translation, *La Théorie de l'Economie Politique*, 1909, Paris: Giard.

Menger, C. (1871) *Grundsätze der Volkswirtschaftslehre*, Vienna: Braumneller.

The market economy model of Walras and his successors

Allais, M. (1967) *Les Conditions de l'Efficacité dans l'Economie* (The Conditions of Efficiency in the Economy), see p. 196.

—— (1971) *Les Théories de l'Equilibre Economique Général et de l'Efficacité Maximale – Impasses Récentes et Nouvelles Perspectives* (Theories of General Economic Equilibrium and Maximum Efficiency – Recent Blind Alley and New Prospects), see p. 196.

—— (1974a) *Theories of General Economic Equilibrium and Maximum Efficiency*, see p. 196.

—— (1974b) *Les Implications de Rendements Croissants et Décroissants sur les Conditions de l'Equilibre Economique Général et d'une Efficacité Maximale* (Implications of Increasing and Decreasing Yields on the Conditions of General Economic Equilibrium and Economic Efficiency), see p. 194.

—— (1981) *La Théorie Générale des Surplus* (The General Theory of Surpluses), see p. 196, especially Part VI, 295–434.

—— (1986) *The Equimarginal Principle. Meaning, Limits, and Generalization*, see p. 196, especially Chapter V, 'Four Significant Mythologies in the Contemporary Literature', 725–35.

—— (1987) *Economic Surplus and the Equimarginal Principle*, see p. 194, 'The Tendencies of the Contemporary Literature', 68.

—— (1989) *L'Economie des Infrastructures de Transport et les Fondements du Calcul Economique* (The Economy of the Transport Infrastructures and the Foundations of the 'Economic Calculus'), Chapter III, 'Quatre Mythologies significatives de la litterature contemporaine sur les Fondements du Calcul Economique', 176–86, and Chapter IV, 'Economie de Marché et Economie de Marchés', 186–92, see p. 197.

Walras, L. (1874–7) *Eléments d'Economie Politique Pure – Théorie de la Richesse Sociale*, sixth edn, Paris: Guillaumin; and 1952, Paris: Pichon et

Durand-Auzias; English translation of the sixth edn W. Jaffé (ed.) (1954) *Elements of Pure Economics*, London: Allen and Unwin (strongly recommended for any work on the E.E.P.P.).

Edgeworth, F.Y. (1881) *Mathematical Psychics: An Essay of the Application of Mathematics to the Moral Sciences*, London, and 1953, New York: Kelley.

—— (1891) 'On the Determinateness of Economic Equilibrium', *Papers Relating to Political Economy*, II, New York, 1963, 313–19.

Launhardt, W. (1885) *Mathematische Begründung der Volkswirtschaftslehre*, Leipzig: Engelmann.

Auspitz, R. and Lieben, R. (1889) *Untersuchungen über die theorie des Preises*; French translation, *Recherches sur la Théorie des Prix*, (1914), 2 vols, Paris: Giard.

Fisher, I. (1892) *Mathematical Investigations in the Theory of Value and Price*, Yale University Press, 1965.

Wicksell, K. (1901–6) *Vorlesungen über National Ökonomie*. English translation, *Lectures on Political Economy*, 1934, 2 vols, London: Routledge.

Hicks J.R. (1939a) 'The Foundations of Welfare Economics', *Economic Journal*, 696–712.

—— (1939b) *Value of Capital. An Inquiry into Some Fundamental Principles of Economic Theory*, London: Oxford University Press.

Lange, O. (1942) 'The Foundations of Welfare Economics', *Econometrica*, July–October, 215–28.

Samuelson, P.A. (1947) *Foundations of Economic Analysis*, second edn, 1948, Cambridge, Mass.: Harvard University Press.

—— (1948) *Economics*, fourth edn, 1958, London: McGraw-Hill.

Arrow, K.J. (1951) 'An Extension of the Basic Theorems of Classical Welfare Economics', *Proceedings of the Second Berkeley Symposium on Mathematical Statistics and Probability*, Berkeley, Calif. 507–32.

—— (1968) 'Economic Equilibrium', *International Encyclopedia of the Social Sciences*, 4, New York, 376–89.

Hutchison, T.W. (1953) *A Review of Economic Doctrines, 1870–1929*, Westport, Conn.: Greenwood Press.

—— (1977) *Knowledge and Ignorance in Economics*, Oxford: Basil Blackwell.

Arrow, K.J. and Debreu, G. (1954) 'Existence of Equilibrium for a Competitive Economy', *Econometrica*, 22, 265–90.

Debreu, G. (1959) *Theory of Value*, New York: Wiley.

—— (1985) 'Theoretic Models: Mathematical Form and Economic Content', Frisch Memorial Lecture, Fifth World Congress of the Econometric Society, MIT, August 17–24.

Mishan, E.J. (1960) 'A Survey of Welfare Economics, 1939–1959', *Economic Journal*, 197–265.

—— (1968) 'Welfare Economics', *International Encyclopedia of the Social Sciences*, 16, New York, 504–12.

Scarf, H. (1962) 'An Analysis of Markets with a Large Number of Participants', *Recent Advances in Game Theory*, Philadelphia: Princeton University Conference, 127–55.

Debreu, G., and Scarf, H. (1963) 'A Limit Theorem on the Core of an Economy', *International Economic Review*, 4 (3), 235–46.

Arrow, K.J. and Hahn F.H. (1971) *General Competitive Analysis*, San Francisco: Holden-Day; Edinburgh: Oliver.

Woo, H.K.H. (1985) *What's Wrong with Formalization in Economics? – An Epistemological Critique*, The Hong Kong Institute of Economic Science.

The concepts of surplus and loss in the literature

Allais, M. (1973b) 'The General Theory of Surplus and Pareto's Fundamental Contribution', see p. 196.

—— (1981) *La Théorie Générale des Surplus* (The General Theory of Surpluses), see p. 196, especially Part IV, 'Les Fondateurs du Concept de Surplus. Jules Dupuit et Vilfredo Pareto' (The Founders of the Concept of Surplus), 157–235. Part V, 'Deux Analyses Significatives. Barone et Hotelling' (Two Significant Analyses. Barone and Hotelling), 237–94. Part VI, 'Vue d'ensemble sur la Littérature concernant la Théorie des Surplus' (Overview on the Literature concerning the Theory of Surplus), 295–434.

—— (1985) 'The Concepts of Surplus and Loss and the Reformulation of the Theories of Stable General Economic Equilibrium and Maximum Efficiency', see p. 196.

Cournot, A. (1838) *Recherches sur les Principes Mathématiques de la Théorie des Richesses*, Paris: Rivière; 1938, published in English as *Researches into the Mathematical Principles of the Theory of Wealth*, 1929, New York.

Dupuit, J. (1844) 'De la Mesure de l'Utilité des Travaux Publics', *Annales des Ponts et Chaussées*, second series, Mémoires et Documents, 116, VIII, 332–75.

—— (1849) 'De l'Influence des Péages sur l'Utilité des Voies de Communication', *Annales des Ponts et Chaussées*, second series, 170–248.

—— (1853) 'De l'Utilité et de sa Mesure', *Journal des Economistes*, XXXVI (147), 15 July, 1–28.

—— (1854) 'Péage', *Dictionnaire de l'Economie Politique*, II, 372–7, Bruxelles: Mèline.

—— (1844–54) *De l'Utilité et de sa Mesure; Ecrits choisis et republiés par Mario de Bernardi*, 1933, Turin: La Riforma Sociale, with a bibliography of Dupuit's works.

Marshall, A. (1890) *Principles of Economics*, Book III, Chapter 6, Section 1, 1947, London: Macmillan.

Pareto, V. (1896–7) *Cours d'Economie Politique*, 2 vols, Lausanne: Rougé; 1964, Geneva: Droz.

—— (1901) 'Anwendungen der Mathematik auf Nationalökonomie', *Encyklopädie der Mathematichen Wissenschaften*, I, Section 2, 1094–1120, Leipzig.

—— (1906) *Manuale d'Economia Politica*, Milan; published in French as *Manuel d'Economie Politique*, 1909, Paris: Giard et Brière and 1966, Geneva: Droz; published in English as *Manual of Political Economy*, 1971, New York: Kelley.

—— (1911) 'Economie Mathématique', *Encyclopedie des Sciences Mathématiques*, Paris: Gauthier-Villars, 591–641; also in *Statistique et Economie Mathématique*, 1966, Geneva: Droz, 319–76; published in English as

'Mathematical Economics', *International Economic Papers*, 5, 1955, New York, 58–102.

—— (1916) *Trattato di Sociologia Generale*, Firenze: Barbera; published in French as *Traité de Sociologie Générale*, 1919, 2 vols, Paris: Payot; published in English as *A Treatise on General Sociology – The Mind and Society*, 1935, 2 vols, New York: Dover.

Barone, E. (1908) 'Il Ministro della Produzione nello Stato Collettivista', *Giornal degli Economisti*, 267–93 and 391–414; published in French as 'Le Ministre de la Production dans un Etat Collectiviste' in F.A. Hayek, (ed.) (1939) *l'Economie Dirigée en Régime Collectiviste*, Paris, 245–99; published in English as 'The Ministry of Production in the Collectivist State' in F.A. Hayek (ed.) (1935) *Collectivist Economy Planning*, London, 245–90.

Hotelling, H. (1938) 'The General Welfare in Relation to Problems of Taxation and of Railway and Utility Rates', *Econometrica*, 242–69.

—— (1939) 'The Relation of Prices to Marginal Costs in an Optimum System', *Econometrica*, 7, April, 151–5 and 158–60.

Frisch, R. (1939) 'The Dupuit Taxation Theorem', *Econometrica*, 7, April, 145–50 and 158–60.

Hotelling, H. and Frisch, R. (1939) 'Papers on the Dupuit Taxation Theorem', *Econometrica*, 145–60.

Hicks, J.R. (1941) 'The Rehabilitation of Consumer's Surplus', *Review of Economic Studies*, VIII (2), February, 108–16.

—— (1942) 'Consumer's Surplus and Index-Numbers', *Review of Economic Studies*, (2), 126–37.

—— (1943) 'The Four Consumer's Surpluses', *Review of Economic Studies*, XI (1), 31–41.

—— (1946) 'The Generalised Theory of Consumer's Surplus', *Review of Economic Studies*, XIII (2), 34, 68–74.

Boiteux, M. (1951) 'Le Revenu Distribuable et les Pertes Economiques' (The Distributable Surplus and the Economic Losses), *Econometrica*, 19 (2), April, 112–33.

Debreu, G. (1951) 'The Coefficient of Resource Utilization', *Econometrica*, 273–92.

—— (1954) 'A Classical Tax-Subsidy Problem', *Econometrica*, 14–22.

Blaug, M. (1962) *Economic Theory in Retrospect*, fourth edn, 1985, Cambridge: Cambridge University Press.

Coase, R.H. (1968) 'Consumer's Surplus', *International Encyclopedia of the Social Sciences*, 3, New York, 354–8.

Collison Black, R.D., Coats, A.W. and Goodwin, C.D.W. (1973) *The Marginal Revolution in Economics, Interpretation and Evaluation*, North Carolina: Duke University Press.

The general theory of surpluses and the model of an economy of markets

Allais, M. (1943) *A la recherche d'une Discipline Economique, (A.R.D.E.) Première Partie, L'Economie Pure* (In Quest of an Economic Discipline, Part I, Pure Economics), first edn, 2 vols, Paris: Ateliers Industria; second edn,

Traité d'Economie Pure (Treatise on Pure Economics), 1952, 5 vols, Paris: Imprimerie Nationale; (the second edition is identical to the first, except for a new introduction); third edn, 1992, Paris: Editions Clément Juglar.

—— (1945) *Economie Pure et Rendement Social* (Pure Economics and Social Efficiency), Paris: Sirey.

—— (1947) *Economie et Intérêt* (Economy and Interest), 2 vols, Paris: Imprimerie Nationale and Librairie des Publications Officielles; second edn, 1990, Editions Clément Juglar.

—— (1952a) 'Introduction' to the second edition of Allais (1943). Imprimerie Nationale.

—— (1952b) 'L'Extension des Théories de l'Equilibre Economique Général et du Rendement Social au cas du Risque) (Extension of the Theories of General Economic Equilibrium and Maximum Efficiency to the Case of Risk), Colloques Internationaux du Centre National de la Recherche Scientifique, XL, *Econométrie*, 81–120. A condensed version was published under the same title in *Econometrica*, 21 April 1953, 269–90.

—— (1964) 'La Théorie Economique et la Tarification Optimum de l'Usage des Infrastructures de Transport' (Economic and Optimum Tariffs for Transport Understructures) *La Jaune et la Rouge* (publication of the Société Amicale des Anciens Elèves de l'Ecole Polytechnique), special issue *Les Transports*, Paris, 108–14.

—— (1967) 'Les Conditions de l'Efficacité dans l'Economie' (The Conditions of Efficiency in the Economy), Fourth International Seminar, Centro Studi e Ricerche su Problemi Economico-Sociali, Milan. Italian translation, 'Le condizioni Dell' Efficienza Nell' Economia' in Franco Angeli (ed.) (1969) *Programmazione E Progresso Economico*, 13–303, original French text in Allais, M. (1967) *Les Fondements du Calcul Economique* (The Foundations of the Economic Calculus), I, Paris: Ecole Nationale Supérieure des Mines de Paris.

—— (1968a) *Les Fondements du Calcul Economique* (Foundations of Economic Calculus), 3 vols, Paris: Ecole Nationale Supérieure des Mines, vol. I, 1967 and vols II and III, 1968.

—— (1968b) 'The Conditions of Efficiency in the Economy', *Economia Internationale*, 399–420.

—— (1968c) 'Pareto, Vilfredo: Contributions to Economics', *International Encyclopedia of the Social Sciences*, 11, New York, 399–411.

—— (1971) 'Les Théories de l'Equilibre Economique Général et de l'Efficacité Maximale – Impasses Récentes et Nouvelles Perspectives' (Theories of General Economic Equilibrium and Maximum Efficiency – Recent Blind Alleys and New Prospects), Congrès des Economistes de Langue Française, 2–6 June, *Revue d'Economie Politique*, 3, May–June, 331–409; Spanish translation, 'Las theorias del equilibrio economico general y de la eficacia maxima – Recientes callejones sin salida y nuevas perspectivas', *El Trimestre Economico*, XXXIX (3), 155, 557–633. English translation; see 1974a.

—— (1973a) 'La Théorie Générale des Surplus et l'Apport Fondamental de Vilfredo Pareto' (The General Theory of Surplus and Pareto's Fundamental Contribution), *Revue d'Economie Politique*, 6, November–December, 1973, 1044–97.

—— (1973b) English translation of above 'The General Theory of Surplus and Pareto's Fundamental Contribution', *Convegno Internazionale Vilfredo Pareto*, Rome, 25–27 October 1973, Rome: Accademia Nazionale die Lincei, 1975, 109–63.

—— (1974a) 'Theories of General Economic Equilibrium and Maximum Efficiency', (Institute for Advanced Studies, Vienna, 1974) in G. Schwödiauer (ed.) *Equilibrium and Disequilibrium in Economic Theory*, Dordrecht: D. Reidel Publishing Co., 1977, 129–201 (English version of Allais (1971) with some additions).

—— (1974b) 'Les Implications de Rendements Croissants et Décroissants sur les Conditions de l'Equilibre Economique Général et d'une Efficacité Maximale' (Implications of increasing and decreasing yields on the conditions of general economic equilibrium and economic efficiency) in *Hommage à François Perroux*, Grenoble: Presses Universitaires de Grenoble, 1978, 605–74.

—— (1975) *De Quelques Contributions Significatives a la Théorie des Surplus d'Adam Smith et Condillac à John Hicks* (On some significant contributions to the surplus theory from Adam Smith and Condillac to John Hicks), Centre d'Analyse Economique.

—— (1978) *Contributions à la Science Economique. Vue d'ensemble 1943–1978* (Contributions to Economic Science – General View 1943–1978), Centre d'Analyse Economique, Centre National de la Recherche Scientifique.

—— (1981) *La Théorie Générale des Surplus* (The General Theory of Surpluses), 2 vols, Economies et Sociétés, January–May, Institut de Sciences mathématiques et Economies appliquées, second edn, 1989, Grenoble: Presses Universitaires de Grenoble.

—— (1985) 'The Concepts of Surplus and Loss and the Reformulation of the Theories of Stable General Economic Equilibrium and Maximum Efficiency' in M. Baranzini and R. Scazzieri (eds) *Foundations and Dynamics of Economic Knowledge*, Oxford: Basil Blackwell, 135–74.

—— (1986) *The Equimarginal Principle, Meaning, Limits, and Generalisations*, Rivista Internazionale di Scienze Economiche e Commerciali, 1987, 689–750.

—— (1987) 'Economic Surplus and the Equimarginal Principle', *The New Palgrave, A Dictionary of Economics*, 2, London: Macmillan, 62–9.

—— (1988) 'L'Economie des Infrastructures de Transport et les Fondements du Calcul Economique', *Revue d'Economie Politique*, 2, 1989, 159–97.

—— (1988) 'Les Lignes Directrices de mon Oeuvre, Conférence Nobel'; English translation, 'An Outline of my Main Contributions to Economic Science, Nobel Lecture' in, *Les Prix Nobel*, Stockholm: The Nobel Foundation, Almquist and Wicksell International, 357–71 and 372–91.

—— (1989) 'Les Lignes Directrices de mon Oeuvre, Conférence Nobel', *Annales d'Economie et de Statistique*, 14, 1–23.

—— (1989) *Autoportraits. Une vie, une oeuvre*, Paris: Montchrestien.

INDEX